The Greens in West Germany

GERMAN STUDIES SERIES

The Greens in West Germany

Organisation and Policy Making

Edited by
Eva Kolinsky

BERG

Oxford/New York/Munich

Distributed exclusively in the US and Canada by
St Martin's Press, New York

**To
Harry and Daniel**

Published in 1989 by
Berg Publishers Limited
Editorial Offices:
77 Morrell Avenue, Oxford OX4 1NQ, UK
165 Taber Avenue, Providence R.I. 02906, USA
Westermühlstraße 26, 8000 München 5, FRG

British Library Cataloguing in Publication Data

The Greens in West Germany: organisation and
policy making. — (Berg German studies series)
1.   West Germany. Political parties: Grunen, Die.
I.   Kolinsky, Eva
324.243'07

ISBN 0–85496–250–6

Library of Congress Cataloging-in-Publication Data

The Greens in West Germany: organisation and policy making / edited
by Eva Kolinsky.
p.   cm. — (Berg German studies series)
"Translations: Eva Kolinsky with the assistance of Lindsay Batson"—P.
Bibliography: p.
ISBN   0–85496–250–6
1.   Grünen (Political party)   2.   Germany (West)–Social policy.
I. Kolinsky, Eva.   II.   Series.
JN3971.A98G723295 1989
88–33995

324.43—dc19

Printed and bound by Billing and Sons Ltd.

Contents

Tables

Introduction

Eva Kolinsky

Since ecology lists unexpectedly won seats in local assemblies and regional parliaments in the late 1970s, the West German Greens — *Die Grünen* — made their mark in post-war political history as the only new and small party to be elected and re-elected to the Bundestag, to enter the European parliament, and even experience a brief taste of government as a coalition partner in Hesse.

The Greens emerged at an interesting political juncture. By 1976, the concentration of the West German party system which had first become visible in the 1953 elections, had reached a peak with less than 1% of the electorate opting for parties other than the three which had dominated parliaments and governments since the end of the Second World War — CDU, SPD and FDP. At the same time, a new generation of West Germans had reached political adulthood. They were socialised in conditions of economic prosperity, of educational opportunities and occupational mobility. Where their parents and grandparents were inclined to underestimate the role the individual could play in political life and would expect the state or the relevant authorities to define the issues and prescribe acceptable actions, the young generation have been more confident that each citizen could contribute to the agenda of policy issues and styles and influence events or decisions. Broadly speaking, the older generations have favoured stability of the political, economic and social order while the younger ones sought to innovate, to expand democratic processes and forge a newly active role for the citizen in the polity. Action groups, citizens' initiatives, informal extra-parliamentary activities and also new small political parties have played an increasingly important role alongside and complementary to the main parties and other traditional channels of participation. Everyone, it seemed, could be directly

1

and personally involved. Preferences were for small groups, based on personal contacts and focused on a locality or neighbourhood and they pursued issues which were regarded as salient but ignored in mainstream politics. Among them, Green themes like environmental conservation and concerns about nuclear and chemical pollutions were particularly relevant as key themes for the young generation, and as widely shared priorities in West German society.

The Greens originated in a political climate in which preferences for new issues and new participatory styles of political action reduced the integrative potential of the major political parties: voters were more willing than in the past to choose between parties and also choose a newcomer party in sufficient numbers to make it politically viable.

However, in order to understand the place of the Greens between conventional participation and confrontation, the affinity between participatory culture and protest must not be overlooked. Centred on a segment of young and educated West Germans, protest which had been blunted by consensus politics since the 1950s, has obtained a new lease of political life. The student movement was the first in a series of so-called new social movements which have combined a critical detachment from conventional priorities or modes of participation and a near-contempt for established institutions of the West German political system with their zeal for new issues and a more fundamental pace of change than citizens' initiatives or, indeed, *Volksparteien* would entertain.

Protest has inspired the Green Party as much as the intent to compete in elections and become a voice for new issues in parliaments. At the heart of the policy intent and electoral appeal of the Greens lies a sting against the styles, practices and conventions of West German parties and parliamentary politics. They at once set out to challenge the consensual, non-partisan climate generated by the *Volksparteien*, and also become part of it through elections and parliaments. Green politics have been confrontational, yet tempered by their integration into parliamentary processes. As a political force, the party is both radical and conventional. The ambiguities inherent in this dual role have shaped — and plagued — the new party from the outset: it is neither a protest party and forum for extra-parliamentary action nor is it merely a parliamentary voice for new movements and issues. Protest and parliamentary innovation merge and also clash. Together they shape the political profile and function of the Greens.

After a decade of party organisation and parliamentary experience, the Greens have developed their own distinctive party style, and have outgrown the birthpangs of party foundation. As can be expected in a new organisation, procedures, policies and elites emerge over a period of time, and in response to the opportunities of playing an active role which are available in the political environment. Internally, the dominant groups, people or interests can assert themselves and define the course and the nature of a party. The external roles of a party at local, regional, national and supranational level, the public and media responses to its activities are no less powerful as social and political forces to define and create the policy orientations and the organisational realities in a nascent political party.

In the case of the Greens, however, one could think that these processes of internal clarification and of conditioning through the political environment have been strangely suspended. In scholarly and journalistic evaluations, the party's claims to articulate otherwise neglected issues, to incorporate into its party organisation as *Basisdemokratie* participatory expectations which have been or would be frustrated in other organisations, and an emphatic commitment to non-hierarchical decision-making, have been readily accepted as characterisations of existing procedures and as party-political realities. The tendency of authors with political affinities to the Greens to adopt as analytical criteria the keywords given out by the party of their choice has been encouraged by the findings of Inglehart and others on the emergence of new values and political orientations. As a party of the young and educated generation, rooted in the participatory culture of the seventies and focused on the new issues, the Greens could be regarded as the organisational equivalent of the changed preferences, values and styles which have been summarily referred to as postmaterialism or New Politics.

With socio-economic and attitudinal changes apparently creating the political space for the party and defining its function and internal structures, a match between Green pronouncements and Green party realities has simply been assumed, not

3

investigated. Thus, the terms 'fundamentalism' and 'realism' for instance can be traced to the party's own language, and a split between the two to its self-perception. Similarly, the affirmation that the Greens involve their members and make parliamentary work public and more accountable relates back to the Green coinage *Basisdemokratie* which implies that a new type of party has been created, troubled only by minor snags such as too much participatory involvement and internal debate, or too much obstruction from a hostile political environment and rival parties.

Where the tools of political analysis have been applied and interpretations been freed from the Green terminology and mode of thinking, discrepancies between the party's self-presentation and its internal organisation or policy-making functions have been unearthed: electorates have proved more diverse, leaderships more elitist, the parliamentary groups more domineering than the myth of the 'anti-party party' has suggested, and the gap between Green and other West German party policies more narrow. Far from being a party with a clear-cut set of policies or an agreed and constitutional internal structure, the Greens are internally controversial, unsettled, and continue to change as they play their role in parliamentary and party politics. More perhaps than parties with established structures and conventions, the Greens have been prone to be shaped by circumstance and the pragmatism of policy requirements or opportunities of the day. The shaping of the Greens is the subject matter of this book: How does the party articulate policies? How does party organisation contribute to its consensus and communicative culture? How have the Greens coped with the cross-pressures of their political environment and the dynamics of personalities and formalised channels?

In the opening chapter, Müller-Rommel and Poguntke survey the emergence of Green parties across Europe. Held together by a similar focus on issues which can be classified as themes of the New Politics, the electoral prospects of Green parties, and their political consolidation vary considerably between party systems and political cultures. In West Germany, the Greens have drawn on the protest milieu on the left which has gathered momentum since the late sixties. Veen's analysis suggests that the reservoir of Green support is distinctive in a number of ways: although it

encompasses a variety of causes, they are all clearly different
from the causes the general public or those who vote for other
parties would regard as priorities. The Green potential is held
together by a common detachment from mainstream political
institutions, underpinned by urban living which allows for easy
communication and the similarity and segregation of orientations and contacts which constitute a milieu. While the socio-
political basis of the Greens is separate and relatively narrow —
urban, young, educated middle class — the party political conditions of their role are more integrated than the notion of a
protest party or New Politics party would indicate. Papadakis
examines the overlap of policy themes between *Volksparteien*
and Greens and detects a two-way traffic of innovation and
adaptation: the Greens have introduced many themes and compelled other parties to respond and incorporate them into their
respective programmes. Increasingly, however, the *Volksparteien* have developed a new flexibility towards policy issues and
initiated themes which were also of relevance to the Greens. In
these cases it was the Greens' turn to follow and adapt to the
pace of their rivals. As the Greens operate in a parliamentary
context and continue to aim for electoral success they are more
and more conditioned by the West German party environment:
the decline of partisan policies and the flexibility of approaches
and preferences which has characterised the *Volksparteien* have
also begun to mould the Greens and to mellow some of their
confrontational traits.

While the first part of the book considers the place of the
Greens in the political environment and the West German party
culture, the second part looks at internal Green policy articulation and party organisation: the failure to transpose the pledges
of grassroot democracy and non-hierarchical communication
into agreed procedures or styles, a participatory Green party
culture, is the recurrent theme of the various case studies. The
party, it seems, is dominated by a plethora of individuals and
factions all with their own priorities and pragmatic channels.

Fogt shows, with special reference to the origins of the party,
the transfer of personnel, leadership practices and policy goals
from the fragmented New Left of the 1970s to the Greens today.
Kostede explains the diffuse and often acrimonious political
climate in the Greens as a result of political and intellectual

disorientation: although intellectuals — educated people — have constituted a significant part of the Green electorate, membership and elite, the Greens lack the sense of direction which could only arise from intellectual clarity about the direction of events today and tomorrow. Since West Germany's intellectuals are unable to focus on the course of history and grasp the needs of the future, parties such as the Greens are deprived of the intellectual-political framework which would harmonise them internally and increase their impact.

In the Greens, the parliamentary groups have taken a lead in policy formulation, and shaped the orientation of the party from the top. Concentrating on German–German issues, Gransow argues that individuals and factions within the parliamentary group initiated the party's policy towards the East and decided when and how the party should try to intensify the links between the two Germanies. It could be regarded as an advantage of such personalised policy-making that actions can be quick and flexible; however, since the Green politicians were neither authorised by the party nor adequately briefed on the current state of German–German relations, the delegations elicited grand-sounding promises and messages of good intent but were effectively ignored, and even duped by the governments of both sides. Scharf, in his case study of local coalition politics in Hesse, reveals a similarly incongruous approach of the Greens which enabled the SPD to utilise coalitions, when they seemed to fit the needs of regional government, and drop them when they did not. With special reference to the policy on women, I argue in my chapter that the party is pillarised and factionalised to such an extent that it lacks a policy consensus of any kind: policies are segmented, and supported only by some groups, leaders, interest sectors. Since an organisational machinery to arrive at agreed policies has yet to be developed, the internal party culture of the Greens is one of acrimony and conflict between competing camps, personalities and styles, not least of women against presumed male values and dominance.

In the concluding chapter, Will-Schinneck presents an inside view of one specific Green policy: to develop a financial network and banking empire for the alternative milieu from which the Green party draws its support. The concepts of eco-bank and eco-polis underline the Green drive for innovative change — in this case with the pragmatic tinge of keeping the monies of the alternative culture inside that culture; the case-study also reveals the precarious basis for policy-making without cross-party consensus or the legitimation by properly constituted decision-making bodies in the party organisation. Individuals have ideas and try to put them into practice. The policy process is uncertain, and the linkage between party goals and new social movements feeble. The personalised nature of policies fuels personal rivalries and inner party conflicts, which often blunt or even obstruct the original intentions, and halt innovation.

It could be argued that internal conflict and a tug-of-war between factions and politicians are the hallmark of all political parties and their processes of policy articulation. In traditional party organisations, congress and other constituted bodies tend to provide a formal framework within which to arrive at a policy consensus, and to bestow upon initiatives some legitimacy as policies for and by the whole party. The articulation processes themselves, and the checks-and-balances of the organisational realisation of a policy consensus also control and integrate functionaries, key bodies like parliamentary groups and, of course, members.

The Greens have none of these safeguards which could tie policies to a party consensus. The party organisation has been outplayed by pressure factions; policies are formulated at random, and frequently by parliamentary personalities. The members, who should have a substantial say if *Basisdemokratie* were to work even if traditional rules of democratic representation were to apply, seem to have been by-passed in a free-for-all of organisational uncertainties and personalised approaches. At the time of writing the most recent example of organisational disarray surfaced at the party congress in Karlsruhe in December 1988. Protracted quarrels over financial accountability and the radical or moderate stance of Green policies led to the resignation of the party leadership with new elections due in February 1989. On the eve of the 1989 European elections, the parliamentary factions and the personalities which dominate them hope to shift the party's image to the centre and gain control over its organisation, finances and policy formulation. Such a one-faction victory could lead to a split of the party and even jeopardise the electoral future of the Greens themselves.

Introduction

After ten years in party politics and parliaments, the Greens have yet to develop an organisational mode to integrate the many conflicting views and arrive at policies which are endorsed by more than one faction. With factions and media personalities firmly in charge of issues and with a narrow elite rotating between offices, the Green party organisation seems little more than a convenient electoral label for a disjointed and divided assortment of policies and a multifaceted opposition.

I
The Greens in the
Contemporary Political
Environment

1
The Unharmonious Family: Green Parties in Western Europe

Ferdinand Müller-Rommel and Thomas Poguntke

Electoral Strength and Parliamentary Representation[1]

After decades of 'frozen' party systems, Green parties have emerged in nearly all Western industrialised societies, although their activities and their electoral success vary considerably between countries and between the local, regional, and national levels within any one country. Green parties clearly transcend frontiers of political systems and cultures, and are found with similar types of organisation and programmes in Europe, the United States, and Japan. Boosted by a lively media interest, Green parties have influenced many areas of political life, such as environmental awareness, nuclear policy, and demands for disarmament among the mass public. The influence of Green parties is illustrated by the fact that a number of major political parties in Western Europe chose to reconsider some of their policies in response to Green party activities. To outline the scope of the Green phenomenon, we shall sketch a political map of the Greens in Europe: since the mid-1970s political parties which we can regard as Green or ecology based have been created in twelve Western European countries: Austria, Belgium, Denmark, Finland, France, Ireland, Italy, Luxemburg, Sweden, Switzerland, West Germany and the United Kingdom. Some of these have entered parliamentary politics, others have remained electorally weak, a political voice rather than a force. Where do we find Green parties and what is their electoral strength?

---

1. The information on Green parties in Europe and their electoral performance has been largely compiled on the basis of newspaper reports and other current affairs information.

In Scandinavia Green parties with national party organisations exist in Finland, Sweden and Denmark. Norway did not see the creation of a Green party, since small left-wing or liberal parties would articulate the relevant issues such as environmentalism or peace.

The history of the Greens in **Finland** began in 1979 with the unpopular decision of the government to drain a lake which was a nature protection area for birds. As a list rather than a formal party organisation, the Greens first nominated candidates of their own for the 1979 parliamentary election, but gained only 0.1% of the national vote. From 1979 until 1983, they consolidated their representation at local level. In the 1983 national election the Green list received 1.5% of the vote. Under the system of proportional representation in Finland, this was enough to win two seats. In the 1987 national election the Green list was again successful and increased its electoral success to 4% of the total vote (Table 1.1).

In **Sweden** Green issues surfaced during the seventies and were articulated by the environmentalist Centre Party. Many Centre party voters were, however, disillusioned by the party's decision in 1980 to support a referendum in favour of nuclear power plants. In 1981 the *Miljöpartiet* was founded with the support of many former Centre party followers. According to a Swedish public opinion poll, the *Miljöpartiet* enjoyed a political electorate of some 4% of the national vote in November 1981. Measured against these predictions, the electoral result in the 1982 general election was disappointing: the *Miljöpartiet* received only 1.6% of the vote and failed to gain seats in the national parliament. Since 1983, the Swedish environmentalists strengthened their ties with other parties in Europe. In the autumn of 1984, the party changed its name to Green Party in order to be more attractive to new social movement followers at the 1985 national election. The electoral outcome was again disappointing; at the time the Social Democrats had adopted several environmental issues and contained the Green vote at 1.5%. In September 1988, however, the Greens finally gained 5.5% and twenty seats in the national parliament.

In **Denmark** a Green party was set up in 1983, but did not receive enough electoral support to appear on the ballot papers for the following national elections. In the local elections of 1985,

Table 1.1. Electoral results of Green parties/lists in national elections in Western Europe

	1978	1979	1979[1]	1980	1981	1982	1983	1984	1984[1]	1985	1986	1987	1988
Belgium[2]	0.8(0)	–	3.4(0)	–	4.5(4)	–	–	–	8.2(2)	6.2(9)	–	7.1(9)	–
West Germany	–	–	3.2(0)	1.5(0)	–	–	5.6(27)	–	8.2(7)	–	–	8.3(44)	–
Denmark	–	–	–	–	–	–	–	–	–	–	–	0.2(0)	–
France	2.1(0)	–	4.4(0)	–	1.1(0)	–	–	–	3.4(0)/3.3(0)[3]	–	1.2(0)	–	–
Finland	–	0.1(0)	–	–	–	–	1.5(2)	–	–	–	–	4.0(4)	–
Great Britain	–	0.1(0)	0.1(0)	–	–	–	0.2(0)	–	0.5(0)	–	–	1.3(0)	–
Ireland	–	–	–	–	–	–	–	–	0.1(0)	–	–	0.4(0)	–
Italy	–	–	–	–	–	–	–	–	–	–	–	2.5(13)	–
Luxemburg	–	1.0(0)	1.0(0)	–	–	–	–	5.8(2)	6.1(0)	–	–	–	–
Austria	–	–	–	–	–	–	3.2(0)	–	–	–	4.8(8)	–	–
Portugal	–	–	–	–	–	–	–	–	–	–	–	–	–
Sweden	–	–	–	–	–	1.6(0)	–	–	–	1.5(0)	–	–	5.5(20)
Switzerland	–	0.8(1)	–	–	–	–	6.4(6)[5]	–	–	–	–	8.3(7)	–
Spain	–	–	–	–	–	–	–	–	–	–	1.0(0)	–	–

1. Results in European Elections
2. Results of AGALEV and Ecolo together
3. 3,4 = Les Verts; 3,3 = Entente Radical Ecologiste
4. Results of VGÖ and ALÖ together
5. Results of GPS and GAS together

however, the Green Party did win enough votes to send several delegates to local councils. In December 1981, a public opinion poll identified 2.3% of the electorate as potential Green voters. However, in the 1987 national elections the Danish Greens received only 0.2% of the total vote. This result was due to the fact that in Denmark two small left-wing parties adopted issues of the 'New Politics' and offered 'Green' programmes. In addition, the Socialist People's Party (SF) and the Venstre Socialist Party (VS) were in close alliance with the anti-nuclear power and the environmental movements and could build on their electoral support.

Green parties have been established in all the **Benelux** countries. **Belgium** is the first country in Western Europe where representatives of Green parties were elected to a national parliament. The two Green parties (AGALEV for the Flemish, and Ecolo for the French-speaking Walloons) had already campaigned jointly in the 1977 and 1978 elections, but it was not until the 1981 general election that they could win 4.8% of the vote and receive four seats in the national parliament. In the 1984 European elections, the Greens in Belgium achieved another electoral breakthrough, winning two seats in the European Parliament. Since then, the two Green parties have become an established element of the party system in Belgium. They received 6.2% (9 seats) in the 1985 and 7.1% (9 seats) in the 1987 national elections.

In **Luxemburg** an 'alternative list' (AL) was founded in 1979 prior to the European and the national elections. The political focus of the AL can be called a protest against the environmental policy of the established parties, and also against the political system as a whole. In both 1979 elections, the AL gained 1% of the vote. Encouraged by the electoral success of the Belgian Greens in 1981, the followers of new social movements in Luxemburg — after a series of acrimonious debates — founded a new Green party in 1983 (The Green Alternative). In the 1984 European and national elections, the party obtained 6.1% and 5.8% of the vote winning two seats in the national parliament. Because of the 'country-vote-proportional representation' for the European parliament, the Luxemburg Green Party however has no seats in Strasburg.

Compared to Belgium and Luxemburg, the story of the

development of the Greens in the **Netherlands** is more complex. Until 1984, the political issues of the new social movements were largely represented by the Radical Party (PPR) and the Pacifist-Socialists (PSP). The Radical Party was formed in 1968 from segments of the Catholic Peoples Party, while the Pacifist-Socialists had split from the Dutch Labour Party in 1957. Since there was fairly strong support for these parties among the followers of new social movements, no Green and alternative list or party were formed. The situation changed in 1984 when the new Dutch electoral law for the European election required that a party could obtain at least 4% of the total vote in order to win representation in the European Parliament. In a bid to pass the 4% electoral hurdle, the Radicals initiated an alliance with those left-wing smaller parties which had remained below 2% in the previous national election. The idea was to reorganise left-wing radical politics in the Netherlands by founding a party alliance with the PPR, the PSP, and the Communists (CPN). After protracted efforts to agree on 'Green credentials', these parties founded the Green *Progressive Akkord* (GPA), taking the Green label because the party executives expected to attract additional voters by calling themselves the Greens. A public opinion survey in 1983 announced that 12.5% of the Dutch voters would support a Green party. The GPA polled 5.6% at the 1984 European elections, while the PPR, PSP, and CPN together had received 5.7% at the national elections in 1982. These results suggest that the GPA's electoral strategy has not been as successful as desired, although it has achieved the immediate aim of getting two candidates elected to the European Parliament, one coming from the PSP and the other from the PPR. In the 1986 national election a small group of 'pure' ecologists nominated their own candidates on a list called 'Green Federation'. This group won 0.2% of the total vote, while the PPR received 1.3%, the PSP 1.2%, and the Communists 0.6% of the vote. Together, these results total 3.3% of the national vote, indicating that the small 'New Politics' parties have lost significantly over the past three years. As in other countries, the Labour Party has absorbed some New Politics issues and may have weakened the electoral potential of the small radical and Green parties.

The Greens in **West Germany** were founded as an electoral

15

and organisational alliance of several political groupings which professed to be alienated by established party and interest structures. It was not until March 1979 that the 'other' political alliance (SPV) was created, primarily to contest the European elections of that year. Following their success in obtaining 3.2% of the vote, they proceeded to form a national party. After a series of lively conferences which demonstrated the political differences among the various groupings, a party *Die Grünen* was founded in January 1980 and a national programme was adopted the following March. Participation in the 1980 federal election, however, was rather disappointing and brought only 1.5% of the vote. Since West German political parties require at least 5% of the vote to qualify for parliamentary representation, the Greens had remained well below. In spite of this poor performance at national level, the Green and alternative lists proceeded to win representation at the state level (Länder) and gain a parliamentary voice. In March 1983 the Greens managed the step into national parliamentary politics; with 5.6% of the vote and 27 seats they entered the Bundestag. In the European election of 1984, the Greens gained an impressive 8.2% of the vote and received 7 seats in the European Parliament. As in Belgium, the Greens in West Germany have since consolidated their position in the national party and parliamentary system. In the 1987 federal election, they received 8.3% of the total vote and presently hold 44 seats in national parliament.

The first 'Ecology List' in Western Europe to be organised on the national level was formed in **France** prior to the 1974 presidential elections. For the first time in French politics, the ecologists nominated their own presidential candidate. Since then, the ecologists have taken policy stands which have been radically opposed to those of the larger established parties. In 1977, three ecological groups formed the *Collectif Ecologie '78* for the purpose of campaigning for the parliamentary elections. The group favoured a decentralised approach and pronounced its distrust of traditional political structures. It was, however, not until January 1984 that the various factions among the *Ecologie* and other new social movements founded the French Green party (*Les Verts*). Electorally, the ecologists have been rather unstable over the past ten years. In the 1974 presidential elections, the ecological candidate polled 1.3% of all votes and held sixth place in the field of twelve. In the 1976 cantonal elections, some local ecological groups obtained relatively high electoral results, and encouraged other ecologists to nominate candidates for the local election in March 1977. The elusive electoral break-through of French ecologists, however, failed to materialise. In the 1978 general election, the ecologists nominated candidates in 201 out of 474 constituencies of metropolitan France. They received the highest vote in Paris and in areas where there was strong local opposition to nuclear power stations (Müller-Rommel/Wilke 1981: 383ff). For the 1979 European elections, the ecologists formed a list called *Europe Ecologie* and gained 4.4% of the vote. In the 1981 presidential elections, the ecologists' candidate obtained 3.5% of the poll, 3.1% of the total electorate, and ranked fifth among the 10 presidential candidates (Nullmeier *et al* 1983: 67). For the 1984 European elections, the French Green Party and another moderate Green list (*Entente Radicale Ecologiste* — ERE) competed for voters. Because of the electoral split neither of the two Green organisations received the 5% of the vote necessary to send Green candidates to the European Parliament.

The foundation of local Green lists in **Italy** dates back to 1980, when some small autonomous ecological groups nominated candidates for local elections in several northern Italian cities. The number of local Green lists increased to 16 in 1983, and for the local administrative elections in May 1985 about 150 Green lists competed with other parties for voters. On the whole, they won 2.1% of the total turnout in three districts where they nominated their own candidates. This result showed that Green lists in Italy gained a total of 141 seats in the representative assemblies: 10 in the regional, 16 in the province, and 115 in city councils. In the June 1987 national election the *Lista Verde*, a joint group of all Green lists in Italy polled 2.5% and won 13 seats in the national parliament (Chamber of Deputies) and 2 seats in the upper house (Senate). Despite this, the Italian Greens have remained incohesive and have been called the 'Green Archipelago'.

The forerunner of the present environmentalist party in **Great Britain** was formed in 1973 under the name People's Party. In 1975 the party changed its name to the Ecology Party and in 1985 to the Green Party. In contrast to most other Green parties in Europe, this party was not as strongly supported by the British environmental and peace movement, which had remained close to the Labour Party or developed their own ethos as non-partisan pressure groups. The Ecology Party maintained a national organisational network, although for electoral purposes the expressions 'Scottish Ecology Party', 'Ecology Party of Wales', and 'Northern Ireland Ecology Party' were used in some areas. In fact, it was the fastest growing party in Great Britain until the formation of the Social Democratic Party in 1981. The Ecologists were for instance quite successful in the 1976 and 1977 local elections. In the 1979 general elections the Party nominated 53 candidates and gained 1.6% of the vote where it contested seats. In the June 1979 direct elections to the European Parliament, they nominted 3 candidates, who gained 3.7% of the vote in their constituencies. The general elections of 1983 and the European elections of 1984 brought low electoral support. This is a likely consequence of the British majority system, where smaller parties stand little chance of winning seats in the national parliament. Even voters who feel close to the Green Party often vote for one of the larger parties since a vote for a small party may be a wasted vote in Britain.

The Green party in **Ireland** was founded under the name 'Green Alliance' in 1981. The party is essentially a network of small, independent groups, either local and functioning in a particular geographical area, or of specialists dealing with a particular issue or aspect of Green Alliance policy. The local and specialist groups are autonomous, and therefore free to adopt the organisational structure they choose. The Irish Greens fielded seven candidates in the 1982 general elections and received only a small number of first preference votes. For the 1984 European elections, the Green Alliance nominated only one candidate in the constituency of Dublin where the party gained 1.9% of the vote. In the 1987 national election they could slightly increase voting support on national level to 0.4% of the total vote.

In **Austria**, two Green parties were founded in 1982: the Alternative List (ALÖ) and the Green Union (VGÖ). Both parties could draw on citizens' movements and political groups which focused on social and environmental issues. The emergence of such groups had been encouraged by the success of the national referendum against nuclear power plants in 1978. The ALÖ and VGÖ differ in ideological terms. While the VGÖ is a right-wing party and even nominated 'fascist' candidates for the 1983 general elections, the ALÖ programme and strategy are similar to those of the West German Green party. The ALÖ has established its strength at local level and has used a network of grassroots organisations and groups to gradually extend its electoral support in district elections. Both parties polled well enough to send Green party delegates to local and district parliaments. In the 1983 general elections the Austrian Greens were not very successful mainly because of conflicts within and among the two parties. The VGÖ and ALÖ entered separate lists and gained 1.9% and 1.4% respectively. With a united Green list and a combined result of 3.3% (VGÖ/ALÖ), the Green Parties would have been able to send 7 delegates to the national parliament in 1983. For the 1986 national elections both Green Parties formed an alliance and received 4.8% of the vote and 8 seats in the national parliament.

In **Switzerland**, the first regional Green party was founded in Zürich in 1978. The party participated in the 1979 general elections with its own list of candidates, and gained one seat in the national parliament because of the proportional representation. In the following years several Green parties were formed in different areas throughout Switzerland. At the same time, alternative left-wing social movements developed in larger cities. In May 1983, most of the decentralised Green parties founded the 'Federation of Green Parties in Switzerland' (GPS) on a national level. One month later, some left-wing followers of the alternative groups established the 'Green-Alternative List in Switzerland' (GAS). Both groups nominated their own candidates for the 1983 general election. The GAS won 3.5% and the GPS 2.9% of the national vote. In 1987 the GPS could increase its electoral support to 4.8%, while the GAS again polled 3.5%.

New Politics Theory

The emergence of Green parties in different social and political settings across Europe has been linked to the impact of socio-economic change on political orientations and issues. This model of explanation has been called the New Politics theory. Although this chapter is not concerned with the theory itself, a brief outline of its main points should be useful to clarify the significance of the Green party developments in a broader perspective.

New politics theory is concerned with the rise of a cluster of new political issues and related changes in participatory dispositions and behaviour. Writers like Inglehart (1971, 1977, 1981) and Barnes, Kaase *et al* (1979) — to mention only the more pioneering ones — have tried to explain these changes primarily by referring to the surge of postmaterialist value orientations. Younger age groups, and particularly those with higher education and a new middle-class background amongst them, have been socialised in a way which makes them emphasise social and self-actualisation needs such as a communicative and personal society, participation at the workplace and in political decision-making freedom of expression, a beautiful environment and the appreciation of creativity (Inglehart 1977: 42). Other authors give more weight to changes in the social structure of modern societies and the related cognitive mobilisation (Kitschelt 1988; Dalton 1984). However, there is no fundamental contradiction between both approaches (Chandler/Siaroff 1986: 303). Value change cannot be explained merely by the socialisation hypothesis which translates period effects into aggregate changes. There is no doubt that shifts towards new politics issue orientations and related behavioural dispositions are intimately related to change in the social structure of advanced industrial societies.

Given its cross-nationally validated anchorage, new politics, it seems, should be regarded as more than just a transitory phenomenon. For the German case the surge of the new politics and the subsequent success of the Green Party has been explained as a reaction to the failure of the political and economic system to provide adequate career prospects for young university graduates (Alber 1989; Bürklin, 1984: 46; 1985a; 1985b: 286–90). Although it is true that New Politics demands represent a convenient focus for such a counter-elite strategy, the argument fails to explain the high proportion of well-paid party militants.

In their 'pure' form, New Politics demands run counter to the dominant political paradigm of the postwar period, which centres around economic and security (old politics) issues (Cotgrove/Duff 1980: 339; Murphy, 1981). Also, the old politics is characterised by the predominance of representative forms of decision-making and conventional political behaviour. Since many New Politics demands are widely perceived as challenging conventional wisdoms of economic policy, sympathy with such policies is likely to rise with growing distance from the production process. Therefore, members of the new middle classes should be disposed to be more favourable to new politics demands — regardless of their actual value orientation (Baker *et al* 1981: 152ff).

This change of the political agenda is accompanied by shifting participatory norms and dispositions among similar social groups. It means the increase of a qualitatively different, i.e. elite-challenging form of political participation which employs protest techniques like unofficial strikes, boycotts, blockades, or rent strikes (Barnes/Kaase 1979). A considerable number of individuals who are prepared to engage themselves in protest action also participate through conventional channels and are hence available for mobilisation by New Politics parties.

New Politics parties should therefore display the essential elements of New Politics on three dimensions: programme, political style, and electoral profile. Being embedded in New Politics should make them distinct from established parties which — though different with respect to ideology and electoral basis — belong to the old politics cluster in terms of conventional political style and a common political agenda.

A New Type of Party

In theory, a new politics party should emphasise the following programmatic goals: Ecological politics, opposition to nuclear power, individualism with a very strong focus on self-determination and self-actualisation (and as a corollary of this, a feminist orientation), participatory democracy with direct citizens' involvement in decision-making, a general left-wing orientation, redistribution of global wealth in favour of the developing

21

nations, and an unambiguous preference for unilateral disarmament.

In addition, the participatory and elite-challenging dispositions of new politics proponents should leave a clear imprint on such a party's organisational structure and political style. In an ideal world, the party organisation of a New Politics party should be marked by a pronounced tendency to guarantee the political autonomy and prerogatives of the grass roots. Also, a New Politics party is likely to lean heavily towards a preference for unconventional political action. Finally, the electoral base of parties that are decisively moulded by the New Politics should correspond to the sociological profile of the New Politics groups of society. In a nutshell, the typical voter of a New Politics party is a young, highly educated member of the new middle class who lives in an urban environment and regards himself or herself as belonging to the political left.

An empirical application of this 'model' to a cross-national data base covering all relevant Western European Green parties can show that most are products of the surge of the New Politics (Poguntke 1987b; 1989). However, it would be an over-simplification to speak of only two groups of parties, those of the New and those of the old politics. Few parties are either completely hierarchical or thoroughly participatory, and some parties may endorse some but not all of the New Politics issues. Furthermore, most issues allow for positions with varying degrees of radicalism.

Green Conservatism

Before we discuss the characteristics of New Politics-orientated Green parties, we should focus on parties that are committed to the ecological cause without sharing other political concerns of the New Politics (Table 1.2).

There are two significant European Green parties that indicate the ambiguity of the ecological theme. As mentioned elsewhere (Poguntke 1987a), conservative answers to the environmental crisis are conceivable, and some of these answers can show a clear slant to the far right. In conservative environmentalism, one line of thought is related to the tradition of conservative

Table 1.2. Green parties: the New Politics dimension

Country	Party	Classification of New Politics variables total +	−	Dimension dimensions total +	−	classification
Austria	ALÖ	13	0	3	0	highly likely
	VGÖ	4	6	0	3	negative
Belgium	AGALEV	15	0	3	0	highly likely
	Ecolo	16	0	3	0	highly likely
Denmark	De Gronne	10	0	2	0	highly likely
Finland	Greens	14	0	3	0	highly likely
France	Greens	17	0	3	0	highly likely
Germany	Greens	18	0	3	0	highly likely
Ireland	Green All.	12	0	2	0	highly likely
Italy	Verdi	9	0	2	0	highly likely
Luxemburg	GAP	12	0	2	0	highly likely
Sweden	MP	16	0	3	0	highly likely
Switzerland	GPS	4	1	1	1	negative
	GAS	7	0	2	0	highly likely
UK	Ecology P	12	0	2	0	highly likely

Summary: We have analysed 15 parties in 12 countries. A high figure in the variables column indicates a high number of New Politics issues in party programmes. The higher the positive dimensions score, the clearer the New Politics dimension is. The most significant result is that in all countries we can identify at least one Green party that is clearly rooted in the New Politics segments of the populace. In two cases, Green parties do not belong to the New Politics family, although their existence can be understood as a reaction to the surge of the New Politics.

conservationism which has always resented the destruction of nature by modern industrial society (cf. Murphy 1985: 145). This tendency is also present — albeit not dominant — within many New Politics-orientated Green parties. The political concerns of these 'conservationists' are usually confined to environmental problems. Consequently, they tend to resist the broadening of the political scope of an emergent Green party. Apart from their concern for the environment, however, they have little in common with the New Politics and their broader set of political issues. Apparently, the Green Party in Switzerland has been dominated by 'conservationists' who have successfully preserved the party's single-issue orientation (cf. Ladner 1989).

Unlike these rather apolitical environmentalists, conservative ecologists have presented encompassing political programmes that can be understood as a reaction to the challenge from the New Politics and the environmental crisis. More radical right-wing versions of ecologism draw on anti-democratic concepts of a 'naturally ordered society' and advocate authoritarian strategies for the solution of environmental problems. One, albeit politically insignificant, example is the German ÖDP of the ex-CDU and ex-Green politician Herbert Gruhl (Poguntke 1987a: 83).

Initially the Austrian VGÖ seems to have belonged to this category of conservative Green parties. Recent developments in Austria indicate, however, that a process of internal clarification has commenced as the VGÖ joined electoral lists with the progressive ALÖ for the 1986 parliamentary election, and moved towards a unified organisation of the two Green parties. This led to the secession of the extreme right wing of the VGÖ, and a consolidation of the New Politics dimension in the new Greens.

Green New Politics Parties: Contrast and Congruence

Although the large majority of Green parties share a wide range of New Politics-induced characteristics, they are by no means alike. On the contrary, there are substantial differences between Green Parties that have led to fierce conflicts in the parliamentary group of the European parliament and brought international Green co-operation for the 1984 Euro-election campaign to the brink of collapse (Müller-Rommel 1985c: 392f).

In the light of these contrasts, it is a legitimate question whether it makes at all sense to speak of one 'new type of party'. However, provided that typologies are a useful heuristic tool if the observed cases have more in common than separates them, political reality as well as empirical analysis provides ample support for our classification (Poguntke 1987b; 1989). After all, experience has shown that despite all controversies, these Green parties have co-operated in many events.

Within the group of New Politics-orientated Green or ecological parties, two subgroups are identifiable: the 'Moderates' and the 'Fundamentalists'. At first glance, the distinction seems to rest on the position of a party on the traditional left–right scale, which is related to reproduce the conflict over the New Politics (Cotgrove/Duff 1980: 344ff; Dalton 1988: 121). However, although this conflict is not unrelated to the left–right continuum, it is primarily motivated by a disagreement over strategies as to how to accomplish the goals that are shared by both groups of parties. Whereas the Moderates believe in the eventual success of piecemeal reform, the Fundamentalists fear the pacifying and demobilising effects of this strategy. The choice of strategy is also related to different concepts of the state and the role of parliamentary politics. Many Green activists adhere to various shades of Marxist-inspired views of the state as an agent of the capitalist system which they in turn hold responsible for the problems of the environment and of society. From this perspective, the real power resides with those who run the industrial system, and politics is primarily seen as a phenomenon of the superstructure.

This interpretation suggests that there is little to be gained from the attempt to attain political control over the state machinery. It would be better to challenge 'the system' directly, through mass movements. This concept of societal 'counter power' (*Gegenmacht*) rests on the conviction that it is possible to effectively limit the power of state and industry through mass mobilisation. Furthermore, it implies that the parliamentary arena is not considered to be the place where decisions are made. Instead, it is primarily regarded as a useful arena to voice political opinions and mobilise people for extra-parliamentary action.

The Moderates, on the other hand, are influenced by the traditional liberal concept of the state as a relatively neutral and powerful instrument in the hands of those who have gained political control over it. Unlike classical liberals, however, Green moderates are considerably more sceptical about the real power of parliamentary politics. They do not deny the power of the industrial system, but believe, nevertheless, in the capacity of the state to influence the course of events.

Consistent with their preference for extra-parliamentary politics, Fundamentalists usually seek to forge broad alliances. Whereas the Moderates keep a close eye on their (parliamentary) respectability, radical Greens are less willing to denounce new social movement activists who get involved in violent confrontations with the police. However, this is primarily a strategic, not a substantive disagreement. Both Green tendencies are opposed to violent action, but the Fundamentalists argue that it is necessary not to isolate extremist activists who share Green goals.

It needs to be emphasised, however, that a preference for one of the opposing positions is not always ideologically motivated. In fact, much of the strategic debate has been marked by a conspicuous lack of theoretical reflection. Frequently, organisational history can provide important clues to understanding the relative importance of competing tendencies. Parties that are products of social movements have frequently struggled their way into political relevance through fierce and sometimes violent confrontations with the police. On the other hand, related bureaucratic and legal action by the state has not always appeared as impartial as it purported to be. A deeply rooted suspicion of the state and an erosion of trust in formalised political procedures is therefore likely to be widespread among movement activists.

Both tendencies, moderation and fundamentalism, are visible in New Politics-orientated Green parties. Besides the reasons discussed thus far, the predominance of one of these factions can also be explained by external, i.e. party system-specific or political factors. In countries where governmental participation is out of reach, responsible opposition may not be very attractive. The German Fundamentalists, for instance, gained influence in the Party after the collapse of the first red–green coalition in Hesse.

The radicalism of a Green party is also likely to be determined by the configuration of the national party system. Where an established left socialist — or even Euro-communist — party occupies the political space to the left of Social Democracy, a newly emergent Green party will find it more promising to embark on a moderate strategy.

Clearly, the distinction between moderate and fundamentalist Green parties is closer to a theoretical construct than to an empirical description. However, if we conceive of these two types as representing the opposite end of a continuum on which all genuine New Politics parties can be situated, the following pattern emerges: The Green parties of Ireland, Great Britain, Belgium (Ecolo), Sweden, Finland and parts of the fluid coalitions of the French Ecologists are closer to the moderate end, whereas the Belgium AGALEV, the Austrian ALÖ, the Swiss GAS, the other tendency of the French Greens, and the Greens in Luxemburg, Italy, and West Germany lean towards the fundamentalist side.

Naturally, most of our categorisations are not on altogether safe ground. Most of the Green parties are of relatively recent vintage, which means that the process of internal ideological clarification — including secessions — is still going on. The organisational existence of some parties is also very fluid because of their small size and all kinds of internal coups seem possible.

Conclusion

Our survey of Green parties and party types has demonstrated that our proposed model represents a suitable tool for identifying parties that owe their 'Gestalt' primarily to shifts towards the New Politics. These parties share the ideological, organisational and sociological properties that are associated with shifts towards New Politics. This sets them apart from established parties which build on the political traditions of the old politics. Even our 'negative' cases are only negative with respect to the whole New Politics syndrome. Their concern with some of these issues, particularly with environmental pollution, can be understood as a response to or a by-product of the New Politics.

The emergence of New Politics parties is likely to create severe difficulties for parties of the left in many countries. For many years, they could attract a good proportion of the young and educated vote which is now defecting to these parties, whereas conservative parties remain largely unaffected. Hence, in countries with non-fragmented party systems, the right is likely to enjoy a structural advantage for a considerable period of time, if the dominant party on the left does not succeed in coming to terms with the New Politics. Given the fundamental conflict involved, compromise is hard to achieve.

At the time of writing, it is difficult to predict which Green tendency will be dominant in the end. Clearly, much hinges on the format of the party system and systemic factors like the electoral system. However, as long as ever-expanding bureaucracies impinge on individual self-determination, as long as the menace of nuclear annihilation is not banned, and as long as one environmental catastrophe is only upstaged by yet another — frequently worse — disaster, it seems highly likely that Green parties of various kinds are here to stay.

References

Alber, Jens (1989), 'Modernization, Cleavage Structures and the Rise of Green Parties and Lists in Europe', in Ferdinand Müller-Rommel (ed.), *New Politics in Western Europe: The Rise and Success of Green Parties and Alternative Lists*, Boulder: Westview

Barnes, Samuel H., Max Kaase *et al*, (1979), *Political Action*, London, Beverly Hills, California: Sage

Baker Kendall *et al*, (1981), *Germany Transformed: Political Culture and the New Politics*, Cambridge, Mass. and London: Harvard University Press

Bürklin, Wilhelm P. (1984), *Grüne Politik*, Opladen: Westdeutscher Verlag

—— (1985a), 'The German Greens: The Post-Industrial Non-Established and the Party System', *International Political Science Review* 6/4, October

—— (1985b), 'The Split between the Established and the Non–Established Left in Germany', *European Journal of Political Research* 13/4

Cotgrove, Stephen and Andrew Duff (1981), 'Environmentalism, Values, and Social Change', *British Journal of Sociology* 32/1, March

Chandler, William M. and Alan Siaroff, (1986), 'Postindustrial Politics in Germany and the Origins of the Greens', *Comparative Politics* 18/3, April

Dalton, J. Russell (1984), 'Cognitive Mobilization and Partisan Dealignment in Advanced Industrial Democracies', *Journal of Politics* 46

—— (1988), *Citizen Politics in Western Democracies*, Chatham: Chatham House

Inglehart, Ronald (1971), 'The Silent Revolution in Europe: Intergenerational Change in Post-Industrial Societies', *American Political Science Review* 65/4, December

—— (1977), *The Silent Revolution*, Princeton: Princeton University Press

—— (1981), 'Post-Materialism in an Environment of Insecurity', *American Political Science Review* 75/4, December

Kitschelt, Herbert (1988), 'Left-Libertarian Parties: Explaining Innovation in Competitive Party Systems', *World Politics* 2

Ladner, Andreas (1989), 'Switzerland: Green and Alternative Parties', in Ferdinand Müller-Rommel (ed.), *New Politics in Western Europe: The Rise and the Success of Green Parties and Alternative Lists*, Boulder: Westview

Müller-Rommel, Ferdinand and Helmut Wilke, (1981), 'Sozialstruktur und "postmaterialistische" Wertorientierungen von Ökologisten'. *Politische Vierteljahresschrift* 22/4, December 92

Müller-Rommel, Ferdinand (1985), 'Das grün-alternative Parteienbündnis im Europäischen Parlament: Perspektiven eines neuen Phänomens'. *Zeitschrift für Parlamentsfragen* 16/3

—— (ed.) (1989), *New Politics in Western Europe: The Rise and Success of Green Parties and Alternative Lists*, Boulder: Westview

Murphy, Detlef *et al*, (1981), 'Haben "links" und "rechts" noch eine Zukunft? Zur aktuellen Diskussion über die politischen Richtungsbegriffe'. *Politische Vierteljahresschrift* 22:4, December

Nullmeier, Frank *et al*, (1983), *Umweltbewegungen und Parteiensystem. Umweltgruppen und Umweltparteien in Frankreich und Schweden*, Berlin: Quorum Verlag

Poguntke, Thomas (1987a), 'New Politics and Party Systems: The Emergence of a New Type of Party?', *West European Politics* 10/1, January

—— (1987b), 'Grün-alternative Parteien: Eine neue Farbe in westlichen Parteiensystemen'. *Zeitschrift für Parlamentsfragen* 18/3

—— (1989), 'The New Politics Dimension in European Green Parties', in Ferdinand Müller-Rommel (ed.), *New Politics in Western Europe: The Rise and Success of Green Parties and Alternative Lists*, Boulder: Westview

2

The Greens as a Milieu Party*

Hans-Joachim Veen

In the 1920s the two German political scientists Heinz Marr and Sigmund Neumann brought the term 'democratic integration party' into contemporary party research (Marr 1968; Neumann 1968 and 1965). This phrase was used to describe parties (for example, at that time, the SPD and the Catholic Centre Party) which were capable of bringing together politically large social groups across the main social, economic and ideological dividing lines and integrating them into relatively closed 'social milieus' (e.g. workers' milieu, Catholic milieu).

These large established milieus have since progressively disintegrated as increasing pluralism and destructuring changed all modern societies. The two people's parties (*Volksparteien*) of post-war Germany, the CDU/CSU and the SPD, no longer have their roots in established social milieus; on the contrary, they have rather 'lost their sociological and ideological context' (Hennis 1977: 188).

Paradoxically the founding of the Green Party was contrary to this trend. The Greens have their roots in a specific, clearly defined social structure, and see themselves as its party-political expression. In this way they are increasingly presenting themselves more as a 'milieu party' than an 'integration party' (with a more neutral focus on ideology and class).

The large social milieus which have emerged since the second half of the nineteenth century were described by M. Rainer Lepsius in an important and perceptive essay as the conservative milieu, the liberal milieu, the Catholic milieu and the socialist/social democratic milieu; political parties were little more than their 'political action committees' (Lepsius 1973: 56ff).

*Translated by Eva Kolinsky with Lindsay Batson

or as Wilhelm Hennis puts it: 'The party political extension of fixed social groups which had already been linked to the numerous organisations below party level' (Hennis 1977: 183). The secret of the decades of stability experienced by the SPD and the Centre Party lay undoubtedly in the extensive congruity between socio-cultural structure and party-political characteristics and in the identity between milieu and party in a highly structured, pre-modern society.

At the same time, however, there were pre-determined limits to their sphere of action and growth. In Imperial Germany and, to a lesser extent, during the Weimar Republic, the parties were concerned internally with integration and the preservation of the milieu and these concerns dominated their external political activities (Lepsius 1973: 66ff). The eventual detachment from these original social roots was inevitable after the Second World War in the wake of the radical destructuring and modernisation processes begun under National Socialism and as a result of the rapid social and industrial changes in the post-war period. The further development of the old milieu parties to modern people's/government's parties, who were to be solely responsible for the first proper parliamentary governmental system in German history, is undoubtedly amongst the greatest constitutional-political achievements of post-war political history.[1] However, the present day highly bureaucratised structure of the large people's parties (*Volksparteien*) which are increasingly regarded as quasi state institutions as far as influence, the cumulation of interests and of decision-making are concerned, has clouded the social roots of parties. This process has found its political science equivalent in their characterisation as 'mass and apparatus parties of modern type' (Mintzel, 1978a, 1978b: 261ff) which loses sight altogether of the original social purposes for the existence of political parties.

The unexpected relevance of milieu also explains the fact that, for a long time, predictions about the survival of the Green Party

---

1. These processes have been analysed in detail for the parties of the Ruhr area and in the Oldenburg region; see Kühr, Herbert (1979) 'Von der Volkskirche zur Volkspartei. Ein analytisches Stenogramm Zum Wandel der CDU im rheinischen Ruhrgebiet' in Herbert Kühr (ed.), *Vom Milieu zur Volkspartei*: 136ff; Naßmacher, Karl-Heinz (1979), 'Zerfall einer liberalen Subkultur. Kontinuität und Wandel im Parteiensystem in der Region Oldenburg, in Kühr, ibid: 30 ff.

were so inaccurate, since neither qualifications of their programme nor the qualifications of their leadership were responsible for or essential to its foundation and growth. It was, above
all the formation of a new socio-cultural, socio-moral and political-ideological milieu which evolved in the course of the far-
reaching social changes that have taken place since the end of
the 1960s. In addition, in the early 1970s a salient issue appeared
which became a political crystallisation point and provided the
impetus which eventually stimulated the Greens to organise
politically. This was the growing ecological crisis and threatening destruction of the environment.

The Greens are today the only newly-formed party to survive,
at least for the foreseeable future. The party has been able to
succeed in spite of the strong process of concentration in the
party systems and against the institutionalised restrictions built
into the German voting system, which up to this point had in
effect doomed to failure all attempts to establish new parties at
national level. This characterises the depth and intensity of the
changes in values, views of life and perceptions of political
issues which have taken place in the last 10 or 15 years. In
society these changes are evident in an indirect and modified
way; in the Greens they are largely reflected directly and without modifications — in *Reinkultur*.

The Green Milieu: Political Topography

The novel social milieu of the Green Party is determined by its
predominant political-ideological concord with respect to
values, life styles, views of life and everyday norms, by the
distinction of its own common culture and, last but not least, by
the density of its organisational network, which stabilises it
institutionally. The concentration of the Green milieu, and
hence its marked detachment from the predominant destruc-
tured structures of society, expresses itself, above all, politi-
cally-ideologically, socio-morally and socio-culturally, i.e. in the
form of a 'community with a common way of thinking'. The
milieu is not quite as distinctive sociologically, although it is
clearly distinguishable as regards education and occupational
structure. This broad statement will be underpinned on the

basis of empirical survey data in later sections of this chapter.[2]

There is little evidence, however, of one of the classical features of a milieu — the spatial and local concentration, as was apparent in the trade union milieu or Catholic milieu, and which is still evident in certain areas to this very day. Previously, local concentration was essential for the effective organisational and communicational cohesion and supervision of the milieu; this is no longer necessary as a result of improved communications and increased mobility. Certain spatial concentrations of the Green milieu are apparent in some cities and university towns, but the local concentration is by no means as extensive as is sometimes suggested. In the Bundestag elections of 1987 approximately 50% of all Green voters came from cities and university towns, whose population makes up only about 40% of the entire electorate. In recent years the Greens have apparently been able to attract more voters in medium-sized towns but not in rural regions.

The Green supporters' milieu can be described as a 'left-wing/alternative milieu' on the basis of the environment and lifestyle typology produced by the Research Institute of the Konrad-Adenauer-Foundation. This typology has broken new ground in structuring society according to value orientations and behaviour preferences (Gluchowski 1987).

The left-alternative milieu is not only the expression of radical secularisation processes in modern society, it is furthermore a specific product of the dialectic of the process of levelling which has occurred in the German affluent society. The left-alternative

2. This discussion is based on the representative statistics prepared by the Federal Statistical Office on the federal election in 1987 and also on data from two surveys which were conducted under the auspices of the Research Institute of the Konrad-Adenauer-Foundation; the first was carried out in March/April 1986 and was based on a representative sample of 5,015 respondents across the Federal Republic, the second was conducted in October 1986 with a representative sample of 3,004 respondents (archive numbers 8601 and 8603). In addition, two further surveys were carried out immediately before and after the federal elections in early 1987 (archive numbers 8701 and 8702) involving 1,053 and 2,025 respondents respectively. The data have been published together with detailed charts and numerous tables in Veen, Hans-Joachim (1987), 'Die Anhänger der Grünen. Ausprägungen einer neuen linken Milieupartei' in Manfred Langner (ed.), *Die Grünen auf dem Prüfstand*. In the context of this chapter, detailed presentation of these data has not been possible, and I shall repeatedly refer to 'Die Anhänger der Grünen'. A major reference point for comparison is the representative survey of 3,000 respondents which had been conducted by the Research Institute in the Spring of 1984 (archive number 8401); these data have been published in Veen, Hans-Joachim (1984), 'Wer wählt grün? Zum Profil der neuen Linken in der Wohlstandsgesellschaft', *Aus Politik und Zeitgeschichte* 35–36.

milieu lacks a common socio-economic interest, similar to that of the working class of the old SPD-milieu, which was held together by an impressive ideological superstructure — the vision of a great socialist future. The left-alternative milieu cannot be defined in socio-economic terms nor is its behaviour determined by economic interest. This results not least from the fact that it is based largely in the upper middle class where high earnings and good family backgrounds are the norm. What is more, the values of the milieu, as I understand it, are devoid of a teleological framework in the sense of a religious or pseudo-religious ideology. The strongly developed ('post-materialistic') emphasis placed on freedom and personal development is not an ideology of this kind but of a more limited scope; it is an essentially secular and even egocentric orientation.

Milieu and Protest

Shortly after the Bundestag elections of 1983 detailed empirical studies revealed that the Greens were much more than just an ecology party or a mere 'melting pot of political protests' (Veen 1984). This does not mean to say, however, that the Greens are not a heterogeneous party as well. They are, even today, a party through which current dissatisfactions, economic and social inequalities, direct concern with the destruction of the environment and various other worries are aired and through which — especially in local and Länder elections — the other parties or 'those at the top' are warned against complacency and passivity on ecological issues. Accordingly, the Greens also attract a mixed bunch of protest voters with highly varying motives, in particular those first-time and young voters who wish to cast a non-ideological vote for ecology and disarmament, and who are far removed from the left-alternative, 'post-materialist' milieu in their value orientations. Certainly, young voters and indeed the majority of the young generation have been socialised to be sensitive to ecological issues. It is possible for large numbers of current protest voters of this kind to turn to the Greens from any of the other parties within a very short space of time in the wake of acute environmental scandals, such as accidents involving nuclear power, etc. Finally the Greens are currently perceived as a protest party by the unemployed and receive a disproportionate share of their vote, particularly from young unemployed and unemployed young academics.

If one were to attempt to quantify the current situational protest potential amongst the present Green voters in comparison with the core potential of milieu voters, a maximum of one-third of today's Green voters could be called protest voters, whilst at least two-thirds could be regarded as core voters belonging to the milieu. This constitutes about 5–6% of the West German electorate as a whole.

The New Milieu and Green Party Support

The following discussion concentrates mainly on the Green supporters who belong to the milieu. For them, voting for the Greens almost without exception means supporting a fundamental and complex alternative to the system (Veen 1987: 68ff). It also indicates, as will be shown later, a fundamental protest against the system in almost all its forms from ecology to the economy and social system, to foreign policy and defence policy, to the concepts of law, society and democracy. This position of principal opposition began to become apparent in its political ideological and alternative structure as early as 1983 (Veen 1984: 7ff). The comprehensive alternative outlook is also based to a large extent on a pronounced ecological consciousness, which has been radicalised to become the sole point of reference for everything and hence demands a radical reform of society, the economy, international relations and last but not least the structure of human needs itself.

In the last few years the left alternative milieu and the Green Party have grown closer together. The milieu is now represented more strongly than ever by the party; in other words, the party has been increasingly successful in exhausting the milieu for its own party-political purposes. The main reason for this was that they were gradually able to attract many previous 'left-wing' SPD voters from the left-alternative milieu (Veen 1987: 73). There is still a latent tendency in many people to be attracted to both the SPD and the Greens and to waver between the two.

However, half of all present Green voters had voted for the party before. This self-recruitment rate of 50% of present voters must take into account the large increase in Green voters between 1983–4 and 1986–7. With reference to 1983–4 the proportion of voters who have remained faithful to the party is considerably greater.

With their increased number of core voters the Greens are attracting increasing numbers of voters between the ages of 25 and 34 but have also made clear gains with the 35 to 44 age group, i.e. the generation of extra-parliamentary opposition. According to official statistics for the Bundestag elections of 1987, 17.4% of 25 to 34 year-olds (an increase of 6.6 percentage points) voted for the Greens (Table 2.1). There was an increase of almost 10% in the age bracket 35 to 44. On the other hand the increase among young voters (18 to 24) has slowed down somewhat in recent years. In the Bundestag elections of 1987 15.5% of young voters opted for the Greens; the increase was below average (less than two percentage points). At the same time the Greens continue to be the party with the youngest electorate. They recruit about two-thirds of their voters from the 18 to 34 age group; if one extends the upper age bracket to 45, this then accounts for 85% of all Green voters.

Despite widely held views to the contrary, more men than women voted Green in the 1987 Bundestag election. Differentiating by age groups, however, shows that since 1986 substantially more young women (18 to 34) than men voted for the Greens.

The shift in the age structure has also led to a broader range in the employment structure (Table 2.2).

The proportion of voters not yet in employment (pupils, students, apprentices and men in military or alternative service) has dropped to approximately 30%. On the other hand the proportion of people in employment (white-collar workers and the self-employed) has risen in recent years to over 30%, as has the proportion of housewives and pensioners.

Compared with the population as a whole, blue-collar workers are under-represented whereas white-collar workers are clearly over-represented. The over-representation of voters not yet in employment is still by far the highest. The population average is 9% and amongst the Green voters it is approximately three times that amount.

Table 2.1. The Green Vote in the regions and the Bundestag by age and gender

	Bundestag elections 1980 1983 %		Länder elections 1983 %				1984		Länder 1985 %		Länder elections 1985 %		1986		Bundestag elections 1987 %
	1980	1983	RPF	SH	HB[1]	HE	BW	SAAR	BE[2]	NRW	NDS	BY	HH	1987
18–24 Years														
Men	5.3	14.2	12.5	11.1	21.9	14.9	18.1	6.2	27.1[3]	11.3	13.6	14.2	22.1	14.5
Women	4.3	13.5	13.0	10.2	17.8	14.8	19.6	5.6	24.0	11.8	16.1	16.3	28.5	16.5
Total	4.8	13.9	12.8	10.7	19.8	14.9	18.8	5.9	25.6	11.5	14.8	15.2	25.2	15.5
25–34 Years														
Men	2.6	11.5	9.1	7.5	19.8	13.7	16.2	4.8	17.6[3]	10.9	14.4	15.1	29.4	16.9
Women	2.1	10.1	6.6	6.5	18.6	12.1	15.3	4.5	15.4	10.3	16.8	16.5	30.3	17.9
Total	2.4	10.8	7.9	7.0	19.2	12.9	15.7	4.7	16.5	10.6	15.6	15.8	29.8	17.4
35–44 Years														
Men	0.9	4.7	3.3	2.3	7.0	5.0	7.2	2.2		4.3	6.4	8.2	17.1	9.9
Women	0.8	4.1	2.6	2.0	7.6	4.4	7.0	2.0		3.6	7.1	8.6	14.4	9.3
Total	0.9	4.4	3.0	2.1	7.4	4.7	7.1	2.1		3.9	6.8	8.4	15.8	9.6

45–59 Years	Men	0.6	2.4	1.9	1.5	3.9	2.1	3.8	1.5	3.8	1.7	2.3	3.3	3.7	3.7
	Women	0.6	2.4	1.7	1.5	3.5	2.3	4.0	1.0	3.6	1.6	3.1	3.8	4.0	3.9
	Total	0.6	2.4	1.8	1.5	3.8	2.2	3.9	1.3	3.7	1.6	2.7	3.5	3.9	3.8
60 Years and above	Men	0.4	1.5	1.2	1.1	2.4	1.4	2.4	1.0	1.5	1.1	1.6	1.9	1.9	2.2
	Women	0.3	1.1	0.7	0.7	2.4	0.9	2.1	0.6	1.1	0.6	1.3	1.8	2.0	1.6
	Total	0.4	1.2	0.9	0.8	2.4	1.1	2.2	0.7	1.2	0.8	1.4	1.9	2.0	1.8
All voters	Men	1.6	5.9	4.9	3.8	8.6	6.3	8.2	2.8	12.3	4.8	6.3	7.3	11.9	8.3
	Women	1.2	4.8	3.7	2.9	7.0	5.1	7.2	2.2	8.4	3.9	6.5	7.2	10.0	7.7
	Total	1.4	5.3	4.3	3.3	7.8	5.7	7.6	2.5	10.1	4.4	6.4	7.3	10.8	8.0

1. Bremen Green List and the Greens
2. Alternative List
3. In the 1985 election the groups 18–29 and 30–44 were chosen to protect the secrecy of the election

RPF	Rhineland Palatinate	BE	Berlin
SH	Schleswig-Holstein	NRW	North Rhine-Westphalia
HB	Bremen	NDS	Lower Saxony
HE	Hesse	BY	Bavaria
BW	Baden-Württemberg	HH	Hamburg
Saar	Saar Region		

Source: Representative statistics from the *Statistisches Bundesamt* or *Statistische Landesämter*

Table 2.2. The occupational structure of West German Party electorates

	Blue-collar workers			White-collar employees			Civil Servants			Self-employed			In education[1]			Unemployed			Housewives, Pensioners		
	80	84 %	86	80	84 %	86	80	84 %	86	80	84 %	86	80	84 %	86	80	84 %	86	80	84 %	86
Population as a whole	14	15	14	21	21	20	6	5	5	6	7	6	11	9	9	1	3	3	41	41	42
CDU/CSU supporters	12	13	11	20	20	18	6	6	5	10	10	8	8	6	6	1	1	2	44	45	49
SPD supporters	19	19	18	20	21	20	6	5	5	2	2	4	12	7	8	1	4	3	40	43	41
FDP supporters	6	4	10	29	28	27	8	8	7	6	14	9	16	8	9	1	0	2	34	38	36
Green supporters	8	16	11	20	20	26	10	6	5	3	2	5	45	36	28	2	5	6	9	16	20

1. Pupils, Students, Apprentices, Men in military and alternative service

Source: Research Institute of the Konrad-Adenauer-Foundation

Archive Nr. 8012: 6,202 respondents
Archive Nr. 8401: 3,000 respondents
Archive Nr. 8601 & 8603: 3,201 respondents
(together)

The broadening of the age spectrum has still not altered the fact that the Greens are the party with the highest level of formal education. Almost 40% hold the German equivalent of 'A' levels (senior matriculation) or a degree and a further 30% have the equivalent of 'O' levels (high school matriculation). People educated in secondary modern schools or equivalent minimum levels are likewise vastly under-represented amongst the Green voters (30%) in comparison with the population as a whole, (Veen 1987: 80).

Hence the Greens are no longer as exclusively the party of student youth protest, people not yet in employment or high income young academics as they were a few years ago.

Value Orientations and Green Party Support

The development of the Green supporters into a group with a common political and ideological outlook has taken shape against the background of the broadening of age, education and employment structures which accompanied the growth of the party. The Green supporters have become progressively more coherent in terms of their political-ideological orientations, values, fears, priorities and principally 'anti' views and manners of behaviour. In 1986 Green supporters, when asked to classify themselves on the political scale, gave answers which varied from clearly 'left' of centre to radically left-wing, and accordingly stressed that they were left of the SPD (Veen 1987: 82–6).

This self-classification has stabilised in recent years. Whilst the CDU is rated by Green supporters to be even further right in the party spectrum than was the case a few years ago or even extreme right wing, the smallest distance relatively speaking is seen to be between the Greens and the SPD. At first glance, such a formal ideological self-evaluation enables one to measure the distances as they are perceived between the parties and will be explained more fully in the course of this chapter. In order to do so, it is necessary to consider the value-orientations of the Green supporters, since these are closely interwoven with the political-ideological views and since the complex left-wing/ alternative milieu consists of a blend of values, everyday norms, political-ideological views and priorities. For the Greens not

Table 2.3. Value orientations and party preferences (1986)

	Purely orientated towards duty and acceptance %	Mixed orientations: more orientated towards		Purely orientated towards personal development %
		duty and acceptance %	personal development %	
Population as a whole	7.2	46.2	37.2	9.4
CDU/CSU supporters	11.6	56.3	30.0	2.1
FDP supporters	9.1	52.4	34.1	4.3
SPD supporters	4.3	42.2	42.8	10.7
Green supporters	0.9	18.4	42.1	38.5

Source: Research Institute of the Konrad-Adenauer-Foundation, Archive Nr. 8601: 5,015 respondents.

only have a common outlook as regards political beliefs, they share a sense of individual values and lifestyles.

Such values as were described (somewhat confusingly) by Inglehart (1977) as 'materialistic' and (more accurately) by Klages (1984) as orientations towards duty and acceptance, are practically non-existent amongst the Greens (Table 2.3). In other words, they have no regard for traditional values; have a low esteem for law and order; and consider the fulfilment of duty, self-discipline, thrift and hard work to be less important virtues than do the rest of the population. On the whole, they reject achievement, wealth and career-mindedness.

On the other hand the 'anti-type' of pure 'orientation towards freedom and personal development' is extraordinarily strongly represented amongst Green supporters — almost 40% of them fall into this category, compared with a population average of only 10%. This orientation towards freedom and personal development means that core values are the unrestricted freedom of speech, individual freedom, personal development, equality for women, a willingness to accept new ideas and the right of co-determination at work. Tolerance, sexual freedom, workers'

Table 2.4. Values in West German society and among Green Party
supporters (1986)

	Degree to which values are perceived to be realised			
	Population as a whole		Green supporters	
	Too much	Too little	Too much	Too little
	%	%	%	%
Hard work	49	24	63	12
Effective economy	49	17	58	16
Meaningful and satisfying work	40	31	29	53
Tolerance	34	40	27	58
Sense of duty	48	27	62	18
Solidarity	35	33	23	55
Capable government	44	19	43	23
Sexual freedom	49	18	33	34
Promotion at work	56	15	54	18
Co-determination at work	42	27	25	51

Source: Research Institute of the Konrad-Adenauer-Foundation, Archive Nr.
8603: 3,004 respondents.

co-determination and solidarity, on the other hand, are deemed
underdeveloped in society;[3] and this likewise contrasts with the
views of the rest of the population (Table 2.4).

This theoretical distinction of the two sets of values is necessary to our analysis, but it alone does not adequately explain the
many possible combinations of these values which exist in real
life. Value types are normally mixed in the population with a
large number of variations. In total more than 80% of the
population possess orientations towards both duty and personal
development in varying degrees. If one attempts to classify
individuals according to their dominant orientations, it is found
that more than half of the population are predominantly orientated towards duty and acceptance, whilst a third are orientated
towards personal development. Those Greens who do possess

3. The terminology has been adapted from Inglehart, Ronald (1977), *The Silent Revolution*
and its further refinement in the critical evaluation of Inglehart by Dittrich, Karl-Heinz
(1984), *Wertorientierungen, Zeitwahrnehmung und politischer Protest* and also Klages, Helmut
(1984), *Wertorientierungen im Wandel*.

mixed orientations do so in proportions which are practically the reverse of those in the population as a whole: 42% are predominantly orientated towards freedom and personal development whilst only 18% are orientated towards duty and acceptance. In this way more than 80% of Green supporters could be described as holding freedom and personal development-orientated values.

The predominance of freedom and personal development orientations is the distinguishing mark of the left/alternative milieu and its socio-ideological core. It also includes the rejection of the predominant orientations, traditional principles and everyday norms of West German society.

Within this left/alternative orientation there is a marked contrast between the emphasis placed on individual self-realisation on the one hand and, on the other, the striving for solidarity, equality, warmth, a sense of belonging and the need to spend one's leisure within a circle of like-minded friends. These kinds of social needs may be meaningfully fulfilled within the small world of the milieu. Often however, the mental conflict for the individual between identification and autonomy remains unresolved.

Aims and Issues

Pessimism about the future is particularly predominant amongst Green supporters, in contrast with the population as a whole. There is a widespread fear of atomic and ecological catastrophes and of war. In the left/alternative milieu the most important political issues are peace, protection of the environment and the banning of nuclear power. These three political priorities vary considerably from the priorities of the rest of the population, for whom, although peace and ecology rank very highly, job security, pensions, economic development and internal security are also prime concerns (Table 2.5).

On the other hand many Greens apparently do not see economic/political questions and the material requirements of the welfare state as problems. On the whole, a high level of economic prosperity is taken for granted. Accordingly economic virtues are underdeveloped amongst Green supporters and are not very highly rated. The importance of the economy is viewed

Table 2.5. Political priorities of party supporters (1986)

| | In October 1986 the following problems were described as very important by: | | | | |
	Population as a whole %	CDU/CSU supporters %	SPD supporters %	FDP supporters %	Green supporters %
To maintain peace	83	82	84	80	92
To secure jobs	81	81	84	83	80
To secure pensions	71	71	76	73	61
To protect the environment	65	58	70	54	90
To maintain a stable economy	63	69	63	67	41
To maintain stable prices	56	60	56	58	37
To protect the public from crime	56	61	54	50	28
To increase the resources spent on the health service	53	49	54	42	68
To ease the burden on families with children	51	48	57	41	62
To be more concerned with social justice	50	40	63	34	65
To improve social benefits	43	32	54	32	59
To increase detente with the Soviet Union	41	37	48	35	50

Source: Research Institute of the Konrad-Adenauer-Foundation, Archive Nr. 8603: 3,004 respondents.

mainly in terms of personal development, satisfying work and the right to co-determination at the workplace.

Socio-political demands, however, are attributed a higher value amongst Green supporters than among supporters of other parties, even higher than among SPD-supporters, who traditionally place great emphasis on social policy.

The fact that questions of internal security and crime prevention are placed almost at the end of the scale of political priorities by the Green supporters whilst it is considered far more important by the rest of the population is hardly surprising when one considers the underdeveloped awareness of the rule of law, as will be further examined below.

The stark difference of opinion between the Greens and the rest of the population is particularly pronounced in the case of opinions about the dangers to peace and about the North Atlantic Treaty Organisation: 50% of Green supporters see the USA as the power which poses the greatest threat to world peace, and only 10% the Soviet Union. This is in clear contrast to the opinions held in the population as a whole (Veen 1987: 97). Further development of detente with the Soviet Union is regarded to be far more important by Green supporters than by the rest of the population.

Almost two-thirds of Green supporters reject NATO as an instrument for maintaining peace in Europe (Table 2.6). The number of Greens who reject it has grown in recent years. In 1986, 60% of the population considered NATO to be necessary for the maintenance of peace in Western Europe, but only 19% of Green supporters did, even fewer than two years earlier.

Apparently the vast majority of Green supporters hope to solve the problem of maintaining peace through the neutralisation of the Federal Republic and Western Europe. Since 1983 the predominant position of the peace movement has declined, but it still plays an important part and, indeed, in the eyes of its supporters the peace movement today is increasingly widening its scope and is no longer restricted to problems of security and disarmament. Rüdiger Schmitt agreed recently in a careful empirical study that membership of the peace movement is closely related to the political support of the ecology and anti-nuclear movements (Schmitt 1987: 110ff). Hence the peace movement today — similar to the citizens' initiatives and ecology move-

Table 2.6. Views of NATO and Party Support

| | Respondents[1] holding the opinion that peace can only be maintained | | | | | |
| | through NATO | | | through a neutral Europe without NATO | | |
	October 1984 %	October 1986 %	Difference 84/86 %	October 1984 %	October 1986 %	Difference 84/86 %
Population as a whole	57	60	+3	20	22	+ 2
CDU/CSU supporters	79	82	+3	7	6	− 1
SPD supporters	49	50	+1	24	31	+ 7
FDP supporters	64	67	+3	16	21	+ 5
Green supporters	27	19	−8	51	65	+14

1. This information was gathered from a sample of 100 respondents.

Source: Research Institute of the Konrad-Adenauer-Foundation, Archive Nr. 8405: 3,060 respondents; 8603: 3,004 respondents.

ments — no longer spans the party spectrum. It feeds into political support for the Greens, and to a lesser extent for the SPD. Approximately two-thirds of adherents to the peace movement prefer the Green Party. 'There are no Greens opposed to the peace movement' (Schmitt 1987: 124).

The two circles of supporters overlap and come mainly from the same left/alternative milieu consisting of younger voters with a left-wing political-ideological stance, a formal higher education and an orientation towards freedom and personal development. The dove of peace against a blue background, the anti-nuclear badge and the sunflower have practically become interchangeable symbols of the complex opposition to the system in the milieu.

It is apparent amongst Green supporters that the previously predominant equidistance in their attitudes towards the USA and Soviet Union as world powers has increasingly given way to an aggressive anti-Americanism, whilst the Soviet Union is increasingly seen as more trustworthy. The Soviet Union tends to be regarded by Green supporters as a far more peace-loving power than the USA. As the vast majority of Green supporters can hardly be accused of simple pro-communism — such a false assumption would belittle the complex sociological and ideological gravity of the left/alternative milieu — one is left with the overriding impression that their opinion of the Soviet Union, although they refuse to admit it, is dominated by defeatism. Opportunistically they favour the power which is assumed to be stronger in world affairs. Peace at any price — in strange contrast to the highly sensitive striving for individual freedom and personal development — is apparently accepted for the sake of pure survival in the face of deep pessimism about the future and an apparent reluctance to assert themselves, perhaps under the private illusion that they would ultimately be able to retreat unharmed into their small world of the milieu.

The Green supporters' political horizon is comparatively narrow. In contrast to the 'man on the street', their view of political problems is reduced to disarmament, neutralism, ecology and socio-political priorities which range from classical socio-political demands through egalitarian concepts of justice to women's equality. The latter is particularly strongly felt by the Green supporters. Paradoxically, these socio-political demands as well as demands for considerable financial support are directed towards a state which they deeply mistrust and reject.

Milieu and Institutional Networks

Green supporters see the state of the Basic Law as an instrument of repression, of the curtailment of civil rights and as a controlling attack on the (in their opinion) individual's limitless free self-determination. Nowhere is the dissatisfaction with the democracy and the internal distance towards the Second German Republic as great as among Green supporters.

Mistrust of the state institutions runs deep. Obedience to the law is often underdeveloped, and on the other hand the conviction is widespread that one is able to violate, not only the 'formal' system of law, which they accuse of 'mere legality', but also the decisions of high courts, in the name of higher legality and 'questions of human survival' (Veen 1986: 105ff). This could be interpreted in terms of the extreme pessimism about the future to be found amongst Green supporters. For when one is ruled by the fear of a world catastrophe in the immediate future, legal boundaries seem to dissipate. However, such an explanation strikes me as too superficial, since the concept of a state of emergency and the playing off of a presumably higher legitimacy against mere legality is part of an unfortunate tradition of anti-parliamentarism and has been empirically evident since the second half of the 1970s, in the case of the disagreements about squatting, for example. At that time there was no predominant fear of an ecological crisis. Is it no more appropriate to recall that in politics, more than anywhere else, ideologies and above all concepts have consequences, that is, they may alter one's view of reality and ultimately become reality themselves? (Bergsdorf 1978).

In this very sense terms such as Galtung's 'structural violence' (1975) and Marcuse's 'repressive tolerance' (1965) have become key terms since the student revolt of the late 1960s in understanding the ideological reality, which greatly influenced whole generations of students — who frequently became teachers of civics — and which became popularised over the years to common knowledge, whilst their political contexts are long forgotten. Today, in the intellectual circles of the Greens, similar attempts are being made to coin phrases in order to defame this republic, partly as a joke, and partly as a systematic plan to introduce them into popular discourse: 'formal democracy', 'majority democracy' or 'legitimacy of legality' — fatal parallels to Carl Schmitt's denunciation of the first republic. (See Guggenberger 1986); Oberreuter 1986; Mandt 1985.)

The accentuated distance towards the system and its institutions corresponds within the left/alternative milieu to the cohesion of organisational networks. In them the internal structure of the milieu is developed. These include, the direct forerunners of the party, the citizens' initiative and ecology movements, as well as the other organisations and action committees which gradually formed in the context of the so-called new social movements, the peace movement, the Third World movement, the civil rights movement, and the women's movement, to name but a few (Schulte 1984; Langguth 1984: 10). To this day they still constitute the milieu to a certain extent in a political/ideological sense and form a rudimentary, disjointed and decentralised organisational structure.

Still more important for the inner constitution of the milieu are those institutions which aim to mould and protect the complete range of individual and social interrelations of life, very similar to the integration of the workers' milieu through the SPD, which in the metaphor of Heinz Marr extended 'from the cradle through the allotments to the grave', from the proletarian adult education group to the savings' clubs, from workers' welfare to the communal cremation society (Marr 1986: 344). The corresponding integration network of the left/alternative milieu is not as extensive, and is being based on life cycles. It ranges from so-called free schools practising alternative reformist pedagogy and other educational institutions, to health food co-operatives, self-help groups, alternative trade, agriculture and services, or from alternative cultural institutions (bookshops, newspapers, magazines) to lawyers' and doctors' collectives. To date, only an alternative undertaker is missing.

The multiplicity and diversity of such institutions reveals the liveliness of a highly complex organism, which is also full of internal quarrels, conflicts, competition and a high degree of internal frictional loss. The milieu has become an entire environment. For many people it satisfies their economic, cultural and social needs, and above all their emotional needs of belonging and security. The price to be paid is then frequently a more or less subtle pressure to conform.

The increase in Green voters in recent years indicates that the party has been successful in reaching the left/alternative milieu; in other words, the milieu has become increasingly explicitly represented by the party — milieu and party have merged into one another.

The Use of Politics

This milieu sees itself as a fundamental political alternative, but today no longer seems, if I have interpreted the signs correctly, to have a predominant outward political orientation which is so intent on actively changing the whole of society. It appears to have become increasingly inward-looking and concentrates on the milieu and its anti-culture as an alternative way of living. In other words, demands for a radical change of the system have been displaced by an orientation towards one's own living environment.

In my opinion this observation is supported by various empirical findings on the subject of political interest, the analysis of the 1987 Bundestag elections and not least by the concrete political judgements of the party itself which, at first glance, appear to be strangely at odds with the basic ideological position of Green supporters.

Firstly, it is noteworthy that the political interest of Green supporters has continually declined in the last three years (Veen 1987: 109). The advantage the Greens always enjoyed over other parties in having voters who were highly interested in politics has declined. Today, political interest amongst FDP supporters and Green supporters is practically the same. A particular feature of the party, which seemed to point to an above average potential for activity and involvement, has gradually deteriorated. The decline in political interest cannot be explained as a result of partisan dealignment, since the political-ideological profile of Green supporters has in fact become sharper.

Views of elections are a case in point. Green supporters attached less relevance to the Bundestag elections of 1987 than other voters, and one-third considered the result as of little importance (Table 2.7). Yet Green supporters were more satisfied with the election result itself than were the SPD supporters. More than one-third said they were ('very' or 'fairly') satisfied with the Greens' performance, and less than two-thirds were dissatisfied with the election result. Indeed, the Greens gained the most in the election with a growth of 2.7 percentage points, but failed to reach their stated election aim, to break the majority of the CDU/CSU-FDP coalition. The fairly relaxed evaluation of the election results is remarkable when one thinks this government, and particularly the CDU/CSU, symbolises everything the Green Party and its supporters reject. It appears rather as though elections have become uninteresting to a considerable number of Green supporters.

As much as Green supporters see themselves as a fundamental alternative, they apparently have very little concept of themselves as a concrete alternative to the government: in 1986 less than 15% of Green supporters considered their party to be capable of governing, even less than in 1983. The belief that

Table 2.7. Importance of the outcome of the 1987 Federal elections

	Extremely important %	Election Results Fairly important %	less/not at all important %
Population as a whole	24	53	23
CDU/CSU voters	33	54	13
SPD voters	21	63	16
FDP voters	28	52	20
Green voters	24	45	31

Source: Research Institute of the Konrad-Adenauer-Foundation, Spring 1987, Archive Nr. 8702: 2,025 respondents.

their party has the best politicians is rapidly declining. Whilst in 1983 almost 40% were of this opinion, by 1986 it was only 20%. Almost as many even considered their party to be 'unrealistic'.

The fact that, at the same time, 90% of Green supporters wish their party would form a coalition with the SPD is not affected by these self-critical judgements. The desire for a coalition only applies in the hypothetical case of being part of the government, in whatever form. It does not tally with the fundamentalist posture of rejecting political co-operation and collaboration which also permeates the Greens.

In the eyes of its supporters the party does also have many very positive aspects, particularly its concern with the future, its representation of the interests of the socially disadvantaged, its honesty and trustworthiness and its concentration on essential problems rather than on gaining and retaining power. This emerged from an image profile of the Greens compiled by the Research Institute in 1986. However, only relatively few Green supporters (29%) believed their own party to be capable of actually governing, of making a political impact and of solving the problems of the future; 21% believed the SPD capable, but the majority (33%) believed that none of the political parties could be effective. The evaluation of the Bundestag elections in 1987, and earlier surveys of regional elections revealed that Green voters, contrary to common belief, are no longer more certain that they would go and vote than voters of the other parties.

Their responsiveness to voting, i.e. the ability of the party to mobilise, has visibly declined. Apart from a small number of fundamentalists who refuse to vote, the reason for this could lie in a decreasing interest in politics or a certain apathy towards anything which occurs outside of their own personal environment.

It seems necessary to modify the commonly held view of the Green supporter as 'homo politicus', strongly interested in politics, highly motivated, easy to mobilise and fundamentally orientated towards change; and to view it in relative terms against the background of the establishment of the party in the political system and the emergence of the milieu in society. Green supporters have become less geared to change and more entrenched in their alternative culture and attitudes.

In the course of the growth and consolidation of their own milieu, at least some of the Green supporters seem to have abandoned those activities which originally were more strongly orientated towards changing the system. The political utopia of the radical alternative to the system appears to many who actually live in the alternative milieu in the meantime (in the sense of Hegel) to have been incorporated. This dialectic of the alternative way of thinking would explain the contradictions to be found amongst a growing segment of Green supporters: the citizens in their electoral milieu (I am not talking about party activists) have become politically self-sufficient and no longer have an economic interest in voting. Whilst more and more voters of the people's parties (*Volksparteien*) are using their vote in a tactical and instrumental manner while maintaining an inner distance to their choice, the Green voters primarily vote 'for themselves'. The act of voting is seen primarily as an act of identification, a political demonstration of the fact that one is different. Voting becomes an ideological and socio-cultural self-assurance of the milieu. Participation in elections does not as a result become unimportant, but it has become detached from expectations of political efficacy or influence. The electoral participation of Green supporters can be seen as a measure of the milieu's collective memory and an affirmation of alternative principles and convictions. From this perspective, parliamentary representation can be seen primarily as the constitutional-political guarantee that one's interests *vis-à-vis* the system continue to be voiced.

Milieu, Party and Democratic System

Nowhere is the need for the symbolic demonstration of one's opinions and for visible identification with one's environment and party as strong as in the left/alternative milieu. Nowhere else are there more heavily symbolic, more diverse and frequently also more imaginative badges, posters, stickers and signs in all shapes and sizes and for all occasions. Spectacular mass demonstrations, sit-ins, festivals and celebrations also serve to establish identity and to aid self-assurance, in addition to their political function. They enable the social components of the milieu to develop in a close environment together with people of the same opinions. Here the milieu becomes tangible and visually distinguishable, in no way uniform, rather diverse and colourful, but nevertheless clearly separate in its deviation from the prevailing standards of outward appearances, in its styles, the colours of its clothes and its accessories.

However, this observation extends beyond external differences to the increasingly noticeable everyday culture typical of the milieu, which is not only notably different from everyday norms in the sense of consumer behaviour and lifestyles, but also with relation to interpersonal behaviour, in scope and appearance, in social rituals in the understanding of work and organisation of free time. Just as the workers' culture was once visible in the solemn, proud procession on 1 May — and still is perceptible in some quarters of cities in the Ruhr — the left/alternative milieu also reveals its distinctive features most clearly in those areas where it is concentrated socially in street processions or where supporters live together contentedly in a restricted space with their own shops, boutiques, cafés and pubs on the corner in old buildings in what were once upper middle-class environments.

The internal integration of the milieu, the establishment and preservation of identity on the one hand, and the external representation of interests on the other, were likewise classical functions of the old integration parties SPD and Centre. In contrast to the Greens, however, they integrated in two ways, primarily inwardly, but also externally, as they enabled their supporters to participate in the system and aimed to integrate them into the middle-class society of their time. However, in the left-wing/alternative milieu today, the second function is not performed for two reasons. Its members do not experience economic problems which would make them dependent on the system, while the refusal to integrate and the emphatically anti-cultural character of the milieu constitute the core of its basic beliefs.

It seems that economic independence, a certain modesty as regards financial needs and accentuated anti-cultural views favour the tendency towards progressive self-isolation and towards sectarianism. This tendency appears to me, if I see it correctly, at the moment not to be predominant for the majority of milieu supporters. Their attachment to the milieu remains rather ambivalent, and, dialectically, integrated in the very system they reject: fundamental opposition to the system and an alternative lifestyle in the comfortable niches of this society go hand in hand.

The apparent inward orientation of the milieu supporters has a completely different political validity than the apparently growing inward fixation of the party (Fogt 1988). Events at the last party congresses and the largely introspective selection of candidates for offices within the party and in parliaments indicate the progression of fundamentalist doctrinaire tendencies among the leaders and office holders of the party.

The tendency towards intellectual and cultural erosion and dogmatic narrowing of the inner variety of the milieu can be traced to would-be revolutionary gestures of a self-styled avant-garde and the intolerant dominance of the self-appointed male and female political commissions in the party leadership.[4]

Robert Michels' oligarchy theory (1911) is confirmed once again: the emancipation of the party leadership from its supporters is apparently also true for a party committed to grass roots democracy. Perhaps this poses the greatest medium-term threat to the survival of the Greens. The discrepancy between

---

4. The observation which Rainer Lepsius made in relation to the internal crises of milieu parties in Imperial Germany turns out to be of fascinating significance if applied to the Greens today: 'In a circular process the scope of action of the political leadership becomes increasingly narrow [as the leadership strata becomes increasingly homogeneous — H.J.V] and focused on the interests of the representatives of the dominant milieu. This tends to alienate those segments of the population whose interests no longer appear to be considered; the concern with the milieu narrows the scope of action of the party and its leadership further.'

the views of the milieu and the aims which have been defined by the party seems to have grown in recent years. It must be borne in mind that there is considerable tolerance, indifference and equanimity amongst Green supporters towards the political activities of their party, as long as Green policy does not endanger the existence of the milieu itself. At the moment only current protest voters could be deterred by the structural argument between 'fundamentalists' and 'realists'. The intense media interest in the frictions meets with little response in the milieu. In this respect a progression of the anti-parliamentarist fundamentalism could reduce the Green electorate to the milieu, but the political existence of the party would only be seriously questioned if the authoritarian behaviour of the party elite were to tangibly affect the anti-authoritarian basic left/alternative views and the self-contained lifestyle in the milieu.

The milieu in its current internal constitution will hardly allow itself to become involved in sectarian total separation and rigorous 'anti' opinions, apart from a few esoterical, radical/autonomous and anarchistic circles which already exist within it.

Were the party to take a strictly fundamentalist course, the political opinions faced by the milieu would either be to refuse to vote or to support the SPD instead, to whom they in any case feel a latent affinity. In my opinion the more probable and more viable development perspective of the Greens would appear to be to constantly balance the ambiguous positions in the milieu and to aim for partial participation in parliament and also for full participation in the system, proceeding in a way at once fundamentalist and realist — not dissimilar to the early stages of the democratic integration parties in Imperial Germany. This delicate state of balance could last all the longer, since, in contrast to the old integration parties, the aim of the Greens is not to integrate into the system and to participate in the government, but to combine non-commitment to parliament with an alternative culture on economically secure foundations.

The consequences for the parliamentary system are serious because the Greens do not achieve the degree of integration of interests which is necessary for parties' ability to govern, to be compehensible and display clarity about political responsibility and inner stability.

The large people's parties are often held in low esteem and in my opinion are measured by the false and out-dated social and ideological yardsticks of how they are embedded in a milieu and by their 'social integration and ability for emotional enrichment' (Hennis 1983: 93). They are criticised for being 'catch-all parties' (Kirchheimer 1985: 20) and are often misjudged in their arduous yet dull efforts at the essential work of aggregating, moderating and integrating. In the last analysis, and without a nostalgic hankering after a lost political home — *Parteiheimat* — catch-all parties have to be viewed positively again (Oberreuter 1983). As a 'modern type of mass and apparatus party', as Alf Mintzel (1978) describes them in his somewhat long-winded attempt at classification, the people's party is, at the end of the day, not the more superficial but rather the more advanced, that is the party type suited to modern society and the democratic political system. Its constitutional-political achievements are fundamental to the governability and the liberal cohesion of a society which is becoming increasingly pluralistic, and to its stabilisation and its ability to make compromises and shape policies. The detachment of the people's parties (*Volksparteien*) from their old contexts was essential for their new responsible function in the parliamentary system of government. This function of parliamentary participation involves 'also the fulfilment of the task of directing the community, and that means primarily being able to govern . . . that is mainly their [the parties', H-J.V.] responsibility' (Hennis 1977: 158).

A parliamentary party which could possibly restrict the ability of parliament to form a majority through boycotting coalitions and hence prevents the alternation of parties between opposition and government, may create a structural asymmetry in the party system and in the government, and contribute to the destruction of the democratic legitimacy of the political system.

References

Bergsdorf, Wolfgang (1978), *Politik und Sprache*, Munich and Vienna: Olzog

Dittrich, Karl-Heinz (1984), *Wertorientierungen, Zeitwahrnehmung und politischer Protest*, Doctoral Dissertation (D. Phil) of the University of Speyer

Fogt, Helmut (1988), 'Zwischen Parteiorganisation und Bewegung: Die Rekrutierung der Mandatsträger bei den Grünen', in Heinrich Oberreuter (ed.), *Wer kommt in die Parlamente?*, Baden-Baden: Nomos

Galtung, Johan (1974), *A Structural Theory of Revolutions: Violent and Non-Violent Action in Industrial Societies*, Rotterdam: Rotterdam University Press

Gluchowski, Peter (1987), 'Lebensstile und Wandel der Wählerschaft in der Bundesrepublik Deutschland', *Aus Politik und Zeitgeschichte*, 12

Guggenberger, Bernd (1986), 'An den Grenzen von Verfassung und Mehrheitsentscheidung oder: Die neue Macht der Minderheit', in Heinrich Oberreuter, *Wahrheit statt Mehrheit?*, Munich: Olzog

Hennis, Wilhelm (1977), 'Parteienstruktur und Regierbarkeit', in Wilhelm Hennis, Peter von Kielmansegg and Ulrich Matz (eds.), *Regierbarkeit*, Volume 1, Stuttgart: Klett-Cotta

—— (1983), 'Überdehnt und abgekoppelt. An den Grenzen des Parteienstaates', in Christian Graf von Krockow (ed.), *Brauchen wir ein neues Parteiensystem?*, Frankfurt: Europäische Verlagsanstalt

Inglehart, Ronald (1977), *The Silent Revolution*, Princeton: Princeton University Press

Kirchheimer, Otto (1985), 'Der Wandel des westeuropäischen Parteiensystems', *Politische Vierteljahresschrift* 1

Klages, Helmut (1984), *Wertorientierungen im Wandel: Rückblick, Gegenwartsanalyse, Prognosen*, Frankfurt: Campus

Kühr, Herbert (1979), 'Von der Volkskirche zur Volkspartei: Ein analytisches Stenogramm zum Wandel der CDU im rheinischen Ruhrgebiet', in Herbert Kühr (ed.), *Vom Milieu zur Volkspartei*, Königstein/Ts: Anton Hain

Langguth, Gerd (1984), *Der grüne Faktor*, Zürich: Edition Interfrom

Langner, Manfred (ed.) (1987), *Die Grünen auf dem Prüfstand*, Bergisch Gladbach: Lübbe

Lepsius, Rainer M. (1973), 'Parteiensystem und Sozialstruktur: Zum Problem der Demokratisierung der deutschen Gesellschaft', in Gerhard A. Ritter (ed.), *Deutsche Parteien vor 1918*, Cologne: Kiepenheuer & Witsch

Mandt, Hella (1985), 'Kritik der Formaldemokratie und Entförmlichung der politischen Auseinandersetzung', *Zeitschrift für Politik* 2

Marcuse, Herbert (1965), 'Repressive Toleranz', in Robert Paul Wolff, Barrington Moore and Herbert Marcuse, *Kritik der reinen Toleranz*, Frankfurt: Suhrkamp

Marr, Heinz (1968; reprint), 'Repräsentations — und Integrationsparteien', in Kurt Lenk and Franz Neumann (eds.), *Theorie und*

Soziologie der politischen Parteien, Neuwied and Berlin: Luchterhand

Michels, Robert (1911), *Zur Soziologie des Parteiwesens in der modernen Demokratie: Untersuchungen über die oligarchischen Tendenzen des Gruppenlebens*, Leipzig: Klinkhardt

Mintzel, Alf (1978, 2nd ed.), *Die CSU Anatomie einer konservativen Partei 1945–1972*, Opladen: Westdeutscher Verlag

—— (1978), *Die Volkspartei*, Opladen: Westdeutscher Verlag

Naßmacher, Karl-Heinz (1979), 'Zerfall einer liberalen Subkultur: Kontinuität und Wandel im Parteiensystem in der Region Oldenburg', in Herbert Kühr (ed.), *Vom Milieu zur Volkspartei*, Königstein/Ts: Anton Hain

Neumann, Sigmund (1965), *Die Parteien der Weimarer Republik: Mit einer Einführung von Dietrich Bracher*. Stuttgart: Kohlhammer

—— (1968), 'Parteiensysteme und Integrationsstufen', in Kurt Lenk and Franz Neumann (eds.), *Theorie und Soziologie der politischen Parteien*, Neuwied and Berlin: Luchterhand

Oberreuter, Heinrich (1983), *Parteien zwischen Nestwärme und Funktionskälte*, Zurich: Edition Interfrom

—— (1986), 'Abgesang auf einen Verfassungstyp? Aktuelle Herausforderungen und Mißverständnisse der parlamentarischen Demokratie', in Heinrich Oberreuter (ed.), *Wahrheit statt Mehrheit?*, Munich: Olzog

Schmitt, Rüdiger (1987), 'Was bewegt die Friedensbewegung? Zum sicherheitspolitischen Protest der 80er Jahre', *Zeitschrift für Parlamentsfragen* 1

Schulte, S. Christoph (1984), 'Die Herkunft der Grünen' in Klaus Gotto and Hans-Joachim Veen (eds.), *Die Grünen — Partei wider Willen*, Mainz: Hase und Köhler

Veen, Hans-Joachim (1984), 'Wer wählt grün? Zum Profil der neuen Linken in der Wohlstandsgesellschaft', *Aus Politik und Zeitgeschichte* 35–6

—— (1986), 'Die neue Spontaneität. Empirische Ergebnisse zur Erosion des institutionellen Bewußtseins bei Jüngeren', in Heinrich Oberreuter (ed.), *Wahrheit statt Mehrheit?*, Munich: Olzog

—— (1987), 'Die Anhänger der Grünen. Ausprägungen einer neuen linken Milieupartei' in Manfred Langner (ed.), *Die Grünen auf dem Prüfstand*, Bergisch Gladbach: Lübbe

3
Green Issues and Other Parties: *Themenklau* or New Flexibility?

Elim Papadakis

Introduction

The proximity and interchange of issues between parties and the flexibility of policy articulation is one of the most striking aspects of contemporary politics. Comparative and longitudinal studies of electoral change have drawn attention to these processes (see Crewe and Denver 1985; Budge, Robertson and Hearl 1987; Dalton, Flanagan and Beck 1985: Daalder and Mair 1983). However, no attempt has so far been made to link them to the development of the Greens in West Germany, whose impact on ideology and programmes is both recent and difficult to assess with much precision. The claim by the Greens that other parties are busily stealing their issues (*Themenklau*) glosses over far more complex processes of policy articulation. In examining some of these processes, certain patterns do emerge. The analysis will focus on the initial and more recent goals of the Greens, with their impact on programmes of established parties, with the importance attributed to certain goals by established parties *prior* to the emergence of the Greens, and with the relationship between these developments and long-term processes of party change.

The Greens, I will argue, are both constrained by these processes and able to influence them. They have been innovative but also rely heavily on established processes for their future survival. They have introduced new themes and rearticulated old ones. In doing this, they have not only gained immense popular support (particularly from followers of new social movements that politicised these themes), but they have helped to reinvigorate the strategies, ideologies and programmes of established parties.

61

Issues of Central Importance to the Greens

The 1987 election programme of the Greens deals, respectively, with democracy and democratic rights, discrimination against women, relations with developing countries, military disarmament and, finally, the links between the environment, the economy and social issues (Die Grünen 1987). It is striking that environmental issues were placed at the end of the programme since the Greens originally entered the parliamentary fray on the basis of an environmentalist campaign, thus reflecting the early wave of support for social movements opposed to nuclear energy and the destruction of the environment (Malunat 1987: 36). Yet if we are to pursue the thesis that contemporary politics is characterised by flexibility of policy articulation and by the proximity and interchange of issues, we may find that the Greens, as much as any other party, seek to broaden their social bases and ideological appeal.

The foundation congress of the Greens in 1980 stressed four basic principles: grassroots democracy; non-violence; social goals; and ecology (Document 1). These general aims emerged directly out of the protest movements of the 1970s. The first sign of preparedness by the Greens to move beyond this ideological framework, to rearticulate old themes in a new political situation was through close co-operation with the peace movement. Despite major successes at regional and state level, based mainly on support from the citizens' initiative and anti-nuclear power movements, the Greens obtained only 1.5% of the vote at the 1980 federal elections.

Their flexibility, their capacity to take on board the issues of peace and nuclear disarmament was crucial in ensuring their short-term survival as a national force. The call by Helmut Schmidt for the placement of Cruise and Pershing missiles in West Germany had, in 1979, aroused little opposition. However, by 1981, major protests were being organised against these policies. The SPD, which until then had enjoyed an almost hegemonic position over the issues of arms control and disarmament (Klingemann 1987: 308), now faced serious competition. This flexible approach by the Greens was extended to other areas, notably through a concern with the economic and social implications of environmental policies. The Greens supported the notion of an ecologically and socially orientated economy. In such a 'dynamically circulating economy' production would be on a 'smaller, more manageable decentralised' scale. The introduction of new technology would be democratically administered and monitored carefully to ensure compatibility with the environment, economy in energy consumption and benefits to the population (Die Grünen n.d.: 7). The SPD has similarly adopted notions of a dynamically circulating economy (Malunat 1987: 38), giving equal priority to ecological, economic and social goals (SPD 1984: 2) and has strongly emphasised the long-term political commitment required for policies of 'ecological renewal' of the economy (SPD 1986: 58).

The Greens, notwithstanding their poor performance at the federal elections in 1980, had begun to achieve some ideological coherence. This was mainly the outcome of the defeat of conservative ecologists by left-wing elements. Although ecology had acted as the common denominator for the mobilisation of new social movements and the formation of the Greens, other issues, reflecting a left-wing orientation, helped to make up the ideologies of the Greens. These included the preoccupation with the rights of women and of social minorities, particularly ethnic and sexual ones, the exploitation of developing countries by the industrialised West, and the call for unilateral nuclear disarmament (Papadakis 1984: 160).

Although the introduction of these issues into the party programme signalled a preparedness to move beyond single-issue politics, this alone would have been insufficient to broaden significantly the electoral base of the party. The issue of peace was perhaps the exception since this did influence many SPD voters to switch their allegiance to the Greens. This is not to underestimate the importance of the articulation of new issues (ecology) and rearticulation of old ones (peace) to the early success of the Greens. What may, however, have ensured their continued success, particularly in overcoming the 5% hurdle at federal elections in 1983 and 1987 was a recognition by supporters and sympathisers that they had used constructively the opportunity to participate in local and state parliaments (Papadakis 1984: 168). To their initial ideological appeal we must therefore add their willingness to broaden the scope of their programme and to combine conventional with unconventional organisational forms. Whatever the shortcomings of these efforts, they have contributed to the interchange of issues and the flexibility of policy articulation across all parties.

The influence on patterns of policy articulation by established parties even applies to economic policy, an area which is often regarded as the Achilles' heel of the Greens' programme. Although support for the Greens is not based on traditional economic concerns, their stance on nuclear power, nuclear weapons and the environment is closely tied in with a radically different understanding of economic progress (see Will-Schinneck in this volume). Established parties have been compelled, as a result, to broaden their own understanding: to make more specific the links between ideology and policy statements, to incorporate concern about the environment, democratic rights and technological developments into their economic programmes. Despite the initial difficulties experienced by the Greens in formulating a coherent economic policy (Papadakis 1984: 178–80), agreement has emerged over the need to combine short-term demands with long-term goals, to 'develop practical and suitable political alternatives which can immediately be put into effect and will mitigate the worst effects of the crisis' (Die Grünen 1983: 10). The Greens have submitted detailed proposals for alternative economic policies in areas including work and technology, fiscal policy, energy, agriculture, forestry, fishing, zoning and community development, traffic, relations with developing countries, employment and so on (Die Grünen 1983, 1986, 1987).

Perhaps more importantly, the Greens have been prepared to break with conventions of consensual politics and to confront in detail the policies of other parties. This goes against the trends identified by recent comparative and longitudinal research on party change. Where Kirchheimer (1966: 190) and LaPalombara and Weiner (1966: 426) drew attention to the emergence of catch-all parties in which ideology played a lesser role, the Greens have attempted to act like 'programmatic parties' whose primary role is that of a 'policy-making agency' (see Epstein 1967: 264). Established parties have not been concerned either with the implementation of their programmes or with the achievement of consistency between ideological assumptions and programmatic statements (Blondel 1978: 121). Contemporary parties in the West have not had real programmes, they have been unable to produce coherent programmatic statements and therefore have had great difficulty linking ideology to policy (Blondel 1978). These weaknesses have been increasingly exposed by the emergence of groups (such as the Greens) that lay far greater emphasis than established parties on participatory democracy. As Blondel has pointed out it might be these groups that produce new ideas and may be much closer to public opinion than parties or pressure groups: 'And if this continues, perhaps parties will slowly find themselves the prisoner of new groups which have the relevant programmes for society. Parties may lose the initiative and merely respond, more or less grudgingly, to the propositions made by new groups' (Blondel 1978: 211). There is a degree of compatibility between this scenario and analyses of party competition in the post-war era.

Whilst not dismissing the possibility of direct confrontation between parties over specific policy issues, studies of party competition have found that 'parties don't often refer to each other's policies' (Budge and Farlie 1983: 274). The tendency has been for parties, in their programmes, to avoid referring directly to issues of contention. This is used as evidence to support the notion, developed by Robertson (1976), of 'selective emphasis' on issues (Budge and Farlie 1983: 270). The analysis of electoral programmes in West Germany between 1949 and 1980, has lent support to the selective emphasis hypothesis, stressing that parties 'advocate issues which work in their favour while other parties try to avoid such themes' (Klingemann 1987: 322). The overall trend, including the West German experience, has been that of a convergence of parties, although we are warned against treating such tendencies as irreversible or inevitable (Budge and Robertson 1987: 416).

The Greens have been able successfully to exploit the reluctance by established parties to conceptualise alternative approaches to tackling pressing problems. The rise of the Greens is in some respects merely a symptom of the gap between changes in the social structure and the failure by established parties to develop relevant programmes for society. The challenge for established parties is to incorporate and adapt to these changes. The challenge for the Greens is to remain at the forefront of the push towards radical reform and innovation. All parties face a difficult balancing act in convincing the electorate that they are able radically to tackle new problems without undermining the gains of the past. It may become increasingly difficult to identify patterns of either convergence or conflict in party programmes.

The Impact on Programmes: Convergence or Conflict?

Evidence from political debates and party programmes suggests the following pattern of conflict and assimilation. The Greens, in order to make their mark on the political scene and to remain at the forefront of demands for changes in policy, have tended to articulate 'new' issues in a highly confrontational manner. Established parties, by contrast, have increasingly begun to include new issues on their agenda. Above all, they have tried to reduce the potential for confrontation by minimising their own differences on 'the New Politics dimension' (Dalton 1984: 131). The Greens, fearful of losing control over this agenda have accused other parties, particularly the SPD, of attempting to 'steal' these new issues (*Themenklau*). The SPD, however, has often drawn attention to the convergence of opinion between its own position and that of a substantial proportion of the Greens over issues such as nuclear energy and nuclear weapons, whereas the Greens, particularly the fundamentalists have emphasised the conflict between the different programmes (see the debate between Jutta Ditfurth and Oskar Lafontaine in *Der Spiegel*, 6, 1987).

The articulation of policies by the Greens contradicts the consensual pattern of party change. It is, however, often difficult to determine whether this is symptomatic of broader social changes or the result of a self-conscious, autonomous and innovative challenge to the prevailing political system. It has been suggested that the Greens are typical of new political movements that challenge conventional processes of political intermediation (Nedelmann 1984). The major difficulties for established parties lie not so much in the type of issue raised by new political movements but in the way it is transformed and reinterpreted, the way in which it is turned, with great intensity, into a moral issue affecting the general population rather than specific categories of voters. Major parties have great difficulty mediating issues which have been transformed in this manner. It makes them far less amenable to solution through compromise: 'The more the political movements transform issues into moral problems, to which they commit themselves with great intensity, the more the parties are unable to mediate them. As moral issues cannot be solved by compromise, they tend to block the political decision-making process as soon as they have been taken over by a political party' (Nedelmann 1984: 1043). A further factor which compounds the differences in approaches to similar issues by the Greens and by established parties is the radically conflicting attitude to popular involvement in decision-making processes. The attempt by the Greens to achieve grassroots democracy threatens the representative style of democratic decision-making in established parties (Nedelmann 1984: 1044).

The Greens, through their proximity to new social movements, also enjoy some of the advantages of more loosely-structured organisations, particularly a capacity to respond more quickly and flexibly to changes in popular mood (see Glotz 1982; Nedelmann 1984). The close relationship between the Greens and the new social movements does not necessarily preclude established parties from accommodating 'new politics' issues and reformulating their policies. This has occurred in the context of emerging divisions among supporters of established parties: between those concerned with so-called old issues of economic and military security and economic growth and those who have questioned existing institutions and priorities on the basis of their concern over the consequences of industrial development and economies that rely heavily on producing weapons of mass destruction.

The gap between the Greens and other parties is frequently interpreted as the outcome of their fundamentalism, their unwillingness to compromise and their unpredictability. Attempts, by the CDU to launch its own peace demonstrations have been described as 'image engineering' and 'clearly not inspired by new politics' since they are 'contradicted' by the deployment of intermediate range nuclear missiles (Poguntke 1986: 82). Similarly, reformist policies on equal opportunities for both men and women are treated as 'symbolic' (Offe 1985: 860). Attempts by established parties to incorporate new issues into old paradigms are correctly described as rhetorical in many instances. Yet there is little doubt that the new issues cut across party lines and may indeed have a substantial impact on Christian Democracy.

There is considerable scope for the CDU, with its share of new middle class supporters, to be pressured into modifying policies and accommodating a new politics perspective. The party, after its 1972 defeat by the Social Democratic–Liberal Coalition, was influenced by a new generation of thinkers and strategists. This influx bore fruit in West Berlin when, in 1981, the Christian Democratic Senate made overtures to alternative projects: it announced that Christian Democracy shared with the projects a commitment to self-reliance, decentralisation and social networks and backed this with substantial offers of funds for alternative projects (see CDU 1982). The possibilities, within the CDU, for pursuing decentralisation, environmental protection and equal opportunities policies for women may be even greater than in the SPD (see Frauenvereinigung der CDU 1985). The SPD is accountable to powerful trade union groups which are highly centralised, often involved in industries which cause considerable damage to the environment, and generally dominated by men. Similar criticisms can be levelled at industrial and commercial interest groups allied to the CDU. Nonetheless, the CDU Minister for Women's Affairs, Rita Süßmuth, has attempted to counter the image of a patriarchal organisation which reinforces the domestic role of women. Her role can hardly be dismissed as purely symbolic since she has been ranked as the third most popular politician in the Federal Republic with an approval rating of 62% and far ahead of leaders both of her own party and the SPD (*Der Spiegel*, No. 52, 1986). This is not to underestimate the powerful countervailing forces in the CDU which oppose moves towards greater industrial democracy, equal opportunities for women and a less confrontational foreign policy. Traditionalists are likely to come into increasing conflict with modernists even in the CDU.

Similar problems confront the SPD — only with greater intensity. In the most comprehensive review of its policies since the 1959 Bad Godesberg Programme the SPD, in 1986, moved even closer to the Greens by insisting that economic growth would have to be linked to the 'quality of life'. The programme called for a new compromise between state intervention and market forces in order to tackle: environmental damage, the emergence of over-centralisation and monopolies, social problems and the destruction of employment. It called for an end to the production of nuclear energy, and a more critical appraisal of the use of technology, citing the potential threats to democracy posed by the development of gene technology, nuclear energy and nuclear weapons. It also set itself the goals of equal representation of women in the Bundestag much stronger representation of European standpoints in foreign policy discussions with the United States, and greater equality in the distribution of resources between rich and poor nations.

At the same time, however, the party was seeking to win the 1987 election with a candidate whose attitudes had more in common with the era of Helmut Schmidt than with the aspirations of the new middle class. Johannes Rau had been a very popular politician in North Rhine-Westphalia, the heartland of working class support for the SPD. He agreed to become Chancellor candidate on condition that no attempt would be made to form a coalition with the Greens. Dazzled by the prospect of a candidate with a higher popularity rating than Helmut Kohl, the party agreed to fight an election on these terms. The campaign centred not so much on Social Democratic policies but on personalities. In the context of deep disagreement over priorities and future goals of the party, it is hardly surprising that a leader was chosen who would try and stand above these differences.

The persistence of these differences and the battle over the middle ground, particularly over the voters who are very interested in and well-informed about politics (see Klingemann 1985: 253), raises questions about future alignments to political parties currently represented in parliament. It also alerts us to the complex interaction of party policies and the conflicts articulated by new social movements. In these respects the development of the Greens is crucial. Without their preparedness to maintain close links with the new social movements and to articulate many of their concerns, there would be much less pressure on other parties to reconsider radically their own policies.

Established parties have responded to the challenge by the Greens. Issues raised by the latter have become 'issues of mainstream politics' (Kolinsky 1987: 329). The catch-all parties, far from being dead and buried, appear to exercise 'a considerable degree of flexibility in incorporating issues of opposition, although they tended to react only after new issues had emerged as focal points of mass concern in extra-parliamentary movements or new political parties' (Kolinsky 1987: 341). Taken literally, the position of the established parties on many issues is now identical to that of the Greens. In health policy similar links are made between health care, the environment and social influences. For the Greens: 'Prevention is better than cure: a preventional ecological health programme is based upon recognition that the largest part of the widespread illnesses caused by modern life can be traced back to the environment or to socially conditioned influences' (Die Grünen n.d.: 44). For the SPD: 'Prevention is better than cure. We want to expand general health-care provision, prevent pollution and contamination of water, soil and air, and to ensure that healthy foodstuffs are grown and put on sale' (SPD 1986: 89–90). In their 1987 electoral programme the CDU and CSU established close links between health care and environmental policy (CDU/CSU 1987: 47). Both the SPD and the Greens have also been critical of the paternalistic attitudes of the medical establishment and called for radical changes in the patient–doctor relationship. Both have criticised 'power relations' and 'economic self interests' in the health care industry, particularly the power and influence of the pharmaceutical industry.

This convergence and flexibility of policy articulation does not necessarily imply similar approaches to politics. Although the established parties have shown immense flexibility in rearticulating new issues, they have not adopted the confrontational approach of the Greens. The latter have referred constantly to the policies of established parties. The first lines of the preamble to their 1987 programme remind the reader that in the 1983 federal election 2.2 million citizens voted for a 'true opposition party' which offered 'a fundamental alternative to the destructive path of the established parties' (Die Grünen 1987: 4). In their 1983 Economic Policy Statement the Greens referred directly to the 'failures' of the employment policies of the established parties as well as to specific instances of economic and environmental mismanagement: 'The large-scale projects, funded at huge costs to the taxpayer, such as the quick breeder reactor at

Kalkar, the airport complex in Frankfurt, or the Rhein–Main––Danube river canal project not only have disastrous consequences for the environment, but are uneconomical as well' (Die Grünen 1983: 4). In 1986 they produced a comprehensive statement on how to transform industrial society (Die Grünen 1986). The 117-page document was structured around a critique of established parties: first, by identifying specific problems, second, by outlining the proposals of the established parties, third, by outlining alternative proposals and fourth, by making specific suggestions on how to achieve their transformative goals.

This approach is particularly threatening to established parties since it raises fundamental questions about their aims and direction. The 'identity crisis' of the SPD (Glotz 1982) has been exacerbated by the entry of the Greens into the Bundestag. This crisis cannot simply be resolved by incorporating items from the programme of the Greens but requires debate over the values and aims of the party. Although support for New Politics issues is widespread within it, any changes in policy are seen as following the path already outlined by the Greens. Issues including nuclear energy and nuclear weapons have been linked by the Greens to a profound questioning of the direction of advanced industrial societies. The involvement by the SPD in such debates has given rise both to a 'process of self-criticism and renovation' (Telo 1987) and to new factional divisions (see Smith 1987: 136–37). The SPD has reacted angrily to the attempt by the Greens to polarise the party system, to suggest that there is no significant difference between the CDU and the SPD (see *Der Spiegel*, No. 19, 1987: 23). Yet in the light of evidence about convergence of party programmes and the non-confrontational approach to specific policy issues, it is easy to see why the Greens have been able to draw attention to their 'totally different' approach to politics.

Political parties face a structural problem in trying to maintain themselves through control of the political agenda. Few problems emerge so long as they are able to set the agenda or to share control of agenda-setting with intermediate non-electoral organisations linked to them (Mair 1983). The major problem for established parties in West Germany is that intermediate non-electoral organisations (particularly those linked to the protest

71

movements of the 1970s) have often developed autonomously and even gone on to form their own political party. Established parties have only gradually come round to addressing the 'problem' of new social movements. The SPD now looks to them as 'major partners in Social Democratic policy' and makes explicit reference to their role in reinvigorating the party:

> Civic initiatives have aroused and heightened people's sensitivity to ecological risks and dangers; the women's movement has drawn our attention to continuing patriarchal structures in society and in politics; the peace movement has renewed our awareness of the mortal dangers of an unstable nuclear deterrence and opened up alternatives to discussion. We refuse to take refuge in conventional wisdoms in coming to terms with the needs, fears and hopes aroused by these concerns. We see the new social movements as providing an opportunity to revitalize the shaping of informed democratic opinion, a major extension to our party-political democracy and an enrichment of political culture (SPD 1986: 34).

The Greens and new social movements have made more difficult the balancing act of modern catch-all parties. Apart from the constraints imposed by 'changing tactical considerations', they need to shift constantly between their 'critical role' and their 'role as establishment support'. Catch-all parties must pay attention to popular grievances and innovations in order to maintain their electoral appeal and 'function as a relay between the population and governmental structure' (Kirchheimer 1966: 189).

The impact by the Greens on the programmes of established parties does not necessarily imply a more confrontationist approach to policy formulation. There will still be a strong tendency to couch the new messages in conciliatory terms. It is also easy to forget that many of the issues are not so much new in content but in the intensity and moral value attached to them by the Greens. The concept of selective emphasis can still be usefully applied to the rearticulation of these issues.

Prior Emphasis on 'New' Issues

Research on party programmes and ideology in West Germany between 1949 and 1980 has revealed fairly consistent patterns of selective emphasis by different parties on particular issues. In promoting its peace policy the CDU has tended to link it with the liberal notions of freedom whereas for the SPD the focus has been on detente and understanding (Klingemann 1987: 307). In the arena of international relations the FDP has emphasised economic cooperation, whereas the SPD has stressed the importance of arms control. All parties make frequent reference to social justice. However, the SPD has been most outspoken in favour of the welfare state *per se* whereas the FDP has targeted such issues as equality of access to education (see Klingemann 1987: 314–15, Table 14.4). 'New Politics' issues such as a concern with the quality of life (art, sport, leisure, the media and environmental protection) were addressed most forcefully by the FDP and to a lesser degree by the SPD and CDU, respectively.

Overall there has been a significant degree of convergence between party programmes. However, the relative importance attached to 'new' issues such as environmental protection is particularly significant to our analysis. The Greens cannot claim originality in selecting certain themes; however, they have turned them into leading issues. In the late 1970s and early 1980s environmental protection even eclipsed economic stability and secure employment as an issue of popular concern (see Kolinsky 1987: 327). Over the period 1949–80 peace occupied only eleventh place and environmental protection occupied twenty-first place on the list of leading issues (Klingemann 1987: 303, Table 14.1).

Nonetheless the established parties had not in fact excluded these issues from their past programmes. Environmental protection had been particularly prominent in the programme of the FDP. Long before the emergence of the Greens the party had drawn attention to most areas of concern including pollution of natural resources, noise, the impact of a profit-orientated mentality, the responsibilities of various levels of government, the international context, the need for planning and the inclusion of social costs in any estimates of environmental damage (FDP 1971: 71–8). The concern of the FDP with environmental policy had a tangible impact on support for the party, particularly from the burgeoning citizens' initiative movement of the early 1970s (Roth 1980: 82). This advantage was lost through the emergence of the protest movements against nuclear power. The FDP, tied into a coalition with the SPD, refused to be carried by the tide of popular protest. Although the party has continued to develop the most stringent criteria on responsibilities for the environment, has called for the inclusion of environmental protection as a basic principle in the Constitution and has placed environmental policy on a par with economic and social policy, it has side-stepped the issue of nuclear energy (FDP 1979).

The FDP like the CDU and CSU remains attached to the social market economy as the cornerstone of its environmental policy (Malunat 1987: 40). The latter, however, were far slower even in acknowledging the environment as a policy issue, although the CSU had, at the executive level, taken the most radical step in this direction by creating the first ever Ministry of the Environment in Bavaria in 1970. This was characteristic of its 'enlightened absolutist' style (Malunat 1987: 34), of support for a strong interventionist state that would iron out any dysfunctions independently of popular protests. The CSU has expressed the greatest faith in technical solutions to environmental problems. Nuclear energy comes under the category of developments that are both essential and can be safely controlled through technical know-how (CSU 1980).

The CDU was the most reluctant of all parties to address environmental issues. It spurned an early attempt to attract the environmental vote by one of its own members of parliament, Herbert Gruhl. Despite massive support from his own electorate and the publication of a best-selling account on the global destruction of the environment (Gruhl 1975), he eventually felt compelled to leave his party. In 1979 he created an alliance between diverse environmentalist groups for elections to the European Parliament, gaining 893,510 votes (3.2% of the national share). Gruhl was a key figure in founding the Greens, although his attempts to restrict the party programme to 'purely' environmental issues were later defeated (Papadakis 1984: 158–63). The CDU went on to develop a strategy similar to the CSU of maximising research effort into developing new technologies and capitalising on environmental protection as a growth industry.

The party has also taken up all the key themes in the debate over environmentalism (CDU 1978: 1984). Although economic growth remains the leading goal, it is stressed that this may

74

have to be reconsidered in situations of 'indefensible damage to the natural environment'. Having established that the 'survival of humanity' depends on technological development the two conservative parties argue: 'Whoever wants to exploit scientific knowledge and technology must consider uses and risks. That is precisely the challenge for a responsible partnership with technology. Not everything that is technically and economically advantageous is from a human perspective either desirable or ethically defensible' (CDU/CSU 1987: 34). The CDU and CSU have attempted to combine ethical concerns, economic progress, technological development and environmental protection.

The SPD has in many respects gone further than the CDU/CSU in addressing environmental policy (SPD 1979; 1984; 1986). Although it tends, like the other established parties, to focus on general principles, it specifies areas which require urgent attention including the replacement of 'environmentally damaging products by environment-conserving alternatives', the promotion of 'the necessary technical innovation and health safeguards', the effective disposal of dangerous materials and the refurbishment of 'old waste-deposits' (SPD 1986: 57).

More than any other party the SPD supports state intervention, the provision of incentives for the production of technologies that comply with environmental safeguards, and the creation of disincentives to production that is environmentally damaging. Unlike other established parties it has turned its back on the nuclear energy industry: 'Social democracy, originally fascinated by the prospects of nuclear energy, has learned that it can be responsibly used only during a short transition period. It will bring about the transition to safe and environmentally acceptable energy supplies without nuclear power. It will reject the invitation to join the plutonium industry' (SPD 1986: 58). Its approach to environmental policy has become far more programmatic. There is also a strong appeal to activists in citizens' initiatives and new social movements.

Central to its attempt to alter radically the structure of the economy (and at the same time to retain economic growth as a core principal) is the notion of *selective growth*: 'A policy of selective growth will reduce the costs of economic activity. Demand for environment-conserving products and processes will increase worldwide, thereby strengthening our economy. A

75

policy to secure these desired developments will also relieve pressure on the state: preventing environmental damage will be cheaper than repairing it' (SPD 1986: 60). The SPD has come closest to the attempt by the Greens to establish inextricable links between ecology and economy.

The Greens also stress that ecology and economy are mutually dependent on one another but have adopted a more confrontational style in their programme. Two factors are particularly relevant to this confrontation: first, the urgency with which they want the implementation of new policies, and second, their ambivalent attitude towards state intervention. The first factor, which reinforces differences between the Greens and the SPD, entails the call for immediate abandonment of the nuclear energy programme, for the withdrawal of the Federal Republic from NATO, for unilateral disarmament and for the withdrawal by the United States of its troops in the Federal Republic. The second factor is more complex.

The Greens have adopted a highly detailed, programmatic approach to the formulation of their policies. A section of their programme on preventing air pollution contains five references to specific problems, followed later by thirteen references to short- and long-term measures (including details of acceptable levels of emission of particular chemicals into the atmosphere) to remedy the situation (Die Grünen 1986: 15–17). These and many other proposals imply a considerable degree of state regulation. The Greens acknowledge this to some extent. However, they diverge considerably from the SPD and are closer to the CDU/CSU in their emphasis on decentralisation and self-responsibility. The basis for such a reorientation would nonetheless be vastly different from that of the CDU/CSU — it would imply the transformation of the social market economy into one which was democratically controlled by the grassroots.

This section has highlighted several important aspects of the articulation of policies. Many of the issues raised by the Greens have featured, to varying degrees, in the programmes of established parties since the early 1970s. However, they were not the leading issues on the political agenda prior to the emergence of the Greens. Although the programmatic style adopted by the Greens has begun to make an impact, for instance on detailed proposals by the SPD for environmental protection, selective emphasis, even on 'new' issues, has remained the predominant approach. The major parties have linked the 'new' issues to established ideologies, to a belief in the free market, to economic growth, to technological and scientific progress, to humanist ethical considerations and to state intervention.

Two tendencies are apparent. First, established political groups have adapted their programmes to include new issues. Economic growth, for instance, has been modified by the SPD into selective economic growth; the social market economy employment policy and technical progress have been linked by the CDU/CSU to flexibility, family life and the 'service to human beings' (CDU/CSU 1987 CDU 1984). Second, established political groups are themselves becoming divided between 'new' and 'old' politics. The incorporation of new issues is not purely cosmetic or rhetorical but reflects new lines of conflict which cut across party boundaries and ideological divisions based on class and religious denomination.

Even though the old divisions still contribute significantly to the differences between parties, the new ones have begun to exert a powerful impact on party programmes and have the greatest potential for contributing to the polarisation and re-alignment of the party system (Dalton 1984). The preparedness of the Greens, for instance, to articulate the conflicts over new politics issues has been an important factor in persuading the SPD to formulate new policies ever since it went into opposition in 1983. This applies especially to the environment and to women's issues (Paterson and Webber 1987: 154). In this respect, the Greens have operated as agents of change, compelling other parties to make up for their failure to respond adequately to new issues. In other respects, the Greens, as much as any other party, are responding to deeper, long-term changes. These processes, though open to tactical manipulation, may also form the basis for polarisation and realignment.

Long-term Processes

The potential for conflict and change in one of the most stable and consensual democratic party systems in the world has become widely recognised. Uncertainty over party change has been linked to the concern with transforming extra-parliamentary opposition into an integral part of the political culture (Kolinsky 1987), the influence of postmaterialist values on traditional party alignments (Inglehart 1984: 68), the erosion of the bases for consensus identified by Kirchheimer (Paterson and Webber 1987), the political realignment of the new middle class and of the younger age cohorts (Dalton 1984), the electoral volatility of the new middle class and the potential for polarisation between the Greens and the SPD on the one hand and the CDU/CSU-FDP on the other (Smith 1987; Offe 1985).

The long-term social and economic bases for change in advanced industrial societies such as West Germany include the dramatic increase in affluence related to economic growth in the 1950s and 1960s, the shift in the structure of the workforce from the industrial working class and the rural sector to the tertiary sectors, the increasing levels of urbanisation coupled with radical changes in leisure activities and lifestyles and the increase in educational opportunities (Baker, Dalton and Hildebrandt 1981; Dalton *et al* 1984). These developments imply changes both in the class structure of society (notably the role of the new middle class in advanced industrial society) and in the structure of public opinion and public influence on decision-making processes (linked, above all, to increasing levels of education and the more extensive dissemination of information via the mass media). The combination of education and new middle-class background is the most salient factor in the challenges to strategies, ideologies and programmes of established parties.

This is not to ignore the importance of other social and economic changes that have altered the basis of industrial societies. Rather, it is to highlight the factor that has threatened most of all the consensual model of party programmes, that forms the basis for electoral volatility and party realignment. The expansion of educational opportunities and the increase in influence of the mass media as a source of information have contributed to the weakening of traditional divisions, particularly among the post-war generations of the new middle class of white-collar employees and civil servants (Baker, Dalton and Hildebrandt 1981; Dalton 1984). These developments have spawned a new type of voter who makes a considered assessment of the past record of a party as well as its likely performance on specific issues in the future (Sjöblom 1983: 398). Voters, far from being apathetic, uninformed or stubbornly loyal, have tended increasingly to scrutinise the behaviour of parties on specific issues:

> Results of recent analyses of West German voting behaviour tend to support the hypothesis of issue politics. In 1983 an analysis of open-ended questions about the good and bad aspects of the CDU/ CSU, the SPD, FDP and the Greens found that more than 90% of the electorate were able to specify both positive and negative political arguments about all four parties. The simple hypothesis was confirmed that voters tended to choose that party for which they could find more positive than negative arguments as compared to other parties (Klingemann 1985: 253).

Although West Germany remains one of the least volatile electoral systems, a strong element of volatility has been detected among the new middle classes (Klingemann 1985: 251). These findings can be linked to the greater interest among new middle-class voters for New Politics issues, to the decline in class voting over the past four decades and to the loosening of partisan ties among post-war generations. Dalton has argued that these processes constitute a realignment of the electorate based on the new middle class and the young (1984: 128).

The erosion of the political consensus identified by Kirchheimer is unmistakable. Paterson and Webber have stressed the preparedness of the electorate, in the light of declining economic growth, to challenge earlier assumptions about the funding of the welfare state, the increase in scepticism towards technological change, the questioning of major aspects of foreign policy, particularly the role of NATO and the presence of the United States, the decline in the potency of anti-communist ideology as a source of political cohesion, and the impact of post-materialist values on 'the old consensus over the desirability of economic growth' (1987: 152). The impact of these significant changes on the consensual mode of politics should not, however, be overestimated. Paterson and Webber note conflicting tendencies but conclude that the influence of the Greens on the opposition strategy of the SPD 'has not been so great as to move the SPD away from an essentially co-operative position' (1987: 163). They draw attention to areas in which polarisation between the SPD and the CDU has occurred, notably over social policy and defence policy as well as support by the SPD for extra-parliamentary protests by the peace movement. However, they also note the powerful elements of continuity: the retention of leadership personnel at the federal level; the importance of the power bases at state and local level which gives added influence to the state premiers in the formulation of electoral programmes; the incorporation of radical tendencies through involvement in the specialist all-party committees of the Bundestag; and the influence of the more conservative trade unions on party strategies.

Despite the dramatic rise in social protests, the emergence of new issues and the successes of the Greens, the established parties have continued to attract around 90% of the votes at both federal and state elections (Klingemann 1985: 230). These paradoxical developments can perhaps be understood as a process of social or ideological realignment, whereby the 'social and ideological bases of party support change, but the number and strength of existing parties remains much the same' (Crewe 1985: 17). The only complicating factor in the West German context has been the emergence of a new party that has made it far more difficult for established parties simply to incorporate new issues within traditional ideological frameworks.

Conclusion

The arrival of the Greens on the political scene has exerted a profound impact on patterns of policy articulation. Although many of the issues raised by the Greens had previously featured in the programmes of established parties, they had not been the most salient ones. The Greens, however, went much further than introducing new issues onto the agenda. Their concern with establishing a new political identity spurred them into making detailed proposals for policy change, for confronting directly the policies of established parties. They exposed and exploited the gap between vague programmatic statements and the implementation of policies directed at practical problems. The established parties have therefore been pressured into a more programmatic approach, into outlining in greater detail the ways in which they propose to tackle specific problems.

The Greens, in directly questioning the fundamental aims and direction of other parties, have highlighted the latent conflict between a new and an old politics. Although the new divisions still have less impact on policy formulation than the old ones, the growth in influence of the former is unmistakable. Established parties have had to become more reflexive, to examine their own assumptions and to reconsider their future direction. These trends are also reflected in the preparedness of parties to question the certainties of the past, to do the unthinkable and analyse in public their own failings (Blondel 1978: 213).

The Greens have also made it awkward for established parties to incorporate the new issues. This is partly due to the autonomous development of new social movements and of a new party whose agenda was not easily subject to control by established parties. It is also linked to the way in which new issues have been transformed and reinterpreted by the Greens. They tend to refer to the survival of the human species (rather than to specific categories of voters), to attach a moral significance to their campaigns and to link these to demands for greater participation (Nedelmann 1984). All these factors highlight the differences between the approach of established parties and the Greens to similar issues. The Greens also enjoy the advantage of being able, through their loose organisational structure, to respond with speed and flexibility to shifts in public opinion, to regional and local pressures.

The Greens have, nonetheless, had to adapt considerably to established patterns of policy articulation. The formation of a party was a response to the constraints imposed on any political organisation, particularly the need to articulate themes through channels which were recognised as legitimate by the mass public. The party has in some respects become a catch-all party seeking to capture the middle ground of politics, to include a wide spectrum of policy issues in its programme. The so-called realist faction in the party has even been prepared to modify certain demands, for instance, to call for the gradual rather than immediate dismantling of nuclear power stations.

The established parties have responded to the challenge of the Greens with immense flexibility and by articulating new issues in a non-confrontational manner. They have stressed the degree of convergence between their own concern and that of the Greens with new issues. The 'selective emphasis' approach is still the predominant one even in relation to new issues. Although they have become more programmatic in their approach, the established parties have played down ideological differences, or at least tied in the new issues with old ideologies, for instance, with economic liberalism or with state intervention. In a sense the combination of flexibility and pragmatically orientated radicalism characteristic of the Greens is itself a reflection of the constraints on new issue politics (see Papadakis, forthcoming). Despite the fundamentalist orientation of sections of the party programme, the overwhelming majority of voters for the Greens are in favour of a coalition with the SPD.

The basis for the successful operation of catch-all parties has none the less changed dramatically. The interchange of issues between parties has become more intense, policy articulation more flexible. In the West German context the contours are being drawn not so much of realignment or dealignment but of a new synthesis. For Inglehart (1984) this means the assimilation of postmaterialist and materialist values. However, this notion could be extended to many other areas, for instance, to the development of greater 'strategic flexibility' in party organisations and in policy directions (even during election campaigns) (Sjöblom 1983). Once new values have been assimilated into party programmes there is a return to the selective emphasis approach. Even among supporters of new social movements there is a tendency to stress the complementarity of parliamentary and extra-parliamentary approaches, to adopt a pragmatic rather than a fundamentalist approach in challenges to established cultural values. The Greens are as likely as the established parties to incorporate or 'steal' issues. In many respects this has strengthened their attack on the consensual pattern of policy articulation and on the political agenda. In others, it has merely complemented and confirmed tendencies towards greater sophistication and towards a new synthesis based on a convergence of issues and of policy articulation.

References

Books and Articles

Baker, Kendall, Russell Dalton and Kai Hildebrandt (1981), *Germany Transformed*, Cambridge: Harvard University Press

Blondel, Jean (1978), *Political Parties, A Genuine Case for Discontent?*, London: Wildwood House

Budge, Ian and Dennis Farlie (1983), 'Party Competition — Selective Emphasis or Direct Confrontation? An alternative View with Data', in Hans Daalder and Peter Mair (eds.), *Western European Party Systems*, London: Sage

Budge, Ian and David Robertson (1987), 'Do parties differ, and how? Comparative discriminant and factor analysis', in I. Budge *et al* (eds.), *Ideology, Strategy and Party Change*, Cambridge: Cambridge University Press

—— and Derek Hearl (eds.) (1987), *Ideology, Strategy and Party Change: Spatial Analyses of Post-War Election Programmes in 19 Democracies*, Cambridge: Cambridge University Press

Crewe, Ivor and David Denver (eds.) (1985), *Electoral Change in Western Democracies: Patterns and Sources of Electoral Volatility*, London: Croom Helm

Crewe, Ivor (1985) 'Introduction: Electoral Change in Western Democracies: A Framework for Analysis', in Ivor Crewe *et al* (eds.), *Electoral Change in Western Democracies*, London: Croom Helm

Daalder, Hans and Peter Mair (eds.) (1983), *Western European Party Systems, Continuity and Change*, London: Sage

Dalton, Russell (1984), 'The West German Party System between Two Ages', in Russell Dalton *et al*, *Electoral Change in Advanced Industrial Societies*, Princeton: Princeton University Press

——, Flanagan, Scott, and Beck, Paul Allen (eds.) (1985), *Electoral Change in Advanced Industrial Societies: Realignment or Dealignment*, Princeton: Princeton University Press

Epstein, Leon (1967), *Political Parties in Western Democracies*, London: Pall Mall Press

Glotz, Peter (1982), *Die Beweglichkeit des Tankers*, Munich: Bertelsmann

Gruhl, Herbert (1975), *Ein Planet wird geplündert: Die Schreckensbilanz unserer Politik*, Frankfurt: Fischer

Inglehart, Ronald (1984), 'The Changing Structures of Political Cleavages in Western Society', in Russell Dalton *et al*, *Electoral Change in Advanced Industrial Societies*, Princeton: Princeton University Press

Kirchheimer, Otto (1966), 'The Transformation of the Western European Party Systems', in Joseph LaPalombara *et al* (eds.), *Political*

Parties and Political Development, Princeton: Princeton University Press

Klingemann, Hans-Dieter (1985), 'West Germany' in Ivor Crewe and David Denver (eds.), *Electoral Change in Western Democracies*, London: Croom Helm

—— (1987), 'Electoral programmes in West Germany 1949–1980: explorations in the nature of political controversy', in Ian Budge *et al* (eds.), *Ideology, Strategy and Party Change*, Cambridge: Cambridge University Press

Kolinsky, Eva (ed.) (1987), *Opposition in Western Europe*, London: Croom Helm and PSI

Kolinsky, Eva (1987), 'The Transformation of Extra-Parliamentary Opposition in West Germany, and the Peace Movement' in E. Kolinsky (ed.), *Opposition in Western Europe*, London: Croom Helm and PSI

LaPalombara, Joseph and Myron Weiner (eds.) (1966), *Political Parties and Political Development*, Princeton: Princeton University Press

Mair, Peter (1983), 'Adaptation and control: Towards an Understanding of Party and Party System Change', in Hans Daalder and Peter Mair (eds.), *Western European Party Systems*, London: Sage

Malunat, Bernd (1987), 'Umweltpolitik in Spiegel der Parteiprogramme', *Aus Politik und Zeitgeschichte* 29

Nedelmann, Birgitta (1984), 'New Political Movements and Changes in Processes of Intermediation', *Social Science Information* 23/6

Offe, Claus (1985) 'New Social Movements: Challenging the Boundaries of Institutional Politics', *Social Research* 52/4

Papadakis, Elim (1984), *The Green Movement in West Germany*, London: Croom Helm

—— (forthcoming), 'Social Movements, Self-limiting Radicalism and the Green Party in West Germany', *Sociology*

Paterson, William and Douglas Webber (1987), 'The Federal Republic of Germany: The Re-emergent Opposition?', in E. Kolinsky (ed.), *Opposition in Western Europe*, London: Croom Helm and PSI

Poguntke, Thomas (1986), 'New Politics and Party Systems: The emergence of a New Type of Party?' *West European Politics* 10/1

Robertson, David (1976), *A Theory of Party Competition*, London/New York: John Wiley

Roth, Roland (1980), *Parlamentarisches Ritual und politische Alternativen*, Frankfurt: Campus

—— (1980), 'Notizen zur Geschichte der Burgerinitiativbewegung in der Bundesrepublik', in Roland Roth (ed.) *Parlamentarisches Ritual und politische Alternativen*, Frankfurt: Campus

Sjöblom, Gunnar (1983), 'Political Change and Political Accountability: A Propositional Inventory of Causes and Effects' in Hans Daalder and Peter Mair (eds.), *Western European Party Systems*, London: Sage

Smith, Gordon (1987), 'The Changing West German Party System, Consequences of the 1987 Election', *Government and Opposition* 22/2

Telo, Mario (1987), 'The Greening of Social Democracy: The SPD Rethinks Economics', *Socialist Review*, 17/1

Documents and Programmes

CDU (1978), *Grundsatzprogramm: Freiheit, Solidarität, Gerechtigkeit, beschlossen auf dem 26. Bundesparteitag, Ludwigshafen*, CDU: Bonn

—— (1984), *Leitsätze für die 80er Jahre: Deutschlands Zukunft als moderne und humane Industrienation, beschlossen auf dem 32. Bundesparteitag, Stuttgart*, CDU: Bonn

CDU Fraktion (1982), *Grosse Anfrage über alternatives Leben*, Drucksache 9/349 Berlin: CDU

CDU/CSU (1987), *Das Wahlprogramm von CDU und CSU für die Bundestagswahl 1987*, Bonn: CDU

CSU (1980), *Umweltpolitik in den 80er Jahren, Positionspapier der CSU*, Munich: CSU

FDP (1971), *Freiburger Thesen der FDP zur Gesellschaftspolitik*, Bonn: FDP

—— (1979), *FDP und Umweltschutz: Umweltpolitische Beschlüsse des 30. Ordentlichen Parteitags Bremen*, Bonn: FDP

Frauenvereinigung der CDU (1985), *Der Beitrag der Frauen in der CDU zur 'Politik Für eine neue Partnerschaft zwischen Mann und Frau'*, Bonn: CDU

Die Grünen (1980), Bundes programme, Bonn: Die Grünen

—— (1983), *Against Unemployment and Social Decline, Purpose in Work—Solidarity in Life*, Bonn: Die Grünen

—— (1986), *Umbau der Industriegesellschaft, Schritte zur Überwindung von Erwerbslosigkeit, Armut und Umweltzerstörung*, Bonn: Die Grünen

—— (1987), *Bundestagswahl Programm 1987*, Bonn: Die Grünen

SPD (1979), *Sicherheit in die 80er Jahre: Ökonomie, Ökologie, Umweltschutz, beschlossen auf dem Bundesparteitag, Berlin*, Bonn: SPD

—— (1984), *Frieden mit der Natur, Für eine umweltverträgliche Industriegesellschaft, beschlossen auf dem Bundesparteitag, Essen*, Bonn: SPD

—— (1986), *Irsee Draft of New SPD Manifesto*, Bonn: SPD

II
The Green Political Environment: Policies and Organisation

4

The Greens and the New Left: Influences of Left-Extremism on Green Party Organisation and Policies*

Helmut Fogt

The destruction of the basis of life and work and the dismantling of democratic rights have reached such threatening proportions that we need fundamental alternatives in the economy, in politics and society. This is why a democratic citizen's movement arose spontaneously (Bundesprogramm 1980: 4).

A Party of the Centre?

Shortly after the federal elections of January 1987 which strengthened the place of the Greens in the Bundestag, the newly re-elected Otto Schily declared: 'In the changed social conditions of the eighties, the Greens are the new centre' (*Deutsches Allgemeines Sonntagsblatt* 8.2.1987). A few weeks later, Lukas Beckmann, then spokesman for the party went a step further: he regarded the Greens as a party with essentially 'conservative values', definitely not 'a party of the left' (*Frankfurter Allgemeine Zeitung* 23.4.1987). Even from outside the Greens, the attempt has received some support to define the Greens as a 'party of the centre'. The chairman of the SPD parliamentary party, Hans-Jochen Vogel for instance, attested the newly elected parliamentary group a 'radically liberal yet largely bourgeois' character and again refused to allocate to them the seats on the far left of the Bundestag (*Deutschland-Union-Dienst* 6.2.1987).

Such efforts to locate their party in the centre have not re-

* Translated by Eva Kolinsky. An extended version of this chapter has been published in Manfred Langner (ed.), *Die Grünen auf dem Prüfstand*, 1987

Table 4.1. The Political Position of the Greens: Left or Right?

	perceptions of the population			perceptions of Green supporters		
	1981 %	1982 %	1986 %	1981 %	1982 %	1986 %
Far left	29	47	53	14	26	36
Moderate left	31	27	28	48	48	41
Centre or right	34	21	18	36	23	22
No answer	6	5	1	2	3	1

Source: Research Institute of the Konrad-Adenauer-Foundation, Archive Nr. 8104, 8211, 8603

mained unchallenged by other Greens. Petra Kelly, for instance, was adamant that her party had nothing in common with 'the bourgeois centre of this country' (*Frankfurter Allgemeine Zeitung* 28.1.1987) and during his time in the party executive Rudolf Bahro called the Greens in clear contradiction to the views of Schily 'a party of the left with a void on the right and in the centre' (*Kommune* 4, 1984: 47). The majority of West Germans share this assessment: in 1986 more than half (53%) regarded the Greens as a party of the far left (Table 4.1). Five years earlier, only 29% had held this view. Today, 28% of West Germans place the party on the moderate left, and just 18% position it in the centre or on the right. Green supporters tend to play down the leftist orientations of their party a little, but among them the proportion of those who regard their party as a party of the radical left has increased sharply — from 14% in 1981 to 36% in 1986.

Despite these developments the public is largely unsure about the new party. In particular the component of left radicalism seems hard to fathom. Even experts appear confused. The report about left-extremist tendencies in the Greens which was produced in early 1986 by the Federal Office for the Protection of the Constitution in relation to parliamentary investigations states initially that former and currently active left-extremists have 'encouraged an orientation of the whole party towards the left'. In a revised version, however, this sentence was replaced by one with the opposite message: 'Left-extremists have been *unable* to gain decisive influence within the Greens' (italics H.F.; *Die Welt* 18.3.1986). This uncertainty about the political orientation of the Greens holds the key to understanding their development and current political situation.

The party itself has never attempted to hide the fact that communists are among its activists. Thomas Ebermann, who had been a leading functionary of the Communist Federation (*Kommunistischer Bund*) in Hamburg and who is today one of the three parliamentary spokespersons for the Greens in the Bundestag declared in 1982: 'It has never been a secret that socialists, communists and Marxists have been active in the Greens and in the *Alternative Liste*' (*Tageszeitung* 10.8.1982). The Greens themselves tend to stress that left-extremists who had been active in the so-called *K-Gruppen* had since undergone a profound change of heart. In 1982, Petra Kelly saw the Greens as a melting-pot beyond partisan divisions: 'I would not wish to exclude communists or conservatives and I do not need to. Because each one learns from the other, they no longer are at each other's throats but have come closer together' (*Der Spiegel* 24, 1982: 56).

Looking at the communist groups which had emerged at the end of the sixties in West German university towns, the political bystander cannot but notice two specific aspects: first, they seemed to aim at abolishing the democratic political order of the Federal Republic and were fuelled by exaggerated ideological dogmatism; second, they seemed to totally lack regard for their fellow human beings or feel inhibitions to use violence against their presumed 'enemies' (among them nearly everything and everyone: the state, 'monopoly capital', 'bourgeois science', mass media, trade unions, etc., etc.). Reports about the internal structure of these conspiratorial political sects suggest that a few 'leading cadres' drove a politically rather naive membership into mental dependency and through some kind of psycho-terror to physical and psychological exhaustion (Wir warn . . .: 1977). Suggestions that such groups might have been able to gain influence on a political party which has for nearly eight years participated in West German parliamentary politics do, therefore, deserve to be taken seriously. By the same token, claims that activists from communist or socialist political sects with their endorsement of violence and their contempt for the constitutional order may have undergone a radical process of rethinking and turned overnight into upright democrats should also be treated with due scepticism.

This chapter is an attempt to trace and evaluate the links between Greens and extremism of the left.[1] How far does the personal influence of former activists of the extreme left reach, and which place do they occupy in the party leadership? Which political goals do they pursue within the Greens, which tactics do they use, and — finally — have they changed their approaches over the years?[2]

1. The term 'left-extremist' is used to denote all organisations and their members whose aims have been classified as left-extremist by the authorities for the protection of the constitution, and who have been the subject of regular observation and reports. See the annual reports: *Betrifft Verfassungsschutz*; also Schwagerl, 1985.
2. I would like to stress that this study does not claim to present an exhaustive evaluation

Left-Extremism and the Origins of the Green Party

It is possible to date the birth of the Greens to the evening of 19 March 1977. On this day, some 2,000 to 3,000 communist demonstrators had confronted police in paramilitary fashion at the perimeter fence of the planned nuclear power plant in Grohnde in Lower Saxony, and fought a battle of unparalleled brutality. More than 300 were injured, and an occupation of the construction site could barely be prevented (*Frankfurter Allgemeine Zeitung* 21.3.77; *Der Spiegel* 14, 1977: 45f).

For two very different groups the day became a decisive event. A couple of communist groups which had already protested violently against the construction of an atomic power station in Brokdorf in the autumn of 1976, felt the need to reconsider their approach. Their strategy of violent escalation had failed. But some moderate environmentalists who participated in the events as demonstrators or as spectators also felt that the struggle against atomic energy could not be continued in this way. Hardly a year later the two groupings rivalled each other in a dramatic race to create alternative parties or electoral lists and put their aims more efficiently into practice. In the event, the organised left won the race.

After Brokdorf and Grohnde, the Communist Federation in particular embraced the idea of an electoral alliance (Langguth 1983: 114f). In July 1977, the organisational preconditions were created: the Communist Federation ousted representatives of other communist factions, notably the KPD and autonomous groupings, from the association of environmentalist citizens' initiatives in the Hamburg region (*Bürgerinitiative Umweltschutz Unterelbe* — BUU) and henceforth dominated it (Mez and Wolter 1980: 17). In October 1977, a BUU majority advocated the creation of an electoral '*Wehrt-Euch-Liste*' (Defend-Yourselves-List) which was officially founded in Hamburg in March 1978 as *Bunte Liste — Wehrt Euch. Initiativen für Demokratie und Umweltschutz* (Multi-Coloured List — Defend Yourselves. Initiatives for Democracy and Environmental Protection).

Under the leadership of the Communist Federation it initially

---

of the political origins, the development and the status of the Greens. It is the intention to highlight one specific aspect of their origin and development — albeit the aspect which can be regarded as the decisive one for the position of the party and its future destiny.

had a membership of some 200 small groups and initiatives with causes as far apart as the rights of tenants, women, pupils, apprentices, environmentalists and anti-nuclear activists, homosexuals, urban districts, foreigners, prisoners, conscientious objectors, and groups from the field of health care, education or culture (Klotzsch and Stöss 1984: 1519; Strohm 1978: 127f; Bading 1982: 122). However, *Bunte Liste* membership soon declined to some 300 individual members (Z — *Organ der Z-Gruppe* — 1.2.1980: 32). In line with Communist Federation preferences, members of the *Bunte Liste* were expected to oppose restrictions to the right to hold demonstrations, to fight 'Berufsverbote', and to hold 'progressive' views on the participation of communists in West German politics and society.

The Communist Federation dominated the *Bunte Liste* in political and personal terms as its 'tireless commitment and organisational talent' (Bieber 1980) reaped the first electoral successes.[3] In June 1978, two women functionaries of the Communist Federation were elected to the district council in Hamburg-Eimsbüttel; one of them, Christina Kukielka is today a Green member of the Land parliament in Hamburg. The alternative electoral movement in Northern Germany was organised by the Communist Federation in Hamburg. To this day, Hamburg along with Frankfurt and Berlin has remained one of the centres of Green policy formulation.

In Lower Saxony, the extreme left played an important part in the emergence of a Green-alternative 'electoral movement'. Assisted by the Communist Federation a number of anti-nuclear initiatives met at the place of the 'battle of Grohnde' to form a clearly left-wing electoral alliance, the *Wählergemeinschaft Atomkraft — Nein Danke* (WGA — Electoral Association Atomic Power — No Thanks). In addition to the Communist Federation, activists from the Socialist Workers' Group were prominent among the membership of the Electoral Association.[4]

---

3. For a detailed account of the *Kommunistischer Bund* and other groups of the extreme left see in particular Langguth, 1983; with special reference to Hamburg also Schiller-Dickhut *et al*, 1981.

4. The Socialist Workers' Group — *Sozialistische Arbeitergruppe* SAG — was founded in 1969/70 by former members of the *Sozialistischer Deutscher Studentenbund* SDS. As part of the so-called *Außerparlamentarische Opposition* APO, both SDS and SAG subscribed to 'openly anti-constitutional aims'. See Betrifft 1968: 85; Langguth 36–46; Hallensleben 1984: ch. 2; Klotzsch and Stöss: 1513–18.

Contrary to Hamburg, political moderates from the citizens' initiative and ecology movements could establish themselves as important competitors to the left in Lower Saxony. In May 1977, an environmental party, the *Umweltschutzpartei* USP was founded near a prospective nuclear dump; this was an altogether bourgeois alliance of traditional conservationists (Klotzsch and Stöss 1984). The new party was headed by Carl Beddermann, a senior official in the financial administration of Lower Saxony who had also been present at the 'battle of Grohnde'.

Another Green party founder was Georg Otto, a senior grammar-school teacher, who advocated a 'free economy', a socialist-type economic model which aimed at overcoming both Western capitalism and Eastern communism. In May 1977 he proclaimed a new party, this time in Hanover. He called it *Grüne Liste Umweltschutz* — Green List Environmental Protection. The following December his group merged with the USP to form the *Grüne Liste Umweltschutz* — GLU — *Niedersachsen*, the Green Ecology List of Lower Saxony.

Several members of the left-wing WGA now joined the GLU and began to influence the new party. On the eve of the Land elections in Lower Saxony in June 1978 the Communist Federation launched a 'mass campaign' to persuade the left to support the Green Ecology List (GLU). The new party was praised as 'a completely fresh political force and it does not have the kind of watertight and ossified power structures which would make it futile from the start to discuss the GLU or to try and influence it from within' (*Tageszeitung* 31.3.1980).

After the Land elections, the moderate conservative GLU executive attempted to curtail the influence of extremist groups in the party and expelled a number of Communist Federation members. The moderate wing, however, was unable to retain control. At the GLU party congress in Liebenau in July 1978, party chairman Beddermann's warnings that the left had gained too much influence were dismissed as unfounded. He resigned in favour of the compromise candidate Georg Otto but not without predicting that the party would 'not be able to rebuff the attempt at infiltration by extremist forces' (*Frankfurter Allgemeine Zeitung* 30.8.78; *Die Welt* 24.7.1978).

In Schleswig-Holstein, the Communist Federation had always been strong. It played a leading role in the environmentalist group *Bürgerinitiative Umweltschutz Unterelbe* (BUU) and was among the founders of two organisations which preceded the Greens in the region: the *Grüne Liste Nordfriesland* (GNLF) which focused on protecting the coastline, and the *Grüne Liste Unabhängiger Wähler* (GLUW — Green List of Independent Voters) in the district of Steinburg, which included the controversial construction site for a nuclear power plant at Brokdorf (Hallensleben 1984: 159). In September 1978, the two Green lists affiliated to form the *Grüne Liste Schleswig-Holstein* (GLSH). In these early days, the GLSH was composed of two equally strong wings, as Uta Wilke, a former member of the Communist Federation and later land chairperson of the Greens explained: 'The conservative wing consisted of environmentalists, the radical socialist wing drew on a number of quite militant action groups against atomic power stations which in turn were strongly influenced by the Communist Federation' (*Moderne Zeiten* 11, 1981: 29). After acrimonious controversies, a small conservative majority succeeded initially to focus the new party on conservationism and environmental issues and excluded members of communist organisations. When a membership meeting of the GLSH in the region voted in September 1978 by a margin of 98 to 78 that extremists should be expelled, 60 of the members present rose to leave the hall. Grouping close to the Communist Federation subsequently formed their own Green party, the *Liste für Demokratie und Umweltschutz* (LDU — List for Democracy and Environmental Protection).

In Hesse, the moderate conservative ecologists initially took the lead. In April 1978, the GLU of Lower Saxony surprisingly succeeded in creating a sister party in the neighbouring region to the South. Two months later, the left caught up: following the example of the *Bunte Liste* in Hamburg, a *Grüne Liste — Wählerinitiative für Umweltschutz und Demokratie* (GLW — Green List — Voters' Initiative for Environmental Protection and Democracy) was founded with support from ecologists, citizens' initiatives, the *Aktionsgemeinschaft Unabhängiger Deutscher* (AUD — Action-Community of Independent Germans) and the Socialist Bureau in Offenbach.[5] Groups of the extreme left were

---

5. The AUD was founded in 1965 by August Haußleiter as a splinter party of the right, but since the late sixties has opened itself towards the left. The 1977 AUD programme advocated 'ecological socialism.' In detail Stöss 1980. The Socialist Bureau was founded in

strongly involved: the Communist Federation, the maoist Communist Party, so-called *Spontis* with their Citizens' Initiative 'Chaos and Swamp' (*Bürgerinitiative Chaos und Sumpf*) whose ideological orientations were more fluid but who had gained notoriety for the use of violence during squatting and in other disturbances in Frankfurt[6].

The rival Green lists in Hesse (GLU and GLW) affiliated on 23 July 1978 and with the organisational assistance of the Socialist Bureau founded the *Grüne Liste Hessen* (GLH). The liaison was to be short lived. Within two weeks, the conservative GLU left the new Green alliance after two prominent socialists had been nominated to occupy the top places of the electoral list for the land elections in October 1978: Alexander Schubert, the head of the city administration and planning office in Frankfurt and a member of the Socialist Bureau, and also Daniel Cohn-Bendit, the former leader of the Paris student unrests of May 1968. Conservative criticism was levelled against 'candidates' whose prime interest was communism, not ecology (*Frankfurter Rundschau* 13.9.1978). Some of the conservative Greens later joined the *Grüne Aktion Zukunft* (GAZ — Green Action Future) which had been founded at national level in July 1978 by the former CDU member of the Bundestag, Herbert Gruhl. Estimates for September 1978 suggested that one in five members of the 1,000 strong Green List in Hesse had earlier been Communist Federation activists (*Frankfurter Rundschau* 13.9.1978).

In the first half of 1978, electoral participation also became a focal point of political discussion in the third centre of the Green-alternative movement, Berlin. The main participants in discussion circles and public meetings originated on the far left: the KPD, the Communist Federation, the Group International Marxists, Trotskyists, the Socialist Bureau, the action group *Rote*

1969 after the collapse of the Extraparliamentary Opposition and the student movement and has been regarded as left-extremist since 1977. See *Betrifft* 1977: 1105; 1982: 92; 1984: 94f; Langguth 1983: 195–9.

6. The *Kommunistische Partei Deutschlands* — KPD was founded in 1970 by former SDS functionaries with Leninist and Maoist orientations. In the seventies, the KPD engaged in several acts of violence; see Langguth 77–84; the so-called *Sponti* groups lack a clear organisational structure but tend to endorse the use of violence. Since the mid-seventies, they emerged in German university towns; Langguth 235; 239. In Frankfurt, the *Spontis* formed the so-called *Putzgruppe* which supported the squatters' movement and were involved in heavy clashes with the police. One of their number was Joschka Fischer who later became Minister of the Environment for the Greens in Hesse. See also Voigt 1986: 486.

Hilfe, the Committee against *Berufsverbote* and a number of affiliated journals and news-sheets. In addition to a group around the lawyers Otto Schily and Hans-Christian Ströbele, several citizens' initiatives were also interested in an electoral alliance — in particular the *Wählergemeinschaft Unabhängiger Bürger* (WUB) which was based in the residential district Zehlendorf and had, surprisingly, won representation in the district assembly in 1975 (Mez and Wolter: 13f).

Eight hundred members of these various groups decided on 24 July 1978 to form a *Wählerinitiative alternativer Listen* (Bühnemann *et al* 1984: 9). Ernst Hoplitschek, one of the key figures of the Green-alternatives in Berlin commented: 'It was common knowledge that activists from the Maoist KPD had been the moving spirits behind the formation of the new list and that they had hoped to gain tactical advantages through such an alliance' (Hoplitschek 1982: 83). At the request of the KPD, the founders' meeting passed a resolution which stressed that communists — regardless of their ideological orientations — should be permitted to participate in the new party list without restrictions. The various citizens' initiatives which had initially been interested, promptly detached themselves from the venture although the chairman of the KPD in West Berlin promised that his people would publicly announce their political affiliation in future — a promise which has not been kept (*Der Abend* 25.7.1978; *Der Spiegel* 28,1978: 83).

When the *Alternative Liste — Für Demokratie und Umweltschutz* (AL) was formally founded on 5 October 1978, the organisations and groups of the communist left in Berlin mentioned earlier were strongly represented. A newcomer was the *Kommunistischer Bund Westdeutschland*, a radical student organisation with a Maoist slant, and other student groups of the so called undogmatic left (Langguth 1983: 91–100). However, only 300 of the 3,000 people present decided to join the new party. The organisational backbone of the *Alternative Liste* remained, as before, the Maoist KPD. Otto Schily, who had been in favour of an electoral alliance distanced himself immediately from the new venture: 'I have the impression that this was a KPD party congress. With this list, I have nothing in common.' He called the *Alternative Liste* a 'KPD under a new name' and warned: 'without a general and decisive detachment from the KPD the

Alternative Liste cannot dispel the impression that it is little more than a branch of the KPD, in order to sell its ideas under a new label' (Bühnemann 1984: 77; 79). The journal *Arbeiterkampf*, published by the Communist Federation, confirmed Schily's fear shortly afterwards: 'The alliance consists largely of members and sympathisers of the KPD, a considerable number of unaffiliated leftists, and the Communist Federation' (*Arbeiterkampf* 8.1.1979). That communist activists worked tirelessly to launch the new organisation was widely acknowledged. Hoplitschek, for instance recalled: 'Everybody who was involved at the time will testify to this: had it not been for the active cadres in the organisation, in the various localities and districts, the *Alternative Liste* would surely not have survived' (Hoplitschek 1982: 85). Given the circumstances under which it was founded, moderate environmentalists in Berlin had no prospects of making their concerns heard through the new party.

From Frankfurt to Saarbrücken: The Emergence of the Greens

The political developments which resulted in creating a Green party at national level were of a completely different type: the godfather of the Greens had been an alliance on the radical right. Under the leadership of Professor Werner Haverbeck, the chairman of the *Weltbund zum Schutze des Lebens* (World Federation for the Protection of Life)[7] a heterogeneous group of people met in the autumn of 1977 in the town of Vlotho/Weser and arrived at a political co-ordination of the environmentalists' movement (Horacek 1982: 124). Prominent representatives of an extremist right with neutralist orientations such as August Haußleiter of the AUD or the artist Joseph Beuys rubbed shoulders with Georg Otto of the Lower Saxony Green List (GLU), with Ossip Flechtheim, a professor of political science at the Free University in Berlin and also a member of the Socialist Bureau, and also Herbert Gruhl who was a CDU member of the Bundestag at the time and, as mentioned earlier, was to emerge as the founding chairman of the *Grüne Aktion Zukunft*, one of the predecessors of the present day Greens. The circle was also in

7. The *Weltbund zum Schutze des Lebens* and the *Achberger Kreis* have been politically close to the AUD and advocate a 'Third Way' between East and West, between communism and capitalism. See Stöss 1984: 1412.

close contact with Rudi Dutschke, the former leader of the West German student movement of the 1960s, who favoured a left-wing organisation similar to the defunct Socialist Students' Federation SDS and himself founded a voters' initiative *Links für Grün* — Left for Green (Dutschke 1977: 20–3).

A German Environmentalist Meeting — *Deutsches Umwelttreffen* — which was organised in Troisdorf near Bonn by the Federal Association of Environmentalist Citizens' Initiatives (*Bundesverband Bürgerinitiativen Umweltschutz* BBU) in June 1978 elected a 27 member committee of the various groups who had participated in Vlotho, and asked them to explore the chances of electoral participation at the European elections in June 1979 and co-ordinate the environmentalist movement accordingly. Representatives of the Communist Federation and of the left-wing Greens (GLH) in Hesse, the *Bunte Liste* in Hamburg and the *Alternative Liste* in Berlin participated as observers in the meeting (Klotzsch and Stöss 1984: 1528f). Against the reservations of the left and its affiliated Green lists, the so called *Sonstige Politische Vereinigung* (SPV — Other Political Association) *Die Grünen* was founded in Frankfurt on 17 March 1979.[8] Among the founding members, conservative and rightist groups such as the GAZ, the AUD, the GLU, the GLSH predominated. Gruhl, Haußleiter and Helmut Neddermeyer were elected joint chairmen. Gruhl made sure that among the 500 delegates at the founding congress only 15 were representatives of the left, among them the subsequent business manager and chairman of the Greens, Lukas Beckmann (Spretnak 1985: 58).

At the European elections on 10 June 1979, the Other Political Association The Greens won 900,000, i.e. 3.2% of the vote. This respectable result persuaded the left to reconsider its position and view the newly founded party with more interest. The conservative environmentalists, on the other hand, had learned from the electoral result that an ecology party of the right was unlikely to pass the 5% electoral hurdle in the German political system unaided. Thus, the two sides came closer together: between June and September 1979 a number of meetings took place in Vlotho and also in Bonn involving a variety of parties

---

8. The name *Sonstige Politische Vereinigung* — SPV was chosen to comply with the law governing the European elections and the participation of non-parties in the elections.

and lists from moderate or conservative Green associations and parties, to left-extremist affiliations such as the *Alternative Liste* in Berlin, the *Bunte Liste* in Hamburg and others, as well as a multitude of local alternative, Green or multi-coloured lists (Tageszeitung 19.7.1979; 20.8.1979; 18.9.1979).

When Herbert Gruhl, the chairman of the conservative *Grüne Aktion Zukunft* announced that a national party was to be founded by November 1979, the left-wing lists and affiliations were caught unprepared. The decisive event which persuaded the left to look towards a national party was the electoral success of a moderate Green list in Bremen which won 5.1% and entered the Land parliament. The *Bremer Grüne Liste* had been founded by two SPD dissidents and won the upper hand despite competition from an *Alternative Liste* under communist control which could score a mere 1.4% of the vote (Willers 1982: 169). These events convinced the 'electoral movement' on the left that it 'would not stand a political chance at national level outside the Green Party' (Bolaffi and Kallscheuer 1983: 74).

The party congress of the Other Political Association The Greens in Offenbach on 3 November 1979, decided to move towards creating a political party of the same name at national level. The official founders' meeting should only be attended by elected delegates from those party organisations at district and regional level which had already existed at the time of the European elections. Discussions with the delegates from the broad political left and from alternative lists were scheduled to be held on the second day of the congress: a resolution to allow them full membership rights was turned down. However, the assembly refused to ban (by 348 to 311 votes) dual membership in the Greens and in communist groups or multi-coloured lists.

Thus, the new party had become accessible to the extreme left although some activists were not immediately prepared to go down this road. The most important controversy over the issue of Green party membership arose within the Communist Federation. At a congress on 1 December 1979, the leadership committee of the Communist Federation — a non-elected body based on self-recruitment — called on the delegates to vote the executive of the *Bunte Liste* in Hamburg out of office since they advocated supporting the new Green party. At that time, the executive of the *Bunte Liste* was directed by the so-called Centre

101

Executive of the Communist Federation whose task it should have been to co-ordinate communist policies in certain areas. However, the Centre Executive (which has since become known as the *Z-Fraktion*) demanded recognition as a separate political group in order to pursue its goal of collaborating in the Green party more effectively. The Communist Federation responded by expelling the *Z-Fraktion* from its ranks, a move which the group itself refused to recognise. From the perspective of the *Z-Fraktion*, a division of labour rather than a split characterised its links with the Communist Federation. It intended to gain the elbow room to join the Greens without, however, renouncing its political convictions. Thomas Ebermann, himself a former member of the Leading Committee of the Communist Federation, explained that the *Z-Fraktion* was interested in

> securing the maximum possible influence in the Green electoral movement, in order to ensure the survival of communism in the present day situation. . . . We advocate the principle of bloc formation, in order to change the negotiating positions vis-à-vis the Green-alternatives, in order to exert more pressure on the Greens, and in order to keep the option of joining the Greens open (*Frankfurter Allgemeine Zeitung* 16.7.1982).

At the time, the *Z-Fraktion* numbered 200 of the 700 Communist Federation members and joined the Greens en bloc. By the end of 1979, some 500 supporters of the *Bunte Liste* in Hamburg had moved towards the Greens (*Frankfurter Rundschau* 30.1.1980).

In Berlin, the *Alternative Liste* decided unanimously on 13 December 1979 to join the Greens. By January 1980, 600 members — the active core of the party — had done so (Bühnemann: 122). Elsewhere, the shift towards the new party was more patchy, but groups of activists from Green and alternative lists with strong communist and left-wing influences joined the Other Political Association The Greens. At the time when *Die Grünen* were created as a national party, its predecessor had some 10,000 members, at least 1,400 of them left-wing members and activists of multi-coloured and alternative lists.

When the new party *Die Grünen* was finally created during the congress in Karlsruhe on 12 and 13 January 1980, 140 of the 1,004 official delegates came from the left and alternative camp, and most of them were also members of one of the communist organisations. The congress was brought under pressure from inside and out: in support of the left-wing delegates, a further 254 so-called autonomous delegates of multi-coloured and alternative lists had arrived in Karlsruhe, among them 100 representatives from the Berlin *Alternative Liste*. The decision to boost the left-wing contingent had been taken at a preparatory congress of left-wing and alternative organisations in Frankfurt (Klotzsch and Stöss 1984: 1535; 1566). Predictably, the congress in Karlsruhe was dominated by disputes about the participation in the Greens of the organised extreme left (*Tageszeitung* 14.1.1980). The potential influence of the left was evident when the demand of the 254 self-styled delegates for full recognition as members of congress was only turned down by a 60/40% majority. After this, the 'alternatives' proceeded to hold their own congress in an adjoining room. A similarly narrow majority voted to ban dual membership in the Greens and other political parties: 548 delegates voted for the motion while 414 preferred that regional parties should make their own decisions; 6 delegates abstained. As it was phrased, the ban on dual party membership did little to obstruct the extreme left since most of its organisations were not constituted as political parties and thus not affected by the ruling. Among the so-called *K-Gruppen*, only the KPD held party status, the others saw themselves as associations or groups (Mez and Wolter: 24).

Based on their 40% control of the vote, the left forced the founding congress in Karlsruhe to shelve the issue of dual membership and allow regional parties to arrive at their own organisational practices. This second concession to the left was supported by 478 delegates and rejected by 397 (*Die Zeit* 18. 1.1980). The loophole in the regulations was used especially in Hamburg and Berlin where dual membership remained permissible even beyond the agreed cut-off point of 30 April 1980. To this day, members of the Greens in Hamburg can also be members of other — including communist — political parties (§ 2 section 1 of the GAL statutes).

The second important outcome of Karlsruhe concerned agreement on a short preamble to the future party programme. The commission which had already prepared a draft party programme, had included some representatives from the left who had prepared their moves well. Originally, the Programme

103

Commission consisted of 11 members: three representatives of the *Grüne Aktion Zukunft*, including Herbert Gruhl, three representatives of the neutralist and generally right-wing AUD including August Haußleiter, three representatives of the *Grüne Liste Umweltschutz*, including Jan Kuhnert who also belonged to the Socialist Bureau, and one representative each of the conservative Greens in Schleswig-Holstein and the *Achberger Kreis*. After massive pressures from the left, and against determined opposition within the committee, four further members were co-opted: all of them representatives of the multi-coloured and alternative left, namely Ernst Hoplitschek of the *Alternative Liste* Berlin; Jürgen Reents of the *Bunte Liste* Hamburg executive; Manfred Zieran of the *Grüne Liste Hessen* and a female spokesperson of the *Bunte Liste* Bonn to represent the North Rhine-Westphalia region (Meyer and Handlögten 1980: 6f).

One of the moderate-right members later claimed that the reshuffle gave the left a majority of 9 or 10 against 5 moderates since the *Grüne Liste Umweltschutz*, the various *Bunte Listen* and representatives of the AUD worked closely together (Taute, 1980: 8f). Since the moderates were unable to develop a common approach they found themselves increasingly on the defensive and forced to defend 'the last bourgeois positions to a point of total physical and psychological exhaustion' (Lüdke 1980: 207). A last attempt at expelling the four co-opted left-wing members from the Programme Commission failed during the preparatory congress in Offenbach in November 1979; at this stage it had already become impossible to command a majority for such a move (*Tageszeitung* 5.11.1979).

In Karlsruhe the most moderate of the three draft preambles to the programme was chosen as the basis for discussion; the left could, however, win the agreement of congress on a number of important modifications. The initial wording read that it was one of the aims of the Greens to 'overcome the totalitarian systems of compulsive economic growth of a Western and Eastern type' (Document 2). This was replaced by the formula, that conditions should be overcome which were dominated by a short-term focus on growth which 'benefited only *segments of the population*' (Italics H.F.). Similarly, a sentence was deleted which suggested that the Greens would oppose not only 'wars and destructions' but also 'revolutions'.

Attempts by the *Z-Fraktion* failed to supplement the renunciation of violence by a clause which would acknowledge a 'right to resistance and social self-defence (*Notwehr*)' against 'acts of violence and repression on the part of the state'. A blanket acceptance of the Basic Law in the party statutes was modified on the insistence of the left; the Greens now advocate 'a further development of the constitutional foundations' if 'these foundations do not offer sufficient scope to realise their political aims'. The changes, although a compromise, appeared to satisfy the left: the *Z-Fraktion* at least felt that they were 'adequately represented through the programme of the Greens' (*Der Spiegel* 29,1982: 36).

The most important result of the founding congress in Karlsruhe was, in the eyes of left extremists that 'the left wing had grown considerably to constitute a sizeable minority within the Greens which can no longer be excluded from the party without endangering its very existence' (*Z—Organ der Z-Fraktion* — 1.2.1980: 6).

After Karlsruhe, the left concentrated its energies on preparing the party congress which was to decide the Green programme and had been called for 21–3 March 1980 in Saarbrücken. A week beforehand, advocates of the extreme left in the Greens organised a meeting in Bielefeld to co-ordinate its approaches (Klotzsch and Stöss 1984: 1568). Events at the Saarbrücken congress showed clearly that the left had grown from a minority into a majority. The left-alternative *Tageszeitung* reported that alternative and multi-coloured lists had won vote after vote (24.3.1980). The organisational experience of the communist activists who had joined the Greens enabled them to skilfully manipulate the agenda, to dominate the party commission which prepared motions and resolutions; they even distributed flysheets to assist delegates with making up their minds and casting their votes (Lüdke 1980: 207; 210). The concerted approach of the left ground to a halt at the election of the three equally-ranked members of the executive when the failure of two leftist factions to agree on one candidate allowed a moderate spokesman of the *Grüne Liste Umweltschutz* in North Rhine-Westphalia, Norbert Mann to win the seat, which appeared to have been earmarked for the left. In the event, this proved a minor setback. The party programme which was

105

accepted in Saarbrücken, contained 'the whole range of themes and demands which had been voiced by the multiplicity of leftist groups after the student movement in 1968' (Grupp 1986: 27). The 'taz' wrote that the resolutions sounded 'more like a summary list of all the demands which the left had ever articulated during the last ten years and advocated in public than like the formulation of political goals based on ecological principles' (24.3.1980). No more than 10% of the Saarbrücken programme was devoted to ecological issues.

The extreme left succeeded in incorporating classical features of Marxist ideology into the Green party programme. Thus we find a version of Marx's theory of impoverishment: 'Our social conditions produce social and psychological poverty of the masses.'[9] The section on the economy stresses 'the exploitation of people by people' as typical for the 'economic crisis of industrial societies'; and blames 'short-term interests in profit' for the 'destruction of nature.' 'Production is not determined by the needs of people but by the interest of monopoly capital'. As a way out, the programme recommends 'that those affected should themselves decide *what* should be produced, *how* it should be produced and *where* this should be done.'[10]

The *Z-Fraktion* seemed particularly happy with this part of the programme: 'The economic programme is not socialist — but the left find open doors to discuss socialist ideas in relation to the concrete demands articulated in the programme' (Z 28. 4. 1980: 6). Subsequent Green programmes on the economy — that passed in Sindelfingen in 1983; the Restructuring Programme of 1986 or the 1987 Electoral Programme — did not modify the anti-capitalist and Marxist tendencies of the early days but developed them in a more concrete, elaborate manner (Document 3).

Concerning the use of violence, the *Bundesprogramm* also changed tack and declared that the renunciation of violence in

9. Thus, Thomas Schmid, a former SDS activist, member of the group *Revolutionärer Kampf* and recently a spokesman for the eco-libertarians in the Greens noted in the Bundesprogramm 'the good old Marxist-Leninist theory of catastrophes, the nearly exalted obsession with collapse, the applause for impoverishment.' 'One should say it openly: there is no doubt that Leninist Marxists had a major hand in formulating this programme . . .' Schmid 1983: 48f.

10. This formula has been adopted from the ideologies of the *Achberger Kreis* (Meyer and Handlögten 1980: 16).

principle did not curtail 'the fundamental right of self-defence and includes social resistance in its many different modes' (p. 5).

The successes achieved by the left in Saarbrücken did not pass unnoticed. Two days after the party congress, the chairman of the Leading Committee of the Communist Federation instructed his followers in a circular: 'I am in favour of massive participation in the Greens' (Z 22.4.1980).

After Saarbrücken: Consolidation of the Left

In the various Land organisations of the Greens which were created or reconstituted after the party congress in Saarbrücken, the left remained an important voice. When the Land organisation of the Greens in Hamburg was founded in 1980, 80 of the 200 or so members also belonged to the *Z-Fraktion*. Two of their number, Ingo Borsum and Jürgen Reents joined the new executive with the highest number of votes, 83 and 77 respectively. In the spring of 1983, five of the eleven members of the executive originated in the *Z-Fraktion* which had remained the 'organisational backbone of the Greens in Hamburg' (Bading: 124).

In competition with the Green land organisation, an independent *Alternative Liste* was founded in Hamburg at the end of 1981. It included some activists from the Communist Federation, some of the so-called non-organised left, former members of the Socialist Studies Group (SOST) and, most importantly two former members of the SPD executive in Hamburg, Christian Schmidt and Regula Schmidt-Bott. Despite extensive power struggles between the *Z-Fraktion* and its new rivals an agreement about a joint electoral list was reached, the *Grün-Alternative Wahlliste* (GAL). In November 1984, a joint Green Land organisation (GAL) was created through the formal merger of the *Alternative Liste* with its 1,200 members, and the Hamburg Greens with its 800 (*Süddeutsche Zeitung* 19.11.1984).

At federal level, the *Z-Fraktion* encountered more difficulties than the party congress at Saarbrücken had led them to expect. In Saarbrücken a working group *Basisdemokratischer Undogmatischer Sozialisten* had been created by members of the Socialist Bureau, of the so-called Grassroot Groups (*Basisgruppen*) and journalists working for the alternative newspaper *Tageszeitung*. All had an undogmatic approach to politics on the left, and all were interested in ensuring that the conservatives who had been co-founders of the Greens would remain in the party and help boost the moderates against attempts from the dogmatic communist and even Leninist factions to set the political tone. The working party called on the *Z-Fraktion* to identify office holders, and to make their meetings open to the public (Grupp 1986: 31f). In early January 1981 a number of prominent Greens launched a petition to collect signatures to demand a 'clear detachment from the Z-group' (*Info Die Grünen*, Hamburg 7.3.1981: 31). For Hamburg, the petition insisted that a new Land organisation be founded. Through the Z-group, they argued 'people had come into the Greens who were former (?) functionaries of the Communist Federation' and who had 'no interest whatever in ecological problems but were only interested in utilising for their own purposes what had been created.' 'The Z-group has managed to occupy all key positions and to alienate everyone from the party who does not agree with them. They have done this through conspiratorial and aggressive tactics, through defamation and ridiculing of political opponents. It was inevitable that the Land organisation would degenerate into a dogmatic sect of the left' (*Info Die Grünen*, Hamburg 7.3.1981: 34). The controversy was discussed at the meeting of the Main Federal Committee (*Bundeshauptausschuß*, BHA) on 21 and 22 February 1981 in Kassel. It passed the (ambiguous?) resolution: 'groups which attempt to force their secretly formulated decisions on the Green party *cannot* exist within the Greens' (Italics H.F.; ibid: 44). A committee was formed to examine whether the activities of the *Z-Fraktion* were compatible with Green party principles; Albrecht Schmeißner and Roland Vogt were among its members. The committee prepared a report which ruled in favour of the *Z-Fraktion* — as a result none of its members has yet been excluded from the party. Since then, the *Z-Fraktion* appears to have extended its influence to the regional executives of Schleswig-Holstein, North Rhine-Westphalia, and Baden-Württemberg and elsewhere (*Süddeutsche Zeitung* 11.3.83; *Die Zeit* 20.12.1985; *Frankfurter Allgemeine Zeitung* 4.1.1984).

While the left sought a foothold in the Greens, events in Berlin took a different turn. The *Alternative Liste* had refused to accept the renunciation of violence which constitutes one of the core commitments of the Greens (*Der Spiegel* 31, 1981: 50–60).

Although a Green Land organisation was created and 80% of its 800 or so members came from the *Alternative Liste*, although a Green executive had been formed and included a former functionary of the splinter KPD, Johanna Mayr, Otto Schily and also Ossip Flechtheim, the organisation never operated independently and agreed not to yield candidates in Land elections to compete against the *Alternative Liste* (*Süddeutsche Zeitung* 12–13.1. 1985). Otto Schily, who had earlier castigated the *Alternative Liste* as too far to the left, rejoined it in February 1980. Commenting on his assessment of two years before he said: 'my views then that the *Alternative Liste* would be dominated by centrally organised communist factions has not been borne out by events. It is possible that the comrades, who are still entangled in dogmatic ideas, can disentangle themselves and find, perhaps [!] a different level of political discussion' (*Tageszeitung* 22.2.1980). One year later, Schily confessed to having 'underestimated the ability of male and female comrades from the former communist party to change their views and learn' and asked 'with a quiver in his voice' that 'the *Alternative Liste* should make their peace with him' (*Der Spiegel* 4.5.1981: 44).

Other observers of the political scene were less optimistic. Rosemarie Stein, a member of the parliamentary group in the district assembly in Berlin-Wilmersdorf for the *Alternative Liste* noted 'with concern how those with several years' of party discipline and organisational practice are beginning to take over' (*AL-Mitgliederrundbrief* No. 12, April 1981: 11). At about the same time, Volker Skierka reported in the *Süddeutsche Zeitung*: 'it has become very clear that the *Alternative Liste* is steered from the background by some 40 or 50 activists who also play a major part in the so-called multi-coloured movement in the Federal Republic' (24.4.1981). One month later, the news magazine *Der Spiegel* reported: 'the direction of the new alternative political party is being determined by comrades, schooled in the tactics of the Maoist KPD and its many defunct branch-enterprises . . .' (4.5.1981: 36).

The Collapse of Left-extremist Organisations

The extent to which left-extremist forces have shifted their activities to the Green Party throughout the Federal Republic is evident from four organisations whose fate we shall sketch briefly: the *Kommunistische Partei Deutschlands*, KPD dissolved in March 1980 after its membership had dropped from 700 in 1976 to 550 in 1978. A core of about 100 comrades continued to work together in an informal group which also stopped functioning one year later. The *Spiegel* commented at the time: 'what had at first glance appeared to be the failure of a self-important would-be avant-garde soon emerged as the rather purposeful dissolution into the multi-coloured and alternative electoral alliances which formed everywhere' (4.5.1981: 44).

The *Kommunistische Bund Westdeutschland*, KBW stopped functioning in February 1985 after its membership had declined from a peak of nearly 3,000 in 1978 to 1,000 in 1981; 500 in 1982 and finally 300 in 1983. At the eve of the 1983 federal elections, the KBW called on its supporters to vote Green. At the time of its dissolution it held financial and property assets worth around 9 million Deutschmark, most of them collected through membership dues. The KBW's legal heir and successor became an 'Association' which absorbed its core. Joscha Schmierer, a former functionary of the socialist student group SDS in Heidelberg was appointed co-administrator of the financial assets; he also had been a member of the KBW executive, and one of its leading theoreticians. The 'Association' decided to make its funds available to the 'left-Green-alternative spectrum' (*Süddeutsche Zeitung* 18.2.1985). The former headquarters of the KBW in Frankfurt (Mainzer Landstraße 147) were now used, among other things, to house the newly launched journal *Kommune* (editor Joscha Schmierer), the Trotskyist Group of International Marxists (GIM) and also the Land organisation of the Greens in Hesse and their district organisation in Frankfurt. Schmierer is reported to have said in 1984 that the members of his cadre party had 'managed to find a foothold in a number of political contexts, in citizens' and peace initiatives or in the Greens and produce solid political work in these contexts' (*Konkret* 12, 1984: 50). One year later, the KBW declared: 'We are today an integral part of the Green-alternative movement.' The collapse of the student movement had split the left to such an extent that it had become 'politically paralysed'. The emergence of the Greens, however, started a 'new process of unification' (*Darmstädter Echo* 18.2.1985).

The Communist Federation (*Kommunistischer Bund*, KB) has

just 1,700 members in 1977, 900 of these in Hamburg. Two years later, no more than a third remained. By increased commitment in the 'electoral movement', it succeeded in 1980 to gain some new members. By 1984, however, it invited its membership to transfer 'individually but jointly' to the Greens (*Betrifft* 1984: 93). At the end of 1986, a remnant of 400 members continued to belong to the KB, 200 in Hamburg alone (*Betrifft* 1986: 116).

In its heyday in 1978, the Socialist Bureau (SB) in Offenbach had 1,200 members throughout the Federal Republic. In 1979, its Council of Delegates called on the membership to support the 'grassroots-democratic and socialist groups' and the multi-coloured, alternative and Green voters' initiatives which had begun to emerge (Langguth 1983: 197). By 1983, membership of the Socialist Bureau had declined to 700 and the Ministry of the Interior reported its imminent collapse (*Betrifft* 1983: 89).

The influx of communist and New Left activists into the Greens continues to be relevant. The 1986 Report for the Protection of the Constitution noted that members of communist groupings (*K-Gruppen*) and Trotskyists continued to regard the Greens and Green-alternative lists as a suitable vehicle in order to move closer towards their revolutionary goals (*Betrifft* 1986: 100). A number of them shifted into the Greens in order to strengthen the eco-socialist wing within the party. On the other hand, a presumed tendency of the Greens towards an 'accommodation with the state' and a proliferation of 'theories hostile to the working class' has provoked sharp criticism within groupings of the New Left.

For the Greens, the fact that 'the bankruptcy stock of a number of communist sects had come into the party' had far-reaching consequences. To quote from a 1984 declaration of the so-called Eco-libertarians, a circle of Greens from the founder generation: the party has 'from the outset been largely dominated by socialist cadres whose goals are anything but Green' (*Grüner Basisdienst* 3, 1984).

The Left in the Green Party Elite

Looking at the personal composition of the Green party elite, and its political origins we can test the influence which members

111

of extremist or radical organisations on the left have exerted on the new party. At the same time we can show the range of political orientations and affiliations which have converged in the Greens.

In this section, we focus on the political background of leading office holders and elected members of parliaments. We have included the 47 members of the Green party executive who have held positions between the founding days of the European party in 1979 and April 1987, and we have also included all the 260 Greens who were elected in the same period into the Bundestag, one of the Land parliaments or into the European parliament.[11] Allowing for the fact that some of the Green elite occupied both types of position, our sample represents 299 individuals.

Parties are not created in a political vacuum: more than half the 300 or so office holders and elected delegates had been active in another political party or organisation prior to their role in the Greens.[12] One in five (20%) had previously belonged to another of the parties represented in the Bundestag; most of them (14%) to the SPD (Table 4.2). Only 5% of the office holders and elected delegates originated from a political party or organisation of the far right — most are no longer influential within the Greens.

At least 33% — 100 of the 299 office holders — were or still are members of a left extremist or radical party or organisation. Thus, this group constitutes the largest ideologically and politically 'pre-shaped' section within the party elite of the Greens. Members of the dogmatic *K-Gruppen* constitute the largest group with 15%, followed by supporters of the non-dogmatic left such as the Socialist Bureau, the *Basisgruppen*, *Spontis*, so-called autonomous groups with 14%. Of the office holders, 5% had been members of the core organisation of the student movement in the late sixties, the *Sozialistischer Deutscher Studentenbund* SDS or a similar group. About the same number had belonged to the official communist party, the DKP or were members of DKP

11. The sample includes some of the designated *Nachrücker*, Greens who have not been elected but who had been next on the electoral list and should rotate into parliamentary office at the half-way stage. The data have been collated from the official handbooks, from biographical sketches normally written by the candidates themselves; from a survey of 84 office holders (42% response) and information collected from Green publications and the press. See Fogt 1986: 16–33; Fogt 1989.

12. It has to be borne in mind that some of these memberships stretch back into the sixties. Members of affiliated organisations have also been counted as members, e.g. of the *Arbeitsgemeinschaft sozialdemokratischer Frauen* ASF, of the *Junge Union* JU, etc.

Table 4.2. The Green Party Elite: Former membership in other organisations and Parties

	Memberships overall[1]	elite positions	Memberships in % of all 299 office holders
	N	N	%
Main Political Parties[2]			
SPD	42	8	14
FDP	8	3	3
CDU/CSU	10	4	3
Parties and Organisations of the Right:			
AUD	12	8	4
Right-extremist organisations	2	1	1
Left-extremist and left-radical parties/organisations SDS and SDS-affiliated organisations	14	5	5
DKP and DKP-affiliated organisations	15	4	5
Dogmatic 'New Left' (K-Gruppen)	43	8	15
Groups with terrorist links	4	1	1
Undogmatic 'New Left' (*Sozialist. Büro Basisgruppen, Spontis, Autonome*)	41	9	14
Left-radical student groups	5	1	2
Total %	100	25	34

1. Taking multiple memberships into account
2. Including affiliated organisations

affiliated organisations such as peace groups or the student groups *Marxistischer Studentenbund Spartakus* (MSB) and *Sozialistischer Hochschulbund* (SHB).

Overall, at least 79 leading representatives of the Greens and their land organisations, i.e. 26% of the office holders, had, during the last fifteen years, belonged to a party or organisation which the Ministry of the Interior has tended to classify as being on the extreme left of the political spectrum and opposed to the constitution. Since the founding period of the party, activists of the extreme left have been strongly represented among the office holders and elected delegates and have managed to expand their personal influence during the lifetime of the Green Party.

Aims and Political Tactics of the Organised Left in the Green Party

Why, we must ask, was the left tempted to participate in the activities of the Greens and what kind of aims or intentions do these groups hold in connection with a party which had originally focused on environmental protection? Broadly speaking, three aims are apparent: First, the hard core of the left hopes to create a new political party with a left-socialist orientation, and uses the Greens as a means to this end. Second, the left is hampered in these aspirations by the presence of the SPD and hopes to weaken and divide it. Third, political discussion and participation appear to have the sole purpose of creating the preconditions for a fundamental change of the economic and social order in the Federal Republic. Within the party, factions such as the eco-socialists, the so-called realists with their interest in the SPD, and finally the fundamentalists are the inner-organisational equivalents of the three broad aims, each vying for dominance despite similarities in origin and intent. There are no 'good' or 'bad' Greens; Greens who are capable of political co-operation — *politikfähig* — and Greens who are not — *politikunfähig*. Rather, the Greens consist of a relatively broad continuum of practical, political, strategic and tactical positions within a basically left-radical internal range of views.

How left-extremist organisations proceeded to influence the Green-alternative electoral movement in the founding days has been described by a former functionary of the *Bunte Liste* Hamburg, Holger Strohm. His experiences can stand for many similar ones: 'It really is not easy to provide proof for the tactics of the Communist Federation. It is never publicly known who is a member and who is not. They remain neutral, they volunteer for work and do their work conscientiously. Since hardly anyone is prepared to take on anything, the Communist Federation slowly moves into many key positions. Due to its strictly hier-archical structure it is at a great advantage compared with the non-hierarchical citizens' initiatives in controlling the involve-ment of its members. No Communist Federation member does anything by chance; only if they already command an absolute majority may it be up to the member himself to decide whether or not to turn up for a vote' (Strohm 1978: 133). In its bid to control the *Bunte Liste*, the Communist Federation in Hamburg used 'manipulation through gossip and slander and even physical assault' (*Die Zeit* 25.1.1980). Twenty-six of the citizens' initiatives which were presumably affiliated to the *Bunte Liste* in 1978, were in fact no more than post-box companies of the Communist Federa-tion (Hallensleben 1984: 94).

The take-over of the *Alternative Liste* in Berlin by the KPD was engineered in a similar fashion. An unnamed letter writer re-ported from the founding congress in 1978 in Berlin:

> When it was time to vote after a general debate a comrade in a red jumper and white shirt rose from one of the front rows. I know him well, he has been active in a number of communist student organis-ations for years. . . . He casually leaned against the banisters, and started to look intently at a big white sheet of paper. This young man did not lose a single vote. At the same time as the white paper in his hand, some 350 hands flew synchronised into the air. In short, he gave the KPD lead . . . (*Radikal* 12, 1978: 6).

To assume that such events may have occurred in the found-ing phase of alternative lists but are unlikely elsewhere, would be mistaken. Joscha Schmierer, former chairman of the KBW 'has to always think of the Green district organisation. How the *Sponti*-gang in Frankfurt tried to catch a glimpse of Cohn-Bendit or Fischer in order to raise their hands at the right time during a vote. How he/she intently studies the facial expressions of the guru of the day in order to gather from a smile or a frown how to keep in line' (*Konkret* 12, 1984: 51).

To this day it has remained one of the characteristic features of Green party meetings that the leaders of the different currents and cliques gather their followers in a corner of the hall for permanent internal voting, and to this day the various groups informally agree how they will vote on various issues, make skilful use of the changing moods of the party faithfuls for their

115

own ends, while the presidencies of the respective meetings steer motions and voters in their own desired direction. Ernst Hoplitschek noted in 1984 that Green party congresses and committees are 'nailed shut with hard-liners who frequently come from the collapsed dogmatic left, and who stage-manage and manipulate party congresses already in their preparatory phases' (*Stuttgarter Nachrichten* 25.2.1984). The principle of public accessibility which the Greens tend to emphasise seems ill-suited to combat and exposes 'a cleverly designed and skilfully handled cadre approach' — on the contrary, the principle of public accessibility seems to encourage undemocratic forces to make extensive use of the ostensibly open meetings (Gert Bastian, *Tageszeitung* 12.1.1984; Fogt 1984: 97f).

At the time of the 1983 federal elections, the Greens decided to subject their parliamentarians to the so-called 'imperative mandate', a measure which flouted the relevant guidelines in the Basic Law about the freedom of elected delegates: 'The Greens in the Bundestag have to abide by the decisions of the Federal Party Assembly (*Bundesversammlung*) and the Main Party Committee (*Bundeshauptausschuß*). Contraventions of these decisions can lead to the expulsion from the parliamentary group' (*Frankfurter Allgemeine Zeitung* 21.1.1983). Immediately after the elections, the *Bundeshauptausschuß* tried to impose a party diktat with a sub-committee of three people charged to 'regularly observe' the parliamentary group and monitor the political performance of elected delegates; after intense protests against the 'political commissars' the sub-committee had to be disbanded (*Süddeutsche Zeitung* 9–10.4.1983; *Konkret* 5, 1983: 14). In November 1983, the *Bundeshauptausschuß* impatiently demanded 'regular reports in writing and attendance of parliamentary party representatives at its meetings'. The threat to stage a demonstration at the parliamentary group was accompanied by the demand that 'full account should be given of all incomes' which had been received by the parliamentarians up to a certain date (*Grüner Basisdienst* 11, 1983: 7).

Similar efforts by the left to employ in the Green party those mechanisms of political control which had been used in the *K-Gruppen* environment were also undertaken in the parliamentary group itself. In December 1986 the member of the Bundestag Henning Schierholz protested that he was not prepared 'to co-operate even for a single day with functionaries such as Jürgen Reents (a former member of the *Z-Fraktion*, H.F.) who act in the manner of Stalinist political-commissars.' In the parliamentary Greens, he detected 'a tendency towards an accumulation of power, political camps and nepotism' and 'a total collapse of political culture' (*Frankfurter Rundschau* 5.12.1986). A few days later, the parliamentary group published a list containing the names of all their members who had defaulted on paying the stipulated proportion of their remuneration into the so-called 'Eco-Fund'. Publishing these details served, as the authors freely admitted, the purpose of putting pressure on elected members of the House who were legally not obliged to any payments (*Frankfurter Rundschau* 11.12.1986; *Frankfurter Allgemeine Zeitung* 11.12.1986). Gert Bastian, who had already clashed with his party about the political scope individual members of parliament were to be allowed, called the blacklist 'a kind of psychological terror bordering on extortion' and severed his links with the Greens in the Bundestag — for the second time (letter to the *Fraktion*, 27.12.1986).

The Emergence of a Left Party Elite

As mentioned earlier, the founder members who came to the Greens from organisations and parties of the extreme left have established a strong position in the party elite from the outset, and continue to play leading roles. Some examples will help to illustrate the structure and cohesion of the elite in the Greens, and the strong place of the left in it. Thomas Ebermann for instance, a founder member of the Greens in Hamburg, was elected to the Land parliament in 1982 and to the Bundestag in 1987. His political friend from Communist Federation days, Rainer Trampert, was a candidate for the *Bunte Liste* in Hamburg in 1978, a member of the programme commission of the Greens and acted as one of three spokespersons for the party from 1982 to 1987. After the 1987 federal elections he joined the Greens in the Bundestag as Ebermann's assistant. Jutta Ditfurth, to give one further example, was a founder member of the left-radical *Grüne Liste Hessen* in 1978 and from 1979 to 1985 held a seat for the Greens on the Frankfurt council. In 1984 she was elected into the federal executive of the party, and re-elected in 1987 for a further two years.

The founder members from the left have used the Greens to create lasting political careers for themselves. The permanent change of personnel in elite positions which seemed to be the aim of statutory regulations such as the well known 'principle of rotation' has not occurred, in particular not among the exponents of the radical left in the party (Fogt 1984). It has become standard practice in the Greens to nominally heed the ban on holding more than one office and move from office to office in a manner which can be called *Querrotation* — sideways rotation. In effect, key offices are always held by the same small party elite. The political leaders change the type of post they occupy and switch back and forth between parliamentary positions and party offices. Or they might take on administrative positions and become business managers of the party or assistants in the Bundestag parliamentary group. In changing functions they also change political levels, moving freely between local, regional, national and European politics.

The countless possibilities of combining offices are well used: of the 260 Green members of parliaments at regional, national and European level, at least one in three held an executive party office immediately before or after their parliamentary mandate. If we include local government, 14% had already held three or more party posts or parliamentary seats. Of the Greens who were elected as members of the Bundestag in 1987, no less than 43% (19 out of 44) had served in the previous Bundestag, in a land parliament or had been members of the Green Party executive.

These processes of self-recruitment have been castigated as 'party internal oligarchies' and the emergence within the Greens of a 'professional party elite' (*Die Zeit* 27.2.1987). One of the founder members, Martin Schata, complained that the Greens were dominated by a 'clique of functionaries with very little exchange of personnel' (*Frankfurter Allgemeine Zeitung* 13.2. 1986). This clique consists mainly of former members of radical or extremist organisations on the left. As early as 1983, a former executive member of the *Kommunistischer Bund Westdeutschlands* (KBW) and subsequently a member of the Green parliamentary group in Bremen, Ralf Fücks noted: 'The virtually dominant type of Green politician is the male (exceptionally: female) seasoned old-left activist between the ages 30 and 40, with his fragments of theoretical knowledge, his political experience, his tactical skills and his willingness to spend half his life in meetings; he has almost naturally assumed control as the Greens became a political force' (*Kommune* 12, 1983: 12).

Conclusion

Since the founding days the activists from the left have, of course, changed their approach in the Greens; this is only to be expected. What this change entails, however, and whether it is a change of direction or merely a change of emphasis without a change of political intent, is less apparent. In their policy goals, these activists have retained three core demands of the extreme left: socialisation of the means of production; the destruction of the German state which is presumed to be dominated by class interests; and revolution as the ultimate long-term perspective of their policy.

Even the so-called 'realists' in the party who are often credited with taking a more moderate approach, underwrite these transformative goals:

> When the Greens are in parliament today, they have to focus on changes which can be carried out today but which prepare the ground for a more fundamental change of the power structure itself. . . . Such a strategic approach does not mean that the Greens have given up the idea of revolution. What they have given up is the idea of riotous uprisings and pseudo-revolutions (Müller and Falkenberg 1984: 34).

The expectation of many political observers that the Greens could be an asset to democratic stability by integrating the extreme left into the democratic process have not been fulfilled. In particular, the 'eco-socialist' camp in the Greens has not undergone an 'inspirational change of heart.' Their programme is little more than an adaptation of classical Marxist ideology to a notion of 'crisis development in late capitalism', this time overshadowed by increasing ecological dangers. This constellation offers novel challenges to the agitation and propaganda of the extreme left. Since the left has begun to utilise the Greens it can meet these challenges calmly and efficiently: 'their' party enjoys considerable electoral support, receives impressive media coverage, and is represented throughout the Federal Republic in parliaments and other elected bodies, and it even scored first successes in winning executive power at governmental level. Indeed, 'in the whole history of the Federal Republic the left has never been as strong as it is today' (Eduard Neumaier in *Stuttgarter Zeitung* 26.8.1985).

References

Bading, Lothar (1982), 'Soziale Bewegungen — politische Strömungen und Verallgemeinerungen — Wahlen' *Marxistische Studien* 5

Betrifft: Verfassungsschutz ed. Bundesminister des Inneren, Bonn (annually)

Bieber, Horst (1980), 'Die Grünen. Dossier', *Die Zeit* 25 January

Bolaffi, Angelo and Otto Kallscheuer (1983), 'Die Grünen: Farbenlehre eines politischen Paradoxes', *Probleme des Klassenkampfes* 51

Bühnemann, Michael *et al* (eds.) (1984), *Die Alternative Liste Berlin* Berlin: Lit Pol

Dutschke, Rudi (1977), 'Subkultur und Partei' *Das da* 11; also in Dutschke (1980) *Geschichte ist machbar*, Berlin: Wagenbach

Fogt, Helmut (1984), 'Basisdemokratie oder Herrschaft der Aktivisten?' *Politische Vierteljahresschrift* 25

—— (1986), 'Die Mandatsträger der Grünen: Zur sozialen und politischen Herkunft der alternativen Parteielite', *Aus Politik und Zeitgeschichte* 11

—— (1989), 'Zwischen Parteiorganisation und Bewegung. Die Rekrutierung der Mandatsträger der Grünen', in Heinrich Oberreuter (ed.), *Wer kommt in die Parlamente?*, Baden-Baden: Nomos

Grupp, Joachim (1986), *Abschied von den Grundsätzen? Die Grünen zwischen Koalition und Opposition*. Berlin: Edition Ahrens

Hallensleben, Anna (1984a), *Von der Grünen Liste zur Grünen Partei*. Göttingen: Musterschmidt

—— (1984b), 'Wie alles anfing . . .', in Thomas Kluge (ed.), *Grüne Politik*, Frankfurt: Fischer

Hoplitschek, Ernst (1982), 'Partei, Avantgarde, Heimat — oder was? Die 'Alternative Liste für Demokratie und Umweltschutz' in West Berlin', in Jörg R. Mettke (ed.), *Die Grünen. Regierungspartner von morgen?*, Reinbek: Rowohlt

Horacek, Milan (1982), 'Zwischen uns und den Etablierten liegen Welten', in Jörg R. Mettke, *Die Grünen*, Reinbek: Rowohlt

Klotzsch, Lilian and Richard Stöss (1984), 'Die Grünen' in Richard Stöss (ed.), *Parteienhandbuch* vol. 2, Opladen: Westdeutscher Verlag

Langguth, Gerd (1983, 2nd. ed.), *Protestbewegung. Entwicklung. Niedergang. Renaissance. Die Neue Linke seit 1968*, Cologne: Wissenschaft und Politik

Lüdke, Hans-Werner (1980), 'Zur Entwicklungsgeschichte grüner Programme', in Hans-Werner Lüdke and Olaf Dinné (eds.), *Die Grünen. Personen — Projekte — Programme*, Stuttgart: Seewald

Mettke, Jörg R. (ed.) (1982), *Die Grünen. Regierungspartner von morgen?*, Reinbek: Rowohlt

Meyer, Rolf and Günter Handlögten (1980), 'Die Grünen vor der Wahl', *Aus Politik und Zeitgeschichte* 52

Mez, Lutz and Ulf Wolter (1980), 'Wer sind die Grünen?', in Lutz Mez and Ulf Wolter, *Die Qual der Wahl*, Berlin: Olle u. Wolter

Müller, Erhard and Gabriel Falkenberg (1984), 'Sechs Thesen für eine systemüberwindende Realpolitik', *Grüner Basisdienst* 5/6

Schiller-Dickhut, Reiner *et. al.* (1981), *Alternative Stadtpolitik*, Hamburg: VSA-Verlag

Schmid, Thomas (1983), 'Über die Schwierigkeiten der Grünen, in Gesellschaft zu leben und zu denken', *Freibeuter* 15

Schwagerl, H. Joachim (1985), *Verfassungsschutz in der Bundesrepublik Deutschland*, Heidelberg: C.F. Müller

Spretnak, Charlene (1985), *Die Grünen*, Munich: Beck

Stöss, Richard, *Vom Nationalismus zum Umweltschutz. Die Deutsche Gemeinschaft/Aktion Unabhängiger Deutscher im Parteiensystem der Bundesrepublik*, Opladen: Westdeutscher Verlag

—— (ed.) (1984), *Parteienhandbuch*, 2 vols. Opladen: Westdeutscher Verlag

Stöss, Richard (1984), 'Die Freisoziale Union', in Richard Stöss, *Parteienhandbuch*, Opladen: Westdeutscher Verlag

Strohm, Holger (1978), 'Warum die Bunten bunt sind', in Rudolf Brun (ed.), *Der grüne Protest*, Frankfurt: Fischer

Taute, Marie-Luise (1980), 'Wie konnte es zu dem Programm-Desaster in Saarbrücken kommen?' *agöp-informationen* 15.5.1980

Voigt, S. Karsten (1986), 'Der Mythos der politischen Kontinuität. Vom Frankfurter SDS zum realpolitischen Flügel der Grünen', *Neue Gesellschaft/Frankfurter Hefte* 33

Willers, Peter (1982), 'Den Tiefschlaf der Altparteien stören', in Jörg R. Mettke, *Die Grünen*, Reinbek: Rowohlt

Wir warn die stärkste der partein . . . (1977), Erfahrungsberichte aus der Welt der K-Gruppen, Berlin: Rotbuch

121

5

The Greens and the Intellectuals*

Norbert Kostede

The Greens, say the intellectuals, are anti-intellectual. Whether left or right, whether modern or post-modern, the intellect keeps its distance. The political left and the socialist representatives of the 'Project Modernity' argue that the Greens are post-modern and too critical of rational approaches. The French post-modernists, on the other hand, wary and without illusions as they are, are critical of the utopianism and the tendency among the German Greens to romanticise nature. The entire intellectual world declare themselves amused about the cosmic tones and spiritual feelings which have characterised Green fundamentalism. They are brimming with polemics against an alleged 'flirting with the world catastrophe'. They attack the Green sense of mission: 'The lack of theory is patched up by moral fervour and eagerness.' Even the intellectuals within the Greens raise similar points when their constant efforts to differentiate, and their political careers, clash with the need of political discourse to simplify matters.[1]

Are the Greens really anti-intellectual? And if they are — is it relevant? Why should a political party which deals in the interests of mankind and is paid in votes be concerned with the peculiar identity problems of a very marginal group of voters? Or does the accusation have to be taken more seriously: is it a warning signal that the Greens in their race to dominate public opinion are already heading for defeat?

Looking at the social structure of the Green Party, its electorate, its membership and its leadership, one is tempted to conclude the opposite: the Greens appear to be a party of

* Translated by Eva Kolinsky

1. Editor's note: The author has been a member of the Green Party since 1979, and a member of the federal executive from 1984–7 when he lost his seat in a shift towards Green fundamentalism. The chapter draws on these personal experiences in Green politics, and has been written from within the Green milieu by a committed participant and an inspired commentator.

intellectuals. Even if the Green electorate has begun to broaden and to include a cross-section of the population, young, urban educated people, intellectuals, clearly constitute its core. This is particularly true for the activists, the parliamentarians and the functionaries of the party. They grew up at a time of educational expansion and student rebellion, and their very biographies seem to disprove the charge of anti-intellectualism. How can a party of the critical intelligentsia possibly be anti-intellectual?

To answer this question, one is easily tempted to take refuge in polemics or point to everyday political controversies. In this chapter, I propose to clarify the link between Greens and intellectuals by making use of the sobering device of theoretical discussion. In two introductory statements, I hope to show that on the one hand the Greens constantly frustrate intellectual expectations and that, on the other, the fact that intellectuals have been disappointed in the Greens does not render the party anti-intellectual. I will then go on to show to what extent anti-intellectual tendencies permeate Green politics and how relevant they are. We shall see that the anti-intellectualism in the Greens is neither of the traditional kind nor indeed is it a label only applicable to the Green Party. In matters of intellectuality, and this will be my fourth point, the experiences of the Greens are similar to those of the intellectuals themselves: they get by — after a fashion.

Politics and Academic Research

'Political parties are anti-intellectual', 'intellectuals are apolitical' — these views and summary judgements contain a grain of truth: the sober distinction between politics and academic research (*Wissenschaft*). Both, the political and the scientific or academic approaches adhere to different norms and follow different rules or logical precepts. Politics concern themselves with power and the legitimacy of democratic decision-making while academic research is orientated towards establishing the truth. If political discourse is constantly compelled to remain comprehensible to everyone, the language of research and academic scholarship can accommodate necessary (and sometimes not so necessary) technicalities which only experts can understand. If the role of the politicians is essentially pragmatic, opportunist, and geared towards utilising mass media, the role of the researcher and scientist is open to esoteric choices, to non-conformist thought, to conceptual specificity and also to being irresponsible.

It is enough to state these dichotomies to invite enraged critical onslaughts. The first variety of criticism is empirical: is this all true? Is not the near juxtaposition of politics and academic research or science breathtakingly simplistic and oblivious to facts? No doubt, this statement is based on a simplified version of the interrelationship between political and academic approaches which is in effect much more complex: politics are also constantly orientated towards establishing the truth; research, on the other hand, is linked to the formation of political power; unconventional thinkers do exist in political life (but at first glance we already notice that they tend to occupy the marginal positions); academic life and research are thoroughly political and a career in either of them demands a high degree of opportunism and exhibitionism. And so on and so forth.

These empirical objections cannot, however, disprove our original thesis. The challenge remains to differentiate without changing the original statement: politics and research are separate and distinctive systems, each with its separate and distinctive role patterns and value orientations. For political parties and also for social movements this means that intellectualising politics and making them more academic whether in the contents of programmes or the language of presentation, will of necessity be penalised by failure and electoral defeat. A political style which is comprehensible to the general public and a straightforward and popular approach to politics have nothing in common with anti-intellectualism. This also applies to the politics of the Greens.

My thesis about the differences between politics and research have attracted another line of criticism: Why, it has been asked, should the Greens as a party of 'a new type' be bound by this distinction? Is it not regrettable to keep politics and research separate? True, in a political environment which is dominated by power politics the commitment to truth is frequently the least convincing and the most likely to lose out. To serve the truth-and-nothing-but-the-truth is always an honourable thing to do even if having the better argument means the Green knight has to fight with his bare hands in the political arena.

All these objections are likely to obscure the view of the advantages to be had from distinguishing clearly between a political and an academic or scientific approach. Historically, we are all too justified to doubt that 'research in the service of the working people — *im Dienst des werktätigen Volkes*' will benefit either the research or the people. The 'betrayal of the intellectual in the name of "class"' committed by Georg Lukács and his recruitment as a propagandist of the 'class-position of the proletariat' had to be paid for with the crudest of dogmatisms. And wherever research has today been conscripted to serve politics — in military research for instance or in the development of high-risk technologies — one cannot help but realise very quickly the disadvantages of blurring the distinctions between research and politics. In short, the critical distance between Greens and intellectuals entails advantages for both sides. To marry the Green Party with one of the schools of research — regardless of which one it may be — would always result in an ill-fated alliance.

An additional note may be useful to clarify the issue further: differences between Greens and intellectuals are sometimes of a most prosaic nature. Whether in academic life, in the realm of culture or in the media, reference to the Green Party has little pay-off. If somebody else controls the purse strings or decides on appointments, it is possible to confuse 'intellectual' with opportunist reservations — but this does not explain, nor indeed does it deflate the diffuse allegations that the Greens are anti-intellectual.

Intellectualism of the Masses and Intellectuals

A political party whose social structure is top-heavy with young, urban intellectuals is by no means a party of intellectuals. The expansion of educational opportunities, technical and scientific progress and the intellectual output of many different types in modern industrial society may not make people into intellectuals but they result in mass intellectuality: the education of an increasing number of people. Using the term 'masses' is neither intended to be condescending nor should it refer only to the growth of a social class. The term 'intellectualism of the masses' is meant to sum up three related developments: first, the high degree of specialisation of intellectual functions in the most diverse economic, administrative, scientific, socio-political or cultural areas of activity. Second, the internal differentiation of respective elites according to qualifications, occupational hierarchies or social status. Third, the increasing similarity between the social situation of intellectuals and average living and working conditions in society.

The last point should not be misunderstood as referring to some kind of 'proletarisation of intellectuals'. Although the vast majority of intellectuals today work in paid employment, I would prefer to characterise the general changes in the class structure as a segmentation of living conditions or a plurality of lifestyles and cultural milieus. Be this as it may, I cannot deny that many of the currently growing number of intellectuals are condemned to a new poverty and to unemployment — without them, the history of the Green Party would not have been written.

These three developments — specialisation, internal differentiation and social similarities — apply to all intellectuals, even to those groups and circles who would like to claim the emphatic term of 'intellectual' for themselves alone. The internal differentiation among intellectuals is rapid and depends in today's society in particular on whether or not somebody can make a public impact via the media at a time when such an impact is difficult to accomplish; many go away empty-handed. The social status and lifestyle of the modern intellectual also no longer match the traditional image of the genius of the eighteenth and nineteenth centuries who would live in affluent bourgeois surroundings or the counter-image of the bohemian café culture which flourished at the turn of the twentieth century. No less out of date is the image of the existentialist post-war intellectual with his grey and threadbare suits. Such myths and scenarios of fictitious lifestyles tend to become fashionable now and again but they are merely nostalgic and contribute nothing to determining the contemporary role of the intellectual.

The aspect which allows us to define the role of the intellectual a little more accurately is the paradox at its heart: intellectuals are specialists in general concerns. They deal with problems which everyone without exception has to face at some point: general questions of contemporary history, general questions of science and technology, general questions of culture and society. In order to make the concept of the intellectual more rational and objective, and also to shorten its leash sufficiently to control its meaning, I would like to venture a definition: intellectuals produce evaluations of their times — *Zeitdiagnosen*. It goes without saying that theirs is a discursive, extremely controversial and competitive branch of business. A vast array of people take part in it: journalists, politicians, artists, writers, social and natural scientists. . . . The very long list of fields from which they come makes it immediately apparent that nobody is involved full-time, as a main occupation, in putting together this puzzle of contemporary history, with the exception perhaps of a few great minds who achieved record editions and an optimal impact.

This notion of the structure and the development of mass intellectuality can be pursued in a number of different directions. The first direction has been hinted at earlier: a political party such as the Greens whose social structure has, to date, been based on mass intellectuality does not possess 'intellectual' calibre on the strength of its support alone. This conclusion draws on well-established insights: workers' parties do not have to be 'proletarian', bourgeois parties do not have to be bourgeois; both are normally petty-bourgeois in spirit, but even this classification of social structure refers today more to resentments than to plausible arguments. In other words, to assume that the social structure of political parties correlates to their programmatic profile or a specific intellectual climate in the party is frequently incorrect. And to assume that the Greens are articulating the interests of the educated masses would not even be a misguided conclusion, it would be sheer nonsense.

The second line of thought can be sketched as follows: the advent of mass intellectuality has deflated the model biography of the intellectual on its very own ground. Let us look at the Greens. Models here would encompass the active ecologist in a citizens' initiative, the resistance fighter at the perimeter fence of a controversial site and perhaps at the access route to a military barracks or similar figures with pacifist and social commitment.

This tendency to have a low regard for the classical biography of the intellectual had surfaced earlier in the student movement of 1968 whose existence in the universities was riddled with dreams about proletarian and revolutionary heroes and activists.

Linked to this tendency — and this is the third aspect I would like to discuss — is something resembling a contemporary *narodniki* effect: does not the typewriter-world of the intellectual amount to little compared with the 'authentic' experiences of an engineer or a nurse or of the small ecologically conscious farmer? Anybody who has observed electoral proceedings in the Green Party will be able to confirm how those passages of a personal biography which relate to 'resistance' or to 'authentic occupational experience' are narrated in excessive detail and how the intellectual parts are contracted into subordinate clauses. Candidates, it seems are fully attuned to the collective models which dominate the procedures of nomination and selection.

Disregarding such opportunist scheming, the positive emphasis on vocational practice and social commitment is not only acceptable, it constitutes an indispensable asset. The reservations against 'intellectuals', 'strategists', 'skimmers', 'generalists' and so forth is not necessarily anti-intellectual. Such reservations are most appropriate in the everyday business of politics since politics are always concerned with specific knowledge and skills and with confidence in the commitment and the integrity of individuals. Intellectual sparkle and an awareness of contemporary history do not, by themselves, make a good politician.

Anti-Intellectual Tendencies in the Greens

The allegation that the Greens are 'anti-intellectual' needs to be examined in detail and could only be considered valid if it were found to apply to the core of Green policies, not to some secondary policy fields. Political parties cannot confine themselves to just 'one theme' even if such a theme should be of key importance, and, at the very least, the competition between political parties forces them to engage in all battlezones of contemporary politics. Despite this broad range of themes, the challenges to cope with the contemporary ecological crisis in the most general sense have constituted the core of Green policy: the destruction of fauna and flora; the pollution of soil, water and air; the damage to the earth's atmosphere; the destructive potential of military and civilian high-risk technologies; the scientific interference with the biological conditions of human living.

These central problems have been the focus of dozens of evaluations of our times — *Zeitdiagnosen* — in the 1970s and 1980s. A theme which, in earlier generations, was the concern of a mere handful of intellectual outsiders, has slipped into the centre of contemporary analysis since the debates by the Club of Rome. Certainly, such evaluations of our times cover an enormous range of themes: economic crises and mass unemployment; the East–West confrontation of political power blocs and the dangers of war; underdevelopment and population explosion; gender specific discrimination and racism; national and cultural crises — and many more. And to explore these themes and how they are interconnected and influence each other, is surely part of the craft employed in presenting a *Zeitdiagnose*, an evaluation of our times. By the same token, the effectiveness of such evaluations has to be measured against their success in identifying the central themes, the task of establishing the centre. To put it in a different way; evaluations of the period face the task of determining which of the many contemporary problems and crises are the central ones and to ensure that public attention will focus on these central themes.

There is considerable room for debate about the theoretical respectability of ecologically orientated evaluations of our times; sociologists have taken to refer condescendingly to 'writings on calamities'. Yet, backed by never-ending waves of global and small-scale ecological crises, these 'writings on calamities' have mastered the task of identifying the central issues: How can industrial and technological expansionism be limited? How can the specific value of non-human nature be recognised and protected? How can the ecological preconditions of human existence be secured? Today, such questions constitute the core of political discourse on contemporary history. Whoever doubts their central importance is simply not up-to-date, even if he happens to be a sociologist.

130

So many answers have been given to these questions, it is nearly impossible to keep track: there are democratic and also authoritarian models of the world, held in balance by ecology; there are socialist models of ecological and economic activity and similar models which subscribe to a market economy; in some cases, the issues have generated their own institutions such as commissions to evaluate ethical implications or the impact of technology; Christian, Taoïst, Aristotelian or discursive moral codes have been created, each with its own ecological focus; there are ecologically slanted educational programmes for executive elites and ecologically inspired teaching for the masses — the permutations are endless and fantasy knows no limits.

The same is not, however, true of politics. This brings us back to our topic. I will attempt to sketch five 'anti-intellectual' reactions to the ecological crisis which can be found within the Greens. Similar reactions are also possible outside the political sphere, but are beyond the scope of this chapter.

Ecological populism: Here, the filtration process which normally controls simplifications in political discourse, has broken down. General terms proliferate. References abound to 'the big multinationals', 'the industrial system', so do scapegoat-definitions such as 'large-scale technology', 'the natural sciences of the modern era'; a tendency to dramatise is also evident in phrases such as 'the apocalyptic mega-machine'. All of these terms have one thing in common: they fail to identify the causes of the ecological crisis, whether they be the more complex ones or those which can be pinpointed accurately. The opportunities for differentiation and specificity which political discourse does in fact offer, are being ignored. Over-dramatising ecological problems in a populist manner — often for the understandable reason to counteract the official tendency of playing them down and making them appear harmless — impedes political credibility: once the respective waves of fear have subsided, the message itself is robbed of its substance. The very real dramatic qualities of the ecological crisis require us to argue in as precise and as rational a manner as possible.

Political surfing: This denotes a kind of surfing from one scandal to the next, from one case of corruption to the next, from one personalisation of ecological conflicts to the other. As legitimate and necessary focal points of political communica-

131

tion, scandals and actors have an important part to play, in particular in relation to the media. But when the arguments never reach deep enough to probe into the system-based causes of the ecological crisis, then 'intellectual' reservations are called for.

Moralism: Here the moral issues tend to be separated from the analytical pursuit of ecological questions; frequent appeals and admonitions stress 'ecological responsibilities' without being aware of the societal structures which prevent or facilitate ecological behaviour, or without clearly identifying them. Ecological moralism usually corresponds to an allocation of guilt on a simplistic good/bad scale, ignores the role of general responsibilities in ecological matters, and leaves no room for relating responsibilities to specific incidents. The familiar figure of the moralist and preacher can also be found in the political counselling, which has come from the humanities. They enlighten us with the idea 'that human beings cannot be allowed to do everything they might be capable of doing'; that 'moderation of human ambition' is called for; we have to look elsewhere, however, if we are interested in identifying the societal causes for such technological excessiveness or the ecological risks under discussion.

Conceptual single-mindedness: To put it succinctly, ecological concepts of this type lack reflection and are therefore ill-suited to determine those consequences which may not be immediately apparent or may only surface in the future. It is, of course, perfectly understandable that single-minded solutions are attractive in the face of the massive and urgent ecological challenges which confront us. Conceptual single-mindedness means calling for 'stop', for a 'reorientation', a complete turn-around in order to stem the dangers of atomic energy, the risks involved in chemical industries or industrialised farming. But such appeals cannot withstand the basic tests of reality — how would they fit into world markets, how could they be incorporated into the labour market? — since they tend to ignore the pragmatic aspects of implementation, and the process of adjustment and amendments which this would involve. One might say that single-minded concepts are essentially naive and not suited to help curb the power of the other side or check the seemingly uncontrollable pressures of the political and industrial system as it stands.

Spiritualism: As spiritualism has become a political issue, ecological protests themselves have lost their political punch. In response to the yearning for a new age and to the renaissance of traditional religiosity one could say that in order to curtail and overcome destructive and aggressive behaviour it is futile to ignore or restrict reason and research; what is needed is their ecological reorientation. Even where the limits of human knowledge themselves are concerned — we may touch on the problem that the consequences of human interference into an interminably complex evolutionary process are beyond our grasp — we still have to remain on the territory of rational discourse, and must resist the temptation to enter the realm of meditation or spiritual insight. In their private individual or collective lives, people are of course free to do as they wish; if approaches which are valid here were to be applied in the public sphere of politics and were to become the basis of political strategies, this would be a recipe for disaster.

There is no question that the anti-intellectual tendencies which I outlined above can all be observed in Green policies and in the political environment of the Green Party. I do not intend to quantify the strength of one of the other of these tendencies; it would be too easy to argue, that neither was strong enough to have a significant impact on the general profile of the Greens. Leaving these arguments and their polemical overtones aside, we can state that the generalisation that the Greens are anti-intellectual, has not been substantiated by our sketch of anti-intellectual tendencies. It has become commonly known that this party includes the most diverse factions and positions. Should, however, the anti-intellectual tendencies which exist in the party gain momentum — in the wake of new ecological catastrophes for instance — the political stability and the future development of the Greens would be under threat. Surely, even an eco-populist or an eco-chiliastic party might 'grow', but its destiny would always remain tied to the fears which sweep through contemporary society at any given moment. Such a party would not constitute a significant factor in policy-making.

To sum up: we are not faced with an anti-intellectualism of a traditional kind as we know it from other political camps: the class-based enmity of the workers' parties, the dull resentments against a 'homeless' intelligentsia, allegedly 'hostile to the state',

133

the vilifications of 'ivory towers' and similar syndromes of a familiar anti-intellectualism. As the masses have become more educated, such traditional anti-intellectualism has become something of a museum piece, at least in the political environment of the Green Party. Any anti-intellectualism in the Green environment is also far removed from the most modern type of anti-intellectualism possible: the ignorance of those political parties and societal camps whose priorities for our times and whose political orientations continue to gravitate around the central axes and issues of past historical eras. People who refuse to face up to the ecological crisis are, of course, also free from the anti-intellectual tendencies which only arise, as we described, in search of answers and remedies.

The Crisis of Social Theory

When intellectuals castigate 'anti-intellectual' developments in politics and society, their own criticism does not leave them unscathed. To altogether discard the anti-intellectualism outlined above as irrelevant aberrations of individuals would be little more than popularised pseudo-psychology and tantamount to saying that human beings tend to be more intimidated and susceptible to irrationality and to anti-intellectual ideologies, the larger the catastrophe which looms in their environment. On the contrary, the new anti-intellectualism of the Greens has to be seen against the backcloth of flagrant deficiencies and contradictions in the thoughts and theories offered by contemporary intellectuals. To put it more bluntly: the evaluations of our times — *Zeitdiagnosen* — which have been presented, lack the stringency which could curtail and contain irrational or anti-intellectual developments.

It would be tempting to illuminate this concluding thesis by looking at the theoretical deficiencies of the literature on the environment. It would be equally tempting to demonstrate the validity of our thesis by examining the criticism of reason and of research which has been proposed by French post-modernists, and which lacks all awareness of the centrality of ecological issues. One could also test our thesis by probing into the traditional orientations in the social sciences which have been as slow to focus on the new centres of conflict as established politicians and established political parties. I will content myself with a brief sketch of three examples, which, I hope, will highlight the flaws in even those evaluations of our times whose conceptual and theoretical acumen is beyond doubt.

Jürgen Habermas, in his 'Theory of Communicative Action' (*Theorie des kommunikativen Handelns*, 1981) chooses to focus on the issue of 'colonialisation of the world in which we live' (*Lebenswelt*): mechanisms of capitalist or bureaucratic rationality, he claims, also determine those aspects of our social environment, which are discursive and based on communication.[2] Habermas concludes in his *Zeitdiagnose* that the real obstacles to communicative action do not lie with the crises of system or with the difficulties of controlling them; for him the 'crises of control have been displaced by the pathology of the everyday environment' (*Lebenswelt*): the process of rationalisation and modernisation which has traditionally been a theme of sociological analysis, now begins to interfere with the key areas such as social integration or cultural reproduction. In all these areas co-ordinated social action has to build on consensus and this consensus cannot be replaced by other means of control like money, for instance, or bureaucratic power. This interference of capitalist or bureaucratic structures with communicative action has been interpreted by some of Habermas' intellectual disciples as the point of origin for the new social movements.

Evidently, this approach contributes towards an understanding of contemporary crises such as juridification, bureaucratisation and others. To strengthen our criticism we have to go further than just to doubt that this approach can illuminate the ecological crises of our era, or indeed explain the emergence of the ecology movement. To concentrate the evaluation of our times on a contradiction between system and *Lebenswelt*, loses sight of the urgency and the centrality of crises in the contemporary world and of the roots of protest potentials. The environmentalist literature of the last ten years or so has identified the juxtaposition of system and environment as the fundamental cause of the contemporary ecological crisis. This is a more

2. Habermas has gained international recognition through his critique of French post-modernism, and also through his spirited defence in the tradition of the European enlightenment of the 'project modernity'.

potent attempt at evaluating our times than Habermas' theory of communicative action, although some of the concepts employed in the studies of environmentalism — terms such as 'the arrogance of man' or the construct 'anthropocentrism' — may fall short of explaining the practices of environmental destruction in an academically sound and theoretically respectable way.

At this point, neo-Marxist approaches to *Zeitdiagnose*, the evaluation of our times come into play: where the dynamics and the tenacity of capitalist systems are concerned, where ecologically and socially destructive trends in the world economy are at issue, the valid insights from this camp cannot simply be discarded with reference to the 'blind spot' of Marxism. Of course, the blind spot of Marxism does exist and has been particularly noticeable when socialist systems of production come under scrutiny. Despite ample historical and documentary evidence, the ecological destructiveness of socialist systems tends to be overlooked and their bureaucratic nature interpreted as a mere 'deviation from the norm'. It is tempting to argue that ecologically responsible actions can only occur if they build on egality and social justice as essential, albeit not sufficient, preconditions. But the question still remains unanswered whether egalitarian politics should mean socialisation or nationalisation as envisaged by Marx or should be understood as securing basic human needs in society. Calling egality a precondition for environmentalism does not by itself clarify its political preconditions.

If traditional Marxism explains all contemporary problems with reference to the societal 'main and basic contradiction' between capital and labour, neo-Marxist thinkers have broken free from this fixation. The recent analysis of fordism by Hirsch and Roth (1986) can serve as an example: 'There is no privileged site for battle, no central conflict which would determine everything.' In this perspective, the fordist state of capitalism has decentralised and particularised crises and protest potentials. It seems to me, that the task of identifying the central aspects of contemporary events which we expect a competent evaluation of our times to accomplish, has been thoroughly misunderstood here: to identify a centre around which crises and conflicts revolve does not mean that everything else — from social inequality or gender-specific discrimination to issues of political repression or threats to the democratic political system — can be discounted and simply be reduced to predictable facets of an all-embracing central conflict. To talk about the centrality of contemporary ecological protest does not mean that all other protest movements should wait until a later date, along the lines of an only-after strategy. The centrality of ecological problems can only mean that without first solving the ecological crisis all other schemes of emancipation in modern society are doomed to failure — since no society will be left in which they could operate. Breaking away from the traditional focus on one central conflict does not mean that identifying the core of current events and crises has ceased to constitute the main task and the over-riding challenge contemporary evaluations of our times have to master.

One of the few 'constructions sites' for contemporary theory, where this task has not been shunned altogether is currently directed by Niklas Luhmann (1986). His theory of a functional differentiation and of the tenacity of systems through their functions responds to the assertion in popular writings on the environment that everything revolves around a juxtaposition of system and environment. In note form: functional systems such as the economy, research and science, politics and law work in an autonomous fashion and follow their own logic and their own momentum. Whether and to what extent their procedures and their products can be accommodated by the (societal and natural) environment is a highly sensitive issue and linked to the functional tenacity of these systems. Events such as industrial pollution, the emergence of high-risk technology, the flood of legislation or the juridification of society exemplify the conflict which may arise and they highlight the difficulties encountered by social systems to adequately perceive the impact of their actions on the (societal and natural) environment and to take corrective action. Since societies which are differentiated by functions do not possess a leadership with overall responsibility or a central system of control, adjustments cannot be ordered from above but have to originate within the system. Luhmann argues, the functional systems of contemporary societies can only respond to environmental pressures and take corrective action if the urgency of ecological problems itself becomes a salient issue for concern and consideration within them.

In discussing Luhmann's theory, one could point to the influences of post-modernism and its criticism of humanism and emancipation; one could also point to the workshop-type approach to social theory which obscures broader issues. In the context of our discussion it is worth stressing that Luhmann cannot account for the role of social inequality in the emergence and the aggravation of ecological crises. Nor can his theory show to what extent the solutions it offers help contemporary citizens to understand their environment and how Luhmann's standard answer to incorporate the analysis of ecological issues into the functional systems could be translated into practical activities. This gap between theory and its realisation is particularly evident in the book in which Luhmann purports to bridge it, his *Ökologische Kommunikation* (1986). His broadside against the Greens that they 'camouflage their lack of theoretical clarity by moralistic fervour' can just as well be turned against him as far as deficiencies of theory are concerned. But such mutual accusations of theoretical deficiencies are, of course ridiculous in an era which is shattering all our established and familiar views of the world and as new questions about the state and the future of mankind begin to emerge.

In order to avoid misunderstandings, let me make myself clear: my comments about the weaknesses and contradictions of these evaluations of our times, the *Zeitdiagnosen* which appear to be theoretically sound and academically respectable are not intended to claim that anti-intellectual tendencies in politics could be traced to these weaknesses and contradictions. It would be too simple to assume that anti-intellectual tendencies would not exist if only a 'correct' *Zeitdiagnose* had been presented. It would also not be permissible to ignore the fundamental difference between such a *Zeitdiagnose* and practical politics: Social theories and evaluations of our times cannot replace the process of experimentation and of learning from experience which political parties and social movements have to undergo; neither can free the parties and movements from the trouble of developing their own workable and effective solutions to the contemporary problems as they perceive them. Evaluations of our times can do little more than aid general orientation. In those instances, however, where such an orientation is not attempted or remains feeble, where evaluations of our times — *Zeitdiagnosen* — even confuse their readers and their public, they miss their chances to stem and to limit irrational reactions and anti-intellectual tendencies in politics and society. Thus, the intellectuals' criticism of Green anti-intellectualism reflects badly on their own approaches.

References

Habermas, Jürgen (1981), *Theorie des kommunikativen Handelns. Handlungsrationalität und gesellschaftliche Rationalisierung*, Frankfurt: Suhrkamp

Hirsch, Joachim and Roland Roth (1986), *Das neue Gesicht des Kapitalismus. Vom Fordismus zum Postfordismus*, Hamburg: VSA

Luhmann, Niklas (1986), *Ökologische Kommunikation. Kann die moderne Gesellschaft sich auf ökoligische Gefährdungen einstellen?*, Opladen: Westdeutscher Verlag

6

A Greening of German–German Relations?

Volker Gransow

The greening of German–German relations is an attempt to create a special Green *Deutschlandpolitik*, or a politics of German–German relations, as the Greens themselves would say.[1] It provides a striking example of how the Greens try to shape a policy field which cannot be regarded as their stronghold. It also shows how the Greens try to solve their general dilemma of the necessary oscillation between 'movement' and 'party'. In other words, that they cannot become an average party like the other established parties *and* that they have to develop specific realist politics and policies, too (Offe 1986: 42). In addition, the exploration of Green politics towards the German Democratic Republic (GDR) will shed new light on the future of the two Germanies. To put it more specifically, the main questions I will address are as follows. First, who are the political actors influencing Green *Deutschlandpolitik*? Second, how has the relation between the Greens and the GDR changed during the years? Third, is a compromise among the various Green currents and factions possible? Fourth, is there a possibility of a rapprochement between the Greens and other major West German parties on these issues?

In order to answer these questions I will give a short description of the relevant Green factions and a sketch of the relationship between the Greens and the GDR. A *Grundsatzpapier*, a basic paper, will be introduced, which gives a rough guideline for the greening of inter-German relations (Document 3).

1. See especially Die Grünen im Bundestag (ed.) (1985), *Deutsch–Deutsch* Bonn: Die Grünen; 'Ansätze und Perspektiven grüner Politik in den deutsch–deutschen Beziehungen' (1986), *Deutschland Archiv* 19/10: 1053–63 (quoted as *Ansätze*; Berschin, Helmut (1986), 'Deutsch-deutsch. Eine Wortkarriere', *Deutschland Archiv* 19/12: 1322–26; Bruns, Wilhelm (1978), *Deutsch-deutsche Beziehungen*, Opladen: Leske; Nawrocki, Joachim (1985), *Relations Between the Two States in Germany*, Stuttgart: Bonn Aktuell; Livingston, Robert D. (ed.) (1986), *West Germany — East Germany and the Germany Question*. Washington D.C.: AICGS.

Another case-study will take a closer look at the trip of a Green delegation to the GDR in the autumn of 1986. The chapter will conclude with a synoptic view of the Green positions in comparison with other major West German parties.

The Greens and their Factions

Within the Green Party, four currents or factions can usually be distinguished: two big groups, the fundamentalists and the realists, and two smaller groups, the eco-socialists and the eco-libertarians (Spretnach and Capra 1986; Langguth 1986). In *Deutschlandpolitik*, however, the spectrum is different, because the discussion of German–German relations takes place mostly on the level of the parliamentary faction, some interested state party organisations (especially the Alternative List in West Berlin, which is affiliated with the Greens) and certain local groups and peace initiatives. According to issues and actors, three main currents can be distinguished (von Bredow and Brocke 1986; Gransow 1985: 14–16):

The first group is centred around a *movement-orientated* approach. The adherents of this position view the Greens in the tradition of the anti-party party or the parliamentary wing of the new social movements the most prominent proponent of this view being Petra Kelly. This group longs for a future in which big international and national economical, political and social systems are dissolved into small units with grass-roots democracy, in which unity between nature and humanity becomes possible. There is a strong distrust for every organisation of society in form of a state. Consequences of this approach are a renunciation of a reunification of Germany and concentration on a non-state level. Partners in the GDR are the new social movements over there, especially the ecology movement and the autonomous peace movement. Even the founding of an East German Green party is thought to be possible (Kelly 1984).

Evidently there are big differences to the second approach, the position of *national politics*. This position developed out of a rethinking of the German national question by members of the new left, namely Herbert Ammon and Peter Brandt (1981). A stronghold of this position was the working group on Berlin and

German politics within the West Berlin Alternative List. Their viewpoints gained currency during the debate about the deployment of nuclear missiles during the early eighties. They try to link the issues of missing national identity, missing sovereignty and security policy. In recent years its proponents have been concentrating on the idea of a peace treaty. They are working on the assumption that a peace treaty with the two German states could be followed by a German confederation and a European system of collective security. Obviously they intend a sort of 'third way' for Germany somewhere between capitalism and 'real socialism' with strong national features. Sometimes the connections of these groups evoke memories of the Nazi past. Ammon and Brandt are not the central targets of this charge, but rather Henning Eichberg, who maintains strong ties with the working-group. Eichberg argues for national separatism, the 'balkanisation of everyone'. He claims that his position is part of a left 'green criticism'. But he also states that nationalism would overcome old distinctions between culture and civilisation, politics and culture, as well as the division between left and right (Eichberg 1981). According to Eichberg, the main enemies are 'Christianity', 'Marxism and communism', and 'capitalist liberalism'.[2] This can indeed be called a 'rightist corollary . . . with 'völkische' or Nazi overtones' (Bodemann 1986: 150) but it would be slander to identify Eichberg's thoughts with basic elements of Green thinking in general.

The third or *realist* approach to the problem of German–German relations adds a further dimension to Green policy orientations — the proximity to other parties. The realist approach is basically internationalist, as one of its main supporters has pointed out (Schnappertz 1984). The internationalist orientation of Green politics leads to the demand for a shape of inter-German relations, in which reunification becomes unnecessary and in which borders lose their separating effects. Therefore a certain closeness to social-democratic ideas about a 'second phase' of *Ostpolitik* is visible. These positions are held by prominent Green politicians like Otto Schily, but also by the Green

2. For a more general analysis of these phenomena see Berman, Russell (1982), 'Opposition to Rearmament and West German Culture', *Telos* 52/1982; Meuschel, Sigrid (1983), 'Neo-Nationalism and the West German Peace Movement's Reaction to the Polish Military Coup, *Telos* 56.

143

members of the parliamentary committee on inter-German relations, Dirk Schneider, and (after his rotation) Henning Schierholz.
This shows that the majority of the parliamentary group from
1983 to 1987 backed the 'realist' approach. In detail, this group
thinks of changing the West German basic law in order to get rid
of reunification goals, of recognising the main demands of the
GDR, and the dissolution of the Federal Ministry for Intra-
German relations. A major problem of this approach seems to be
the lack of specific Green components and small distance to
some advanced social-democratic ideas.

The Greens and the German Democratic Republic

The Green Party was founded on a federal level as late as 1980,
three years before the Greens were first elected to the Bundestag, the parliament of the Federal Republic of Germany. In the
early eighties, times of heated discussion about the NATO
double track resolution and the deployment of US missiles in
West Germany and Western Europe, the main Green concern
with ecology was complemented by the issue of peace. Therefore peace issues were dominating the first contacts between the
Greens and East Germany on an official level as well as on the
level of personal meetings between Green politicians and participants in the autonomous peace movement in the GDR. After
some prominent Greens had demonstrated for disarmament in
the centre of East Berlin and had written a letter to Honecker, a
delegation of the party steering committee and the parliamentary groups received an invitation from the East German General Secretary Erich Honecker. On 31 October 1983 Honecker
met with the Green delegation: Gert Bastian, Lukas Beckmann,
Petra Kelly, Otto Schily, Dirk Schneider, and Antje Vollmer.
They talked primarily about disarmament and about the independent peace groups in the GDR. Honecker signed a 'personal
peace treaty', promised to release GDR prisoners, and regarded
the meeting as a 'beginning'. He had no objections to a short
demonstration of the Green delegation. He was also informed
that some Greens would participate in actions of East German
pacifists, which were to take place on 4 November 1983.[3] Shortly
after the meeting, which most Greens regarded as a success, a

member of the East German politbureau travelled to Bonn to warn the Greens that a participation in the independent peace activities would not be permitted. This illustrates the difficulties the ruling East German Socialist Unity Party (SED) has with a movement-orientated approach to German–German relations.

On 4 November the GDR leadership took a tough line: West German Greens were not allowed to enter the GDR and East German demonstrators were imprisoned. In spite of internal divisions, the Greens reacted with public protest. Relations deteriorated quickly after November 1983, especially because some peace demonstrators in the GDR remained in prison and because a considerable number of members and office holders of the Green party and the affiliated West Berlin Alternative List were turned back at the border and refused entry into the East Germany.[4] In this situation the office of the 'realist' member of parliament, Dirk Schneider, led by Jürgen Schnappertz, started new activities. It attempted to:

— integrate the parliamentary group into day-to-day activities of the Bundestag in respect to the two Germanies;
— serve as a place of coordination;
— build an archive;
— seek scholarly advice.[5]

In 1984 the GDR continued the policy of refusal of entry, but released some of the imprisoned adherents of an independent peace movement in the GDR. In Bonn, representatives of the Permanent Mission of the GDR met with members of the Green parliamentary group. There were also meetings between high-ranking East German functionaries and Greens in West Berlin. Partly as a result of these contacts, the next Green delegation travelled to the GDR in January, 1985. This delegation consisted of women only and was mostly concerned with questions of gender relationships. It received top publicity in the East German media (von Bredow and Brocke 1986: 54). During 1985 the

3. This account is based on 'Vorläufiges Gedächtnisprotokoll des Gespräches mit Erich Honecker' (1983), Bonn: Die Grünen im Bundestag. Unpublished manuscript.

4. See Schneider, Dirk (1983), 'Chronologie der gescheiterten Aktion am 4.11. in Ostberlin', Bonn: Die Grünen im Bundestag. Unpublished manuscript.

5. See the *Arbeitspapier* by Schnappertz, Jürgen (1984), 'Zur deutschlandpolitischen Arbeit der Fraktion', Bonn: Die Grünen im Bundestag. Unpublished manuscript.

Green parliamentary group also expressed its disagreement with the politics of German–German relations pursued by the Federal Government and the other major parties by proposing the dissolution of the Ministry of Intra-German Affairs and advocating recognition of GDR citizenship and 'self-recognition' of the FRG. It increased its efforts to write a 'basic paper' with a group of advisors and grassroots activists. In early 1986, the number of refusals of entry had decreased, although not to zero. Leading Greens could enter East Berlin now and participate in seminars run by autonomous peace and ecology movements. Another indication of a certain relaxation of tension was the visit of Horst Sindermann in Bonn. Sindermann, president of the People's Chamber (*Volkskammer*) of the GDR and member of the SED's politbureau, visited Bonn, invited by the Social Democrats. Nevertheless, he met with the Green parliamentary faction for a long talk, after which he issued an invitation for a new Green visit to East Berlin (*Neues Deutschland* 22/23.2.1986). In the summer of 1986 the 'basic paper' was published (and perhaps also read in East Berlin). Shortly thereafter, the next Green delegation travelled to the GDR. The trip was regarded by some Greens as a success, by others as treason — I shall deal with both the 'basic paper' and the trip below. After the Greens had been informed by the GDR that it would not give in to the Western demands that East Germany should ban asylum seekers from transit to West Berlin, the Greens had to learn (from the SPD!) that the East German government had already complied. The Green press service castigated these moves as 'horse-trading on the backs of asylum seekers' (Die Grünen im Bundestag 1986: 591).

The main German–German events of 1987 were an SED/SPD paper and a visit by Erich Honecker to Bonn. The SED/SPD paper was written by members of the SED's Academy of Social Sciences and the SPD's Basic Values Committee. It called for a culture of political struggle, for dialogue in spite of all diversity, and dealt with the reform capability of both sides. The Green specialist Jürgen Schnappertz published a commentary in which he acknowledged the importance and quality of the paper. After that, however, he criticised it for its neglect of a movement-oriented type of politics in East and West (Schnappertz 1988).

Honecker's visit was the first trip of an East German head of state to the FRG. Generally it was supported by the Greens, as the statements by Karitas Hensel and Wilhelm Knabe in the Bundestag showed (Hensel 1987). Hensel and Knabe were in charge of the parliamentary group's *Deutschlandpolitik* after their election in 1987. Knabe, however, added a sharp attack and argued that an agreement on environmental issues signed by Honecker and Federal Chancellor Kohl was inadequate in ecological terms and in forging German–German relations (Knabe, 1987).

Towards the end of 1987 and the beginning of 1988 there was another setback for Green–GDR relations. The GDR leadership started a crackdown on the autonomous peace and human rights movement. Imprisonments and expatriations were harsh over-reactions to protests of the independent movements, of people seeking exit visas, and the increasing popularity of Gorbachev. GDR authorities hit especially hard after some human rights campaigners unfolded a banner at an official commemoration of Karl Liebknecht and Rosa Luxemburg in January 1988. The banner quoted Luxemburg: 'Freedom is always the freedom of those who think differently.' More than 100 people were arrested, and movement activists like Stephan Krawczyk, Vera Wollenberger and others were expelled to the West. Shortly afterwards a lot of Greens were refused entry to East Germany because of their solidarity with the GDR movements (Die Grünen im Bundestag 1988: 115). The SED's daily accused even Roland Jahn, a former GDR peace activist and prominent Green, of being a paid agent of Western intelligence services.[6] Roland Jahn was quoted by the *New York Times* concerning the Green Party's treatment by the East Germans: 'First they cuddled them, now they are kicking them in the shins' (20.2.1988). In this respect, the state of Green–East German relations seemed in early 1988 to be as ambiguous as ever. It would be hasty to draw conclusions on the links between the Greens and the GDR without first evaluating the Green visit to the GDR of September 1986, and the policy outline laid down in the 'basic paper', the *Grundsatzpapier*.

6. See the unsigned article (1988), 'Wer steuert die sogenannte DDR-Opposition?', *Neues Deutschland* 17.2.

Green Perspectives on German–German Relations: The Grundsatzpapier

It took the parliamentary group of the Greens two years (from 1984 to 1986) to develop a *Grundsatzpapier*, a policy document outlining German–German relations. Various drafts were discussed during numerous meetings in Bonn and West Berlin, which were organised by Jürgen Schnappertz and Lothar Probst, who are also responsible for the final version (see Document 3). Initially, the participants of these discussions included activists from the three party factions mentioned earlier. Some members of the Bundestag and of the House of Representatives in West Berlin, journalists, and scholars of various disciplines also took part in the discussions. In the concluding phase, only the movement-orientated and the realist factions remained. The neo-nationalist group was frustrated and therefore dropped out. The rightist working-group on Berlin and the German question even left the party in 1987 (*Frankfurter Allgemeine Zeitung*, 6.11.1987).

In 1986, the paper was documented in *Deutschland Archiv*, the leading West German journal in matters of GDR research and *Deutschlandpolitik*. It addresses itself to four key issues:

1. Green understanding of the politics of German–German relations;
2. historical preconditions and political starting points of German–German relations;
3. political strategy of German–German relations;
4. suggestions for concretisation of a German–German dialogue.

The first part deals with the Green notion of politics as centred around human ways of life, around the satisfaction of elementary needs and the needs for more ecology, non-violence, individual and social autonomy. This fulfilment of needs is singled out as the core theme of any German–German dialogue. Dialogue in a Green understanding is not restricted to the state level, but concerns all human beings.

The second part deals with the Nazi legacy, the restoration of capitalism in the FRG and the Stalinist construction of socialism in the GDR. In addition, it calls for an integration of German–German relations into a process of overcoming present military alliances in East and West.

The third part explains the politics of full recognition of the GDR and self-recognition of the FRG. This includes:

— recognition of GDR citizenship;
— establishment of official contacts between the German Federal Assembly and the People's Chamber;
— a regulation of the Elbe border according to international principles;
— dissolution of the Salzgitter monitoring centre;
— dissolution of the Ministry for Intra-German Relations.

This means the acceptance of most GDR demands for status improvement and in some cases even more (*Neues Deutschland* 14.10.1986). Therefore the authors link these measures to the expectation that the GDR will increase communication possibilities and help to free the Elbe from pollution (Ansätze 1986: 1058–9).

The last part is a plea for a degree of re-integration of politics into society by using the term 'field of dialogue' instead of 'field of politics' (ibid). There are five fields of dialogue:

— peace;
— environment;
— women and gender questions;
— culture;
— science and technology.

This selection indicates the fields of dialogue where the Greens presume to have special expertise. Each field of dialogue shall have meetings on the level of everyday life. 'Peace' includes common demonstrations and actions as well as free exchange of publications. 'Ecology' shall not be restricted to debates among experts. 'Women's dialogue' means also an extension of informal connections. 'Culture' contains, for instance, the establishment of *regional* cultural centres in the FRG and GDR, and 'science' shall deal with alternative technologies.

In conclusion, the paper appears to be a compromise between

realist and movement-orientated thoughts, whereas there is no reference to nationalist ideas. It contains the most important realist point (full recognition of the GDR as a precondition for any substantial improvement of German–German relations), but also the fundamentalist concerns about politics as a way of life, human rights and central Green issues, like peace, ecology, and gender relationships. Last but not least, it provides ideas for concrete steps on the local, regional, and federal state level. This means that the Greens do not have to delay implementation until they are a governing party at the federal level, but could start right now.

From the vantage point of the governing coalition, the paper is not readily acceptable, especially because it contradicts constitutional principles, like the pledge of reunification contained in the Basic Law and contained in the rulings of the constitutional court on the two Germanies.

The Social Democrats, however, may find points of convergence. But because the paper stresses the grassroots democracy and decentralisation, it is different enough to be regarded as essentially Green.

The GDR values the idea of full recognition, whereas the demands for non-controlled dialogue among peace and ecology activists in the two Germanies appear to be more painful to the East German government.

The GDR Delegation

The 'basic paper' has a notion of dialogue, which includes both society and state. Because of this formula it could function as a bridge between the movement-orientated and the realist factions, leaving the nationalist wing aside. It could also attract readers in the GDR — in the party government as well as in the alternative culture, which is drawing closer to East European dissidents (Fricke 1984; Woods 1986). Thus some obstacles to a further development of a Green policy of German–German relations had been removed, when the Greens heard in August 1986 of the timing and the agenda for their visit to the GDR. They had barely two weeks for preparation, but decided to take the chance. They wanted to achieve 'three essentials': dialogue at social *and* state level; an end to the refusal of entry permits and no impediments to contacts with people from the independent movements. Specifically they hoped to agree on:

— a symposium on environmental questions;
— a seminar about peace policy;
— a regionalisation of Green–GDR contacts.

The delegation consisted of nine persons:

— Annemarie Borgmann (spokeswoman of the parliamentary group);
— Thea Bock (from the Green-Alternative List, Hamburg; an expert on chemistry and waste);
— Uli Fischer (a member of the committee on foreign relations in the Bundestag);
— Hannegret Hoenes (spokeswoman of the parliamentary group);
— Lothar Probst (responsible for German–German relations in the parliamentary group);
— Claudia Roth (press spokeswoman);
— Henning Schierholz (member of the committee on inter-German relations in the federal assembly);
— Jürgen Schnappertz (research fellow for the parliamentary group).

Thus, the delegation included some policy experts and also members of the realist and movement-oriented factions (albeit a realist majority).

The group arrived in East Berlin on 1 September 1986, and they met first with Horst Sindermann, president of the People's Chamber, who was their official host. Sindermann appeared friendly, but somewhat unprepared. He assured the Greens that there would be no restrictions imposed on the transit of asylum seekers, mostly from Third World countries and promised a decrease in the number of refusals of entry. The second high-ranking partner was Hans Reichelt, the Minister for Environmental Affairs with whom they discussed the different viewpoints in respect to Chernobyl, nuclear power, and the protection of the environment, finally reaching an agreement about a symposium on environmental affairs. They also met with Hermann Axen, a member of the SED's politbureau. The main topic for discussion with Axen was peace policy.

The Green delegation then went on to talk to the president of the office for nuclear security to discuss nuclear power, and finally visited a waste dump in the north of the GDR, which was regarded as highly dangerous. They found good reason for this assumption. In their 'spare time' they visited members of the autonomous movements. The trip was brought to a close by a press conference in East Berlin in which the delegation characterised the trip as a success and referred to concrete results of their talks: two symposia about peace and ecology. They reported that the GDR had promised not to send asylum seekers home and not to close its doors to Green party members. The image of success was reinforced by big media coverage in the two Germanies and by favourable reports in the West German liberal press.[7]

Some weeks later, however, the image had changed somewhat. As mentioned above, the GDR had given in to the Bonn government and banned asylum seekers. The Greens could barely avoid the feeling that they had been used by the GDR to strengthen its bargaining position against the federal government (Schnappertz 1986). Second, the refusals of entry decreased, but didn't stop. Especially members of the West Berlin Alternative List were still barred from visiting the GDR. Third, the members of the delegation came under attack at home. The Green-alternative daily *Die Tageszeitung* printed a 'report from East Berlin', which stated that this trip had been 'treason to the grassroots movements in the GDR' (*Tageszeitung* 12.9.86). A well-known West Berlin Green-alternative 'nationalist' politician spoke of 'green bankruptcy in the GDR' (Schenk 1986a; 1986b) and accused the delegation of opportunism towards the GDR. This controversy cooled down, however, when East Berlin dissidents published a letter criticising the Green trip, although they refuted the accusation of 'treason' and mentioned instead meetings of the Green delegation with dissidents and other politically independent people.

As a matter of fact, the Green delegation had pursued the 'three essentials' (two-level dialogue; protest of the entry re-

---

7. Reports in *Neues Deutschland* 2–6.9.1986; *Stuttgarter Zeitung* 6.9.1986; *Frankfurter Rundschau* 6.9.1987; *Süddeutsche Zeitung* 6.9.1987; *Die Zeit* 5.9.1987.

fusals; contacts with independents) and reached two of their three goals: to hold symposia or seminars on the environment and on peace. There is, however, some justification in the critical storm. The delegation had dispensed with symbolic actions and had restricted the contacts with East German alternative groups to an 'informal' level. Nevertheless, they had demonstrated the possibility of a two-level policy among the two Germanies *and* the uniqueness of Green positions. To that extent the visit was a success in spite of its hasty preparation and the difficulties in dealing with seasoned Communist politicians. It will be interesting to see *how* the future symposia will be organised. The Greens will have to insist on the participation of members of the autonomous peace and ecology movements from East Germany or they risk losing the trust of their supporters — the Basis — in West Germany and in West Berlin. By mid 1988, however, there was no sign that a symposium or seminar would in fact take place.

Greens and Other Parties

In order to compare the positions of the Greens on German–German relations with the viewpoints of the coalition government (CDU/CSU/FDP) and the Social Democrats, a synopsis of ten inter-German issues and responses is shown in Table 6.1.[8]

This overview confirms the observations that 'this is a "catchall" party with a difference: a real opposition in the West German political system' (Cohen and Arato 1984: 328). On the other hand, there are some convergences with SPD positions. The Greens have another chance of 'cultivating political space' (Markovits and Meyer 1985) before the SPD takes over these issues in order to have better starting points for the electoral campaign of 1990. The Free Democratic Party pursues contacts with the East German Liberal Party and is in favour of official relations with the GDR's People's Chamber. The Christian Democrats have begun to modify their position and speak more

8. Adapted from Bismarck, Philipp von *et al* (1986), *Zur Teilung Deutschlands und Europas*, Bonn: Europa Union; also Martin, Ernst (1986), *Zwischenbilanz Deutschlandpolitik der 80er Jahre*, Stuttgart: Bonn Aktuell; and *Ansätze* (1986).

153

Table 6.1. Policy issues and party positions

Issue	Government Parties (CDU/CSU/FDP)	SPD	Greens
1. Support for alternative GDR movements	Unclear	Unclear	Yes
2. Change of Basic Law	No	Maybe	Yes
3. Recognition of GDR citizenship	No	Maybe	Yes
4. Upgrading of missions to embassies	No	Unclear	Yes
5. Dissolution of Salzgitter monitoring centre	Unclear[1]	Yes	Yes
6. Elbe border in the middle	No	Yes	Yes
7. Agreement on chemical warfare	No	Yes	Yes
8. Agreement on nuclear-free zones	No	Yes	Yes
9. Dissolution of Ministry for Intra-German Relations	No	Unclear	Yes
10. Increase in communication	Yes	Yes	Yes

1. Yes if conditions 6–10 were to be met

of a reunification as a perspective on a distant future which would require the consent of *all* (East and West) European neighbours (Wilms 1987). Thus, the Greens have a chance of influencing debates within the government and in parliamentary politics. A new breakthrough in German–German relations could even be helpful to the Christian-liberal government in their search for electoral majorities and policy innovation.

Conclusion

The future of the Greens will not be decided by the Greens only. There are other important factors: changes in the social structure of the electorate, the politics and policies of the other parties, and ups and downs of issues. But an equally decisive factor is the Green capability of solving the dilemma of changing *and* preserving its identity. On the basis of Green politics on German–German relations I draw the following conclusions:

1. The Greens who are interested in the relationship between the two Germanies differ slightly from the majority of the party. The two main currents are movement-orientated and realist. The nationalist influence is shrinking. The eco-socialist and eco-libertarian factions are unimportant in this respect.
2. The relations between the Greens and the GDR are characterised by tension. The GDR leadership has major problems with a movement-orientated understanding of the political process from its point of view, or 'an interference with domestic affairs'. Nevertheless, it acknowledges not only the realism of the Green program as reflecting demands of the GDR, but also the stability of the Green factor in West German politics. *If* there is a pro-Gorbachev faction in the GDR leadership, it will doubtless follow the Soviet leader's open position towards the Greens.
3. A compromise among the Green factions and currents is indeed possible. This may be achieved more readily in the policy field of German–German relations, because the number of people involved is smaller than in other areas. The compromise which has been reached between the movement-oriented and the realist factions does not extend to the Green nationalists.
4. There are sharp differences between the Greens and all other major West German parties in questions of *Deutschlandpolitik*. But there are some convergences with SPD positions. And there might even be a chance to influence the government's rethinking of German–German relations.

The Greening of German–German relations demonstrates aptly that the Greens are not yet completely capable of *solving* their identity dilemma or 'adolescence crisis', but that they can *manage* it. They were able to develop a fully-fledged oppositional approach to *Deutschlandpolitik* which does *not* touch on the rationale of the relations between the two Germanies. This rationale is 'status improvement' from the side of the GDR, and 'increase in communication' from the side of the FRG (which may preserve the all-German nation, but not necessarily). The Green contribution to the politics of German–German relations is presented at a time when improvements in the links between the two Germanies seem to be more and more contingent upon East Berlin (McAdams 1986: 153) but when the GDR is also entering a period of social uncertainty as the repercussions of the Gorbachev reform plans are not yet fully visible (Gransow 1987).

In this situation, a (partial or total) implementation of the Green *Deutschlandpolitik* in any possible form would lead to the insight that the politics and policies derived from the Basic Treaty between the two Germanies in 1972 are exhausted (Plock 1986). A new Basic Treaty would be needed to bring the two Germanies closer together.[9] A Green contribution to this renewed *Deutschlandpolitik* could show that the Greens are still good for surprises, even in German–German relations.

References

Books and Articles

Ammon, Herbert and Peter Brandt (eds.) (1981), *Die Linke und die nationale Frage*, Reinbek: Rowohlt

Berman, Russell (1982), 'Opposition to Rearmament and West German Culture'. *Telos* 52

Berschin, Helmut (1986), 'Deutsch-deutsch. Eine Wortkarriere'. *Deutschland Archiv* 19/12

Bismarck, Phillip von *et al*, (1986), *Zur Teilung Deutschlands und Europas*, Bonn: Europa Union

Bodeman, Y. Michal (1986), 'The Green Party and the New Nationalism in the Federal Republic of Germany', in Ralph Milliband *et al* (eds.), *The Socialist Register 1985–6*, London: Merlin

Bredow, Wilfried von and Rudolf H. Brocke (1986). 'Deutschlandpoli-

9. A conservative-liberal specialist in questions of German identity has come to this conclusion, even without including the possibilities of red-green coalitions or the possible influence of Green ideas on the dominant political culture; see Weidenfeld, Werner (1987), 'Zweiter Grundlagenvertrag könnte neue Impulse geben', *Deutschland Archiv* 20/2: 148–53.

tische Ansätze der Partei der Grünen', *Deutschland Archiv* 19/1

Bruns, Wilhelm (1978), *Deutsch-deutsche Beziehungen*, Opladen: Leske

Cohen, Jean L. and Andrew Arato (1984), 'The German Green Party', *dissent* 3

Eichberg, Henning (1981), 'Balkanisierung für Jedermann?', *Befreiung* 19–20

Fricke, Karl Wilhelm (1984), *Opposition und Widerstand in der DDR*, Cologne: Wissenschaft und Politik

—— (1985), 'Dominant and Alternative Political Cultures in Germany', unpublished paper presented at the Fifth International Conference for Europeanists, Washington D.C.

Gransow, Volker (1987), 'East German Society at the Turning Point?', *Studies in Comparative Communism*, XX/1

Kelly, Petra (1984), *Fighting for Hope*, London: Chatto and Windus/ Hogarth Press

Langguth, Gerd (1986), *The Green Factor in German Politics*, Boulder: Westview

Livingston, Robert G. (ed.) (1986), *West Germany–East Germany and the German Question*, Washington D.C.: American Institute for Contemporary German Studies

McAdams, James A. (1986), 'Inter-German Detente: A New Balance', *Foreign Affairs* 65/1

Markovits, Andrei S. and David S. Meyer (1985), 'Green Growth on the West German Left: Cultivating Political Space', paper (unpublished) presented at the IPSA Conference in Paris

Martin, Ernst (1986) *Zwischenbilanz. Deutschlandpolitik der 80er Jahre*, Stuttgart: Bonn Aktuell

Meuschel, Sigrid (1983), 'Neo-Nationalism and the West German Peace Movement's Reaction to the Polish Military Coup', *Telos* 56

Nawrocki, Joachim (1985), *Relations Between the Two States of Germany*, Stuttgart: Bonn Aktuell

Offe, Claus (1986), 'Zwischen Bewegung und Partei' in Otto Kallscheuer (ed.), *Die Grünen — letzte Wahl*, Berlin: Rotbuch

Plock, Ernest D. (1986), *The Basic Treaty and the Evolution of East–West-German Relations*, Boulder: Westview

Schenk, Wolfgang (1986a), 'Grüne Pleite in der DDR', *Kommune* 10

—— (1986b), in *Die Tageszeitung* 15.10

Schnappertz, Jürgen (1984a), 'Festgefahren', *Kommune* 10

—— (1986), Flüchtling in systemischer Definition', *Kommune* 9

—— (1988), 'Dialog als unendliche Geschichte oder als Lernprozess? Über die Ambivalenzen des SED-SPD papiers', *Deutschland Archiv* 1

Spretnak, Charlene and Fritjof Capra (1986, revised ed.), *Green Politics*, Santa Fe: Bear & Company

Weidenfeld, Werner (1987), 'Zweiter Grundlagenvertrag könnte neue

Impulse geben', *Deutschland Archiv* 20/2

Wilms, Dorothee (1987), *The German Question*, Washington: Konrad Adenauer Foundation

Woods, Roger (1986), *Opposition in the GDR*, London: Macmillan

Documents and Programmes

Die Grünen im Bundestag (1985), *Deutsch–Deutsch Wider die Mauern auch in den Köpfen*, Bonn: Die Grünen

—— (1986), *Pressemitteilung* 591

—— (1988), 'Erklärung gegen die Abschiebungen aus der DDR', *Pressemitteilung* 816

Hensel, Karitas (1987), 'Grüne zum Abschluß des Honecker Besuchs', *Die Grünen im Bundestag Pressemitteilung* No. 816

Knabe, Wilhelm (1987), 'Zwei deutsche Staaten als Chance begreifen', *Das Parlament* 31.10

Schnappertz, Jürgen (1984b), 'Zur deutschlandpolitischen Arbeit der Fraktion', Bonn: Die Grünen im Bundestag, unpublished manuscript

Schneider, Dirk (1983), 'Chronologie der gescheiterten Aktion am 4.11. in Ostberlin', Bonn: Die Grünen im Bundestag, unpublished manuscript

'Vorläufiges Gedächtnisprotokoll des Gespräches mit Erich Honecker' (1983), Bonn: Die Grünen im Bundestag, unpublished manuscript.

7

Red–Green Coalitions at Local Level in Hesse

Thomas Scharf

The differences of political approach and programmatical orientation which divide Greens and the SPD at the federal and regional levels of the West German party system have been well publicised, while the existence throughout the Federal Republic of a number of local level coalitions between the two parties has been virtually overlooked.[1] This is surprising since the divisions between the Green Party and the SPD at the local level are potentially just as great as those at higher system levels, given the fundamental divergence of the Greens' perception of local politics from that of the established parties (Loreck 1987; Herbers 1987; Traunsberger and Klemisch 1987). I have briefly outlined the origins and nature of this conflict before focusing attention upon the factors which underlie the local red–green coalitions in the state of Hesse. In no other region has the scope of co-operation between the Greens and SPD been so wide-ranging, with coalitions extending from the local level to the inauguration in 1985 of the Federal Republic's first ever red-–green regional government. The unique dynamic of the rapprochement of the SPD and Greens in Hesse has witnessed the transformation of the state's Greens from a party of fundamental opposition to one willing to assume responsibility for the implementation of its reformist policies. Indeed, the evidence suggests that the most unstable element of local red–green coalitions in Hesse has stemmed from the difficulties experienced by SPD local party organisations in coming to terms with the introduction of a new politics agenda to the region's party systems.

1. The list of major towns and cities in the Federal Republic (beyond Hesse) with experience of red–green alliances/coalitions includes Nuremberg, Hanover, Brunswick, Oldenburg, Wuppertal, Leverkusen, Bielefeld, Solingen and Saarlouis. In a number of cities alliances were mathematically possible, but failed to come about: Hamburg, Munich, Cologne Düsseldorf.

The Greens and the New Local Politics

The origins of the Green Party are inextricably linked to the socio-economic transformation of West German society during the post-war period, marked by an increase in the activities of the welfare state, a movement away from a production-based towards a service-sector-orientated economy and a general improvement in levels of education. The transformation process has supported the creation of new social groups that are no longer bound by traditional socio-economic ties to the established political parties. The distance of a new middle class and of groups excluded from the benefits of modernisation from the production process makes them more susceptible to the negative effects of industrial growth (Alber 1985: 213ff) and has contributed towards the change in basic political values that has led to the development of a 'New Politics' agenda (Baker, Dalton and Hildebrandt 1981). The value change, most prevalent amongst the well-educated younger generations (Bürklin 1981), coincided with the apparent failure on the part of the Federal Republic's established parties to offer solutions to the New Politics problem areas and led directly to the growth of the protest forms (anti-nuclear movement, women's movement, environmental protection groups, citizens' initiatives) from which the Greens derived.

For our purposes, however, it is necessary to establish that the process of socio-economic change, which has weakened traditional party ties and instigated the value change, has occurred highly unevenly throughout the Federal Republic; not only between its regions, but within its regions and local communities. This uneven development has affected local party systems accordingly and offers a partial explanation for the widely varying levels of electoral support for the Greens. Whereas the party performs well in those areas which have witnessed a rapid process of socio-economic change, the decline of traditional social milieus accompanied by new value orientations (*Dienstleistungszentren*), it has been less successful in communities in which the processes of modernisation and value change have been slower.

The uneven character of the socio-economic transformation in the Federal Republic is symbolised in the case of Hesse by the

160

diverging social and economic structures of the North and South, which is reflected in the disparate local party systems of the two areas. Whereas the economy of the Rhine-Main area, centred on Frankfurt, is increasingly dependent upon service sector industries and its local party systems reflect the growing influence of the New Politics values of its highly mobile electorate, the modernisation process has been delayed in the North of the region, the economy of which is still largely reliant upon the production of industrial and agricultural goods. In the North of Hesse the relative slowness of socio-economic change supports the continued existence of traditional social milieus and subsequently of local party systems less marked by a New Politics dimension. The heterogeneous nature of the modernisation process means, however, that there are departures from the regional norm in both North and South Hesse.

Although the debate over New Politics issues preceded the widespread entry of the Greens to the local parliaments of the Federal Republic, only with their election is it possible to talk of the existence of a 'new local politics'. In the post-war period, local authority self-administration in West Germany has been regarded essentially as unpolitical in the majority of its local communities, typified by the widespread existence of all-party administrations. There were signs that the unpolitical nature of local politics was changing during the 1970s, especially in the large towns and cities of certain Länder (including Hesse), but with the parliamentarisation of the Greens as a party of the New Politics, the consensual element of the Federal Republic's local politics is in decline. Not only are the issues which the Greens represent at the local level new to the party systems, but also the ideology of the Green Party, with its global orientation, and the style in which they portray issues transcend the traditional scope of local politics.[2] Local problems are viewed by the Greens in their regional, national and sometimes international contexts, as reflected in the party slogan *Global denken, vor Ort handeln* (think globally, act locally), with the consequence that the established local political actors sometimes resort to consti-

2. A principal source of information on Green/Alternative local politics is the periodical *Alternative Kommunalpolitik* (AKP), which was also responsible for producing a practical guide to local politics (Handbuch 1985). See also Erklärung 1984 and particularly Swatzina 1987.

tutional and legal means to maintain the local orientation of local politics. In addition, the Greens' participatory structures and their perception of their parliamentary role engender conflict. The organisational forms of the Greens, their direct democratic aims and intended parliamentary function as the voice of the extra-parliamentary protest movements, contrast fundamentally with the conventional party structures and representational roles of the established parties at local level.

Local alliances between Greens and SPD should be viewed against this antagonistic background. Whether the Greens will be regarded as suitable political partners varies inevitably from case to case depending upon the characteristics of the local party system and the nature of the new politics debate within it. In Hesse there have been two distinct phases of red–green co-operation at local level, following the local elections of 1981 and 1985. I intend to illustrate the differing contexts under which the two sets of alliances operated whilst paying particular attention to the learning process undertaken by the region's Green Party.

The First Local Red–Green Alliances in Hesse

The rapprochement between the Greens and SPD in Hesse has its historical roots in the alliances established in a number of localities following the local elections of 22 March 1981. Various Green lists had campaigned previously in national, regional and European elections in Hesse, but the local elections provided the Green movement with its first elected representatives as shown in Table 7.1 (Klotzsch and Stöss 1984: 1523ff). The 1981 elections occurred at a time of clear polarisation between the Greens and SPD at both the federal and regional levels. The Green Party in Hesse had developed largely as a response to the modernistic, large-scale projects of the SPD/FDP Land government led by Minister President Holger Börner; specifically the intention to add a new runway to Frankfurt Airport (Startbahn-West) and the planned extension of the region's nuclear energy programme, which encompassed the construction of the Federal Republic's first nuclear reprocessing plant. In a political context characterised by the mobilisation of public protest against these schemes and by the disintegration of the SPD/FDP federal govern-

Table 7.1. Local Elections in Hesse 1981 and 1985: the Green Party vote and seats won

| | Local Council Elections | | | | | | District Council Elections | | Local Elections | |
| | *Stadtkreise* | | *Gemeinden* | | Together | | *Kreise* | | | |
Year	%	Seats	%	Seats	%	Seats	%	Seats	%	Seats
1981	4.5	15	1.0	58	1.7	73	4.3	36	4.3	109
1985	8.0	33	4.0	400	4.9	433	6.8	96	7.1	529

1. The table excludes the percentage vote and seats gained by local Green/Alternative lists in Hesse.
2. Local elections: the percentage figure represents the Green Party vote in Hesse's *Stadtkreise* and districts. The number of seats won comprises those Green Party representatives in the councils at *Stadtkreise*, district and *Gemeinde* level.

Source: *Hessisches Statistiches Landesamt*

ment, Green/Alternative groups gained 4.7% of the overall vote in the 1981 local elections and entered a number of councils with upwards of 163 representatives (see Woyke and Steffens 1987: 108; Hassler 1981a and 1981b).

As a result of the elections, red-green majorities existed on paper in a small number of Hesse's local councils, most notably in the towns of Marburg and Kassel and in the district of Gross-Gerau (*Frankfurt Rundschau* 23.3.1983). In each case an agreement was reached between the Greens and the SPD, the durability of which varied according to specific local factors. The red–green alliance in Marburg, with the additional support of the FDP, survived for only three months providing a typical example of the problems inherent in early forms of co-operation in Hesse. Once an SPD stronghold, Marburg was governed from 1976 until 1981 by a Grand Coalition. Having pledged to end the coalition with the CDU, the Social Democrats were forced to enter negotiations with the Greens and FDP after an election result which granted neither major party an absolute majority on the town council.[3] Although the three parties still lacked the necessary absolute majority, they hoped that the tacit support of the Communist Party (DKP) Fraktion would ensure a

3. Distribution of seats on Marburg town council following the 1981 local election: CDU 25, SPD 22, DKP 5, Greens 4, FDP 3 (Source: HSL). See Kuhnert 1981, Kleinert 1982, Kuhnert/Kleinert 1982, Bullmann 1985: 189ff.

degree of stability.

The Marburg Greens sought to exploit their strategic position, recognising that alternatives were open to the SPD if negotiations failed: 'Despite objections in principle to the so called "established parties" there was general agreement that a Grand Coalition would create the worst possible overall conditions for alternative local policies in Marburg and one would have to fear that the destruction of the character of the town might become even more extensive than in previous years' (Kleinert and Kuhnert 1982: 136). In order to prevent the SPD from continuing the Grand Coalition following the election of its candidates to the council executive, the Greens attempted to secure an agreement which would bind the parties together for the duration of the electoral period. In this way it was hoped that contentious planning proposals could be influenced in their early stages, albeit without the assumption by the Greens of executive responsibilities themselves (Kleinert and Kuhnert 1982: 139).

The Greens were also aware that they could directly influence the New Politics debate within the town's SPD. A refusal to enter into negotiations would stifle the discussion of New Politics themes in the SPD and allow the party's old-politics-orientated right-wing to reconstruct the Grand Coalition in the absence of alternative partners.

Agreement was reached between the Greens, SPD and FDP after five months of talks, but ultimately without the active support of the Greens' grassroots. This followed a period of conflict between the Green district party, dominated by traditional environmentalists, and its local politics working group, which was open to non-members. Both groups had originally participated in the talks with the SPD, but the final agreement was only signed after the working group's representative had been dropped from the negotiating committee, with the result that the alliance had little active support from the town's Green spectrum.

Criticism of the alliance from within Marburg itself came less from those Greens opposed to co-operating with the SPD out of principle than from a grassroots element disappointed both with the manner in which agreement was reached and with the programmatical content of the agreement. In return for the provision of access to the planning process, there was a marked absence of significant concessions to the Greens in several key policy areas. The actions of the Marburg Greens attracted a different type of criticism from its regional party, however, as recorded in the minutes of a session of the party's regional steering committee (*Landeshauptausschuß*): 'Other members accuse the Marburg Greens of serious infringements of Green principles by for instance entering into an alliance over four years with the SPD and the FDP which specifically stipulated that alliance partners had to honour the agreement. In such a fashion, our radical, alternative and clear positions can not be fought for and put into practice' (LHA 1981). The absence of regional party support was, however, not a decisive factor behind the collapse of the Marburg alliance. When it seemed likely that the DKP would vote with the CDU and bring about the rejection of the 1982 budget, SPD mayor Hanno Drechsler came under pressure from within his own party to end the alliance. The participation of Green councillors in a demonstration against the visit of Minister President Börner to an award ceremony in the town only provided the SPD with the symbolic excuse necessary to reconstitute the Grand Coalition. As one commentator noted: 'The red-Green co-operation together with the FDP had failed although not a single case has become known of inextricable programmatic disagreement' (Bullmann 1985: 190). The course of the alliance between the Greens and SPD in Kassel, the first major city in the Federal Republic to be jointly administered by the parties, was unlike that of Marburg, if only because the co-operation survived the electoral period from 1981–5 intact (Rehrmann 1985).

The stability of the Kassel alliance can be attributed to a series of interdependent factors. First, the SPD in Kassel had addressed itself to the issues of the New Politics at a relatively early stage, establishing an element of consensus with the Greens in those areas which might otherwise be regarded as representing an uncompromisable part of the Greens' 'identity'. 'Programmatically, the Social Democrats in Kassel had overtaken the SPD at the regional or federal level by four or five years. The SPD in Kassel understood already in the second half of the seventies that economy and ecology have to be considered together' (Eichel and Hilgen 1985: 11). The SPD's perceptiveness to New Politics themes, characterised by a rejection of its own Land government's plans to extend Hesse's nuclear energy programme and by opposition to the NATO twin-track decision linked to support for the creation of a nuclear-free zone in the city, led some members of the Kassel SPD to the view that the red–green alliance offered the best means of implementing party conference resolutions (Peter and Sprafke 1985: 37).

Second, there was no significant opposition to the prospect of entering an alliance with the SPD from within the Kassel Green Party (Bullmann 1985: 193), which stemmed partly from the character of the local Social Democrats and partly from the nature of the agreement reached. The scope of the *punktuelle Zusammenarbeit* — collaboration on specific issues — between the Kassel parties was far narrower than that of the agreement reached in Marburg, although it was extended to include broader policy areas.

Third, the dominance of the left-wing of the Kassel SPD was itself a stabilising factor behind the city's red–green alliance. Whereas the Marburg SPD could fall back upon a certain tradition of co-operation with the CDU were negotiations with the Greens to fail, the Kassel party's close trade union links and traditional absolute majority on the city council would have been endangered by a deal with the CDU. In 1981 there was felt to be no political alternative to a red–green alliance.

The Kassel alliance survived under these conditions, although the emergence of significant policy differences ensured that there was always a source of friction between the partners. Significantly, the Greens discovered that their failure to assume an executive post meant not only that the SPD could exploit its hold over the city administration to delay the implementation of policy concessions to the Greens, but also that the Greens experienced difficulties in profiling their specific contribution to the city's local politics since the SPD alone was responsible for policy implementation (Weist 1985: 28ff).

The course of the red–green alliance in the district of Gross-Gerau was similar in a number of ways to that in Kassel, but the local conditions which led to its creation were of rather a different nature. Primarily as a result of the successful mobilisation of protest against the Startbahn-West proposals, the Greens in Gross-Gerau secured the Hessian party's highest percentage vote in the 1981 local elections (Table 7.2). A significant propor-

Table 7.2. Local Elections in Hesse 1981 and 1985: Green/Alternative[1] Vote and Seats Won in Gross-Gerau District

	%		Seats	
Gemeinde	1981	1985	1981	1985
Biebesheim	–	6.9	–	2
Bischofsheim	–	7.8	–	3
Büttelborn	25.2	12.2	9	5
Gernsheim	–	–	–	–
Ginsheim-Gustavsburg	–	7.1	–	3
Gross-Gerau	12.6	9.6	5	4
Kelsterbach	15.2	9.8	6	4
Moerfelden-Walldorf	25.2	17.0	11	8
Nauheim	10.4	8.8	3	3
Raunheim	–	10.9	–	4
Riedstadt	–	8.2	–	3
Rüsselsheim[2]	16.5	7.5	10	5
Stockstadt	–	–	–	–
Trebur	–	6.9	–	3
Gross-Gerau District	11.0	9.0	44	47

1. The Green/Alternative spectrum in the Gross-Gerau district comprises the following electoral lists:
   Biebesheim: DIE GRÜNEN, Bischofsheim: Grün-Alternative Liste, Büttelborn: Unabhängige Wählervereinigung "Grüne Liste Büttelborn", Ginsheim-Gustavsburg: Grüne Liste, Gross-Gerau: Grüne Liste (1981) and DIE GRÜNEN (1985), Nauheim: Grüne Liste, Raunheim: Wählerinitiative, Riedstadt: Grüne Liste, Rüsselsheim: Freie Wählergemeinschaft, Trebur: Grüne Liste. The data suggest that Green electoral mobilisation tends to decline once environmental or other new political issues have disappeared. (e.g. Startbahn-West). Electoral support for the Greens is not linked to the existence of ecologically controversial installations but only to the protest climate which may surround them.
2. Whereas the *Freie Wählergemeinschaft* belonged to the Green spectrum in 1981 there is some doubt over whether the Green label can still be applied.

Source: Compiled by author from HSL (Ed.) *Die kommunalwahlen am 10. März 1985.*

tion of this vote came from former supporters of the SPD which, despite its opposition to the runway project and nuclear energy programme of its own Land government, subsequently forfeited its traditional absolute majority on the district council. In this case there was no alternative to an alliance of Greens and SPD, despite the willingness of the CDU to participate in a Grand Coalition (Weirich 1982: 437).

The negotiating process in Gross-Gerau was simplified by the fact that the SPD and Greens shared a common social and political background, several Green councillors having themselves been former SPD members. Whereas in Kassel the two parties' councillors were attracted from contrasting social milieus (Bullmann 1985: 194), the Green representatives and followers in Gross-Gerau comprised a broad cross-section of the local population, politicised in the protest movement against the Startbahn-West. A further source of cohesion was provided in this district by the existence of a number of red–green alliances in its communities.

The combined opposition of Gross-Gerau's Greens and SPD to the runway development was undoubtedly the overriding feature of the alliance, but the co-operation extended during the course of the administration to cover other areas of local policy-making; primarily to the New Politics areas of environmental and social policy where the two parties appeared to hold similar positions (Bullmann 1985; 191).

The Changing Political Context in Hesse

In the three cases examined above, the specific local factors which led to the creation and subsequent durability of red–green alliances varied considerably. In the absence of political alternatives the stability of the Kassel and Gross-Gerau alliances was guaranteed by the programmatical similarities of the Greens and SPD on key New Politics issues. In Gross-Gerau an additional unifying factor was provided by the common social background and protest experience of the two parties' representatives. In Marburg the alliance was undermined by internal divisions between the new politics left and old politics right of the SPD, by the lack of a consensus in the Green Party, and by the existence of an alternative coalition partner.

In the two alliances that survived the 1981 to 1985 electoral period intact, it is possible to identify the beginnings of a shift by the Greens from their New Politics structures, based on their experience of co-operating with an SPD administration. Since the coalitional practices at the local level of the West German party system have traditionally been orientated less towards policy-making than towards the distribution of executive posts, the Greens' ideological refusal to accept such positions reduced the effectiveness of their bargaining stance when it came to extracting policy concessions from the SPD.[4] By the time a prominent Green Party member tried (unsuccessfully) to gain election to an executive post in Gross-Gerau the party had lost its leverage over the SPD (*Frankfurter Rundschau* 29.3.84). The principal feature which Hesse's first phase of local red–green alliances shared was the absence of a favourable regional political context in which they could operate, since neither of the respective Land parties openly supported such alliances in their early stages. The Greens were not represented in the state legislature when the agreements were reached and they were dominated by a faction opposed to any form of co-operation with the SPD. The SPD was itself doubly sensitive to local alliances with the Greens: not only had the Green protest been inspired by the policies of an SPD-led regional government in the first place, but the existence of red–green alliances could be treated by conservative critics as a slight on the personal authority of Minister President Börner.

A second phase of red–green coalitions which followed Hesse's local elections in 1985 should be viewed, however, against a background marked by significant changes within the Hessian Green Party and by a series of developments at both the federal and regional levels of the West German party system.

The Hesse Green Party of 1985 was far removed from that of the early 1980s in which the inner-party debate was propelled by the fundamentalist Frankfurt line, which regarded even local level alliances as a betrayal of Green principles. The shift towards the adoption of a reformist strategy resulted primarily from events surrounding the 1983 regional election in Hesse, called early by Börner after he had failed to attract Green support for his minority SPD government following the regular regional election of 1982 (Franz *et al* 1983). It had proved difficult for the realist majority in the *Landtagsfraktion* to fulfil the fundamentalist strategy assigned to it by the party membership (Grupp 1986:

---

4. The lack of interest shown by Greens in executive posts can simplify the negotiation process as one SPD party worker explained: 'Sie (Die Grünen T.S.) sind keine Postenjäger. Deshalb kann man sich häufig leichter einigen als mit CDU oder FDP' — 'They (the Greens) are not jostling for positions. It is therefore often easier to come to an understanding with them than with the CDU or FDP,' (quoted in Loreck 1987: 76). The Kassel Greens underestimated their bargaining strength when it came to electing the city mayor in 1981 (Weist 1985: 28).

56). In a re-election which had followed the collapse of negotiations between the SPD and Green Alternative List (GAL) in
the Hamburg state legislature in autumn 1982, the Social Democrats had exploited a wave of public sympathy which accompanied the party's removal from the Federal Government
and were able in December to regain the absolute majority they
had lost in June (Müller-Rommel 1983). The SPD hoped, rather
optimistically, for the same outcome in Hesse. In both the
Hamburg and Hesse re-elections the Green share of the vote
declined, but whereas the GAL's strategy resulted ultimately in
its loss of leverage over the SPD, the Green Party still held the
balance of power in Hesse, despite the loss of one quarter of its
1982 percentage vote (Bürklin *et al* 1984).

At successive party conferences following the 1983 regional
election the reformist wing of the Hesse Green Party asserted its
superiority, beginning in Petersberg-Marbach on 1 October 1983
when a three-to-one majority voted in favour of entering negotiations with the SPD, the expressed aim of which was to
co-operate on a 'prolonged basis' with a minority SPD government.[5] This clear decision, supported at subsequent party conferences in Usingen and Lollar, essentially marked the end of
the power struggle between Green reformists and fundamentalists in Hesse. As a result of the Marbach decision the fundamentalist wing of the Hesse Green Party established its own
organisation, the Radical Ecologist Forum, as a form of opposition to both the established parties and the inner-party majority, but has been unable to regain the dominant influence it
had in the early 1980s. The new strategy adopted by the Greens
in the wake of the Hamburg and Hesse regional elections was
accompanied by a tactical shift within the Hessian SPD, its
national party in opposition to the CDU/FDP government in
Bonn and in the process of reconsidering previous policy commitments. At a regional party conference in Baunatal in November 1983 Börner seized upon the Greens' Marbach resolution
and stressed the necessity both of integrating the protest el-

5. The key element of the Marbach resolution is a recognition that Green demands
'können unter den derzeitigen Machtverhältnissen parlamentarisch nur in kontinuierlicher
Zusammenarbeit mit der SPD-Fraktion des Landtages durchgesetzt werden' — 'can only
influence parliamentary decisions if a steady collaboration with the SPD group in the Land
parliament is maintained, at least while the present distribution of power continues,'
(Marbach 1983). See also Kerschgens 1985: 119ff and Grupp 1986: 54ff.

ement into the party system and of establishing a credible
political alternative to the conservative-liberal trend:

> We do not want to create a situation in which the fundamentalist
> opposition in the ecology movement once again rules the roost. To
> prevent the Greens from assuming responsibility and to reject with-
> out discussion their offers of constructive talks, would mean
> strengthening the irrational forces in the Green camp. We have to
> succeed in integrating the young generation and the new electoral
> strata into our democratic state (*Frankfurter Rundschau* 7.11.1983).

The fact that the right wing of the Hesse SPD, identified with
the disputed policies from which the Greens derived, laid the
foundations for a future deal with the Green Party at the Land
level is significant. Had such a step been undertaken by a
left-wing leadership this might have been a permanent source of
inner-party dissent and likely to undermine the stability of any
compromise agreement reached with the Greens (Wentz 1987:
154ff).

There were already indications, however, that the SPD's new
strategy in Hesse would not be fully accepted by either its voters
or its membership. Whilst 83% of prospective Green voters
favoured a coalition with the SPD in a 1983 survey, 47% of
potential SPD voters actually supported the creation of a Grand
Coalition in Hesse and only 24% indicated support for an
alliance with the Greens (Bürklin *et al* 1984: 244ff). The same
study also showed that the advocates of a Grand Coalition were
disproportionately anchored amongst the SPD's old politics
electorate, whilst its New Politics followers favoured the Greens
as alliance partners. By co-operating with the Greens at the
Land level the SPD ran the risk not only of alienating part of its
traditional electorate, but also of encountering opposition from
its old politics orientated local party organisations. The deep-
seated animosities of many Social Democrats towards the
Greens could only be overcome, temporarily, by the creation of
local level coalitions after the 1985 local elections in Hesse, when
Green support was required to secure the election of SPD
candidates to key executive posts (Meng 1987: 18). The Mar-
bach/Baunatal conference resolutions established a basis for the
lengthy negotiation process between the Green and SPD *Land-
tagsfraktionen* culminating on 7 June 1984 in the joint approval of

Hesse's annual budget and the toleration by the Greens of a minority SPD government. Although the period of toleration lasted for less than six months, faltering ultimately over the question of the nuclear installations in Hanau, the foundations had been laid for a full coalition between the parties in late 1985.

The outcome of the Hessian local elections of March 1985 was regarded as a means not only of testing the level of popular support for a possible red–green Land coalition (Weist 1987: 133), but also of creating a network of local red–green coalitions which would support the implementation of the policies agreed by SPD and Greens in the *Landtag*, particularly in those areas in which the Greens had secured significant concessions from the SPD: energy, social and transport policy, waste management and local government reform.[6]

The 1985 Local Elections in Hesse: Parliamentarisation of the Green Party

For the local elections of 10 March 1985 the Greens entered party lists in each of Hesse's 21 districts and 5 *Stadtkreise*, gaining representation in all but 4 districts with an overall vote of 6.8% (Table 7.1). It is indicative of the rapid spread of the Hessian Green Party's local level organisation that whereas official party lists had only been entered in 36 localities in 1981, by 1985 candidates were fielded in 186 of the state's 421 local communities (Hassler 1985b: 160). As a result of these elections some 540 council seats were won by the Green Party itself, although account should also be taken of a further 135 seats gained by local Green/Alternative groups.[7]

These figures provide an insight into the degree of parliamentarisation of the Hessian Green Party. Local electoral success creates a number of structural problems for a party with a relatively low active membership and a high dependence upon

6. The agreement reached between Greens and SPD in Hesse runs to 112 pages, covering all aspects of regional policy-making (Vereinbarung undated). For sections with local relevance see waste (19ff), transport (27ff), energy (39), women (57ff), social policy (79ff), democracy and law (99).

7. Figure represents those Greens elected to councils of Kreise, Stadtkreise, Gemeinden and Umlandverband Frankfurt based on HSL and correspondence with GAK (Grüne und Alternative in den Kommunalvertretungen Hessen) of 24.2.87.

the state's parliaments. Taking the number of official Green Party councillors alone in Hesse (540), about one in eight of the party's membership of 4,200 held a council office in 1987. In addition, however, a significant proportion of the remaining membership was involved in other tasks related directly to parliaments; encompassing those Greens elected to neighbourhood councils (*Ortsbeiräte*) in the larger towns and cities, parliamentary business managers, council committee members, party members holding executive positions and those sitting on non-elected bodies. In the case of Frankfurt and Wiesbaden alone 47 Greens were sitting on neighbourhood councils (30 and 17 respectively). In 1987 the Hesse Green Party also had 4 members elected to or serving on the Bundestag and ten in the regional parliament in Wiesbaden. In addition, a considerable number of Greens from the region are employed as assistants to parliamentary groups or work elsewhere in the party organisation.

It would be difficult to calculate precisely the degree of parliamentarisation of the Hessian Green Party, but it is evident that the party's parliamentary arm is increasingly overshadowing the work of its local level organisation. This imbalance in turn influences directly the tactical debate between the party's reformist and fundamentalist wings.

Since local politics in the Federal Republic are reformist by nature, with key decision-making competences and financial powers lying at higher levels of government or with extra-parliamentary interest groups, the fact that a large proportion of the Hesse Green Party's active membership is involved directly in the everyday compromises demanded of local politics serves to reinforce the inner-party dominance of the realist wing. Even party fundamentalists are subjected to the necessity of reaching compromises in order to realise their policy goals, a dynamic which Joschka Fischer has called the 'realism of concrete practice' — *Realismus der konkreten Praxis* (Fischer 1987/88: 8).

Furthermore, the integration of the Greens into Hesse's local party systems has corresponded with a broadening of the scope of the party's local policy-making and a movement away from its New Politics structures. Whereas the Greens were initially able to maintain the global orientation of their ideology at the local level, the party is increasingly directing its activities

173

towards the traditional issues of local politics (budgetary and economic policy, personnel matters) whilst the established parties are shifting to occupy former Green areas, primarily that of environmental policy: 'The strategic approach to local politics and its focus on social change is virtually restricted today to Green parliamentary groups in large cities; the small and very small parliamentary parties hardly have a chance to advance 'global' concepts as they struggle to cope with mountains of everyday political- and paperwork' (Seliger 1987/88: 20). A re-appraisal of any New Politics organisational structures has been forced upon the Greens by their local level experience. With a large proportion of the Hesse party's active membership currently involved directly in parliamentary work there is a marked lack of members, particularly in the more rural areas of the state, capable of maintaining a viable party organisation. In the Gross-Gerau district during the 1981 to 1985 electoral period, the success of the Green Party, based on local opposition to the Startbahn-West proposals, led to the election to various councils of 60 of the party's district membership of 100 with the result that it was difficult to find candidates for party executive positions (Groebner 1984: 20). Under such circumstances it is not possible for the Green membership to exercise the degree of control over its elected representatives envisaged in early party programmes. Such links that exist between parliamentary group and party tend to be rather weak and are characterised by what one commentator has called a 'tacit division of labour' (*stillschweigende Arbeitsteilung*, Swatzina 1987: 3), with local politicians rarely finding the time to attend party meetings and party workers displaying only a minimal interest in the council activities of its representatives. In order to professionalise the party organisation by providing a permanent link between party and *Fraktion*, it seems inevitable that the Greens will overturn a further organisational principle which bars members from holding public and party office concurrently. Such a move is already supported openly by prominent members of the Hesse party (Fischer 1987/88: 8).

The integration of the Hessian Greens' realist majority into the state's local parliaments and the declining degree of polarisation between the New Politics structures and themes of the Greens and those of the established parties ensures that the

Greens are regarded increasingly as suitable alliance partners by the SPD at the local level. An examination of a second phase of local coalitions between the Greens and SPD in Hesse shows, however, that the declining salience of the new–old politics dimension has occurred at differing rates throughout the state.

Second Phase Red–Green Coalitions in Hesse

The outcome of the Hessian local elections of 1985, in which the Greens and the SPD increased their shares of the vote, was treated by both parties as an affirmation of public support for their joint strategy, and provided the necessary impetus for the resumption of talks to co-operate in the Landtag. The result of the negotiations was the inauguration at the regional level of the first red–green coalition of the West German party system (Grupp 1986; Meng 1987; Weist 1987). The new Land government could in turn rely upon the support of a loose network of local red–green coalitions, made possible by the local elections, to implement its new waste management policy and to encourage the decentralised provision of energy (Bullmann 1987: 66).

The negotiations which took place between the Greens and SPD in Hesse's local communities in 1985 were stimulated by the open support of their respective regional parties. Whilst Holger Börner called upon SPD groups in local assemblies to enter alliances with the Greens wherever mathematically possible (*Frankfurter Rundschau* 12.3.85) in order to safeguard the strategy on which so much of his personal credibility rested, the necessity of displaying a willingness to compromise appeared increasingly critical to the Hessian Greens following the party's twin election disasters of 1985 in the Saarland and in North Rhine-Westphalia. In both regions the Greens failed to gain the 5% of the vote required to gain representation in the state legislatures; in both cases the Greens had adopted fundamentalist strategies (Berger *et al* 1985; Kimmel 1985; Feist and Krieger 1985). Red–green majorities existed on paper in 8 of Hesse's 21 districts, in several large towns and cities and in a number of small communities. After the elections, however, it soon became obvious that such alliances were not universally desired. Although the Greens were generally willing to begin

175

negotiations with their SPD counterparts, a number of Social Democrat *Fraktionen*, especially in Hesse's smaller communities, sought their partners elsewhere. In the Lahn-Dill district, for example, the SPD reached swift agreement with an independent voters' group (*Freie Wählergemeinschaft*) at the expense of a possible alliance with the Greens. The concession of three honorary posts on the district council executive was preferred by the SPD to the prospect of entering into lengthy talks with the Greens on the basis of their 24-point catalogue of demands (*Frankfurter Rundschau* 20.3.85). In the case of Darmstadt the alternative to a potential red-green alliance was provided by a Grand Coalition of SPD and CDU. Following a period of internal strife the Darmstadt SPD was in conflict with its regional party (*Frankfurter Rundschau* 11.7.84) and resisted the pressure towards a red–green alliance. The local SPD view of the Greens was expressed by mayor Günther Metzger: 'The Greens include hard-line communists who want a fundamental change of our social order, our state and our town — with these people we must have nothing in common' (*Frankfurter Rundschau* 22.3.1985). In other cases alliances between SPD and Greens foundered when individual SPD councillors, so-called U-Boats, failed to give their support to new administrations backed by Green votes, thus ensuring the continuation of CDU rule. This was the case in the district of Limburg-Weilburg and in the town of Offenbach, although in the latter a relatively stable red–green coalition developed at a later stage (*Frankfurter Rundschau* 4.10.86).

Generally, the smaller the community, the less was the inclination of the SPD to enter into negotiations with the Greens. In a survey of localities in which alliances between the SPD and Greens were theoretically possible, the Hesse Green Party's umbrella organisation for local politics (GAK) discovered only two cases in which a written agreement had been reached: 'In smaller communities, the SPD tends to be thoroughly conservative and despite good intentions of the Greens collaboration is not normally possible' (GAK 1986: 2). It is in these smaller communities, though not only given the experiences of Lahn-Dill, Limburg-Weilburg and Darmstadt, that the differences between the New Politics orientation of the Greens and traditional local politics are still most pronounced in Hesse. Only in Hesse's larger councils — at the district, large town and city level — were the Greens treated as a potential ally by the SPD, whose left-wing had ensured that New Politics issues already featured on local agendas.

Characteristics of Coalition Agreements

In the wake of the 1985 local elections in Hesse red–green coalitions were established in the towns of Wiesbaden, Marburg (again), Giessen, belatedly in Offenbach and in the districts of Marburg-Biedenkopf, Wetterau, Darmstadt-Dieburg and Bergstrasse as well as in a number of smaller towns. Although the policy content of the agreements varied considerably according to local factors, one feature shared in common by the more stable coalitions was the inclusion of Green Party members in local council executives. In two further cases in which red–green alliances had been possible (the districts of Main-Kinzig and Giessen), the Greens failed to assume executive posts and had little permanent influence over the decision-making process, although compromises were reached periodically with the SPD over specific issues.[8]

Despite the recognition that executive participation would be an essential factor behind the stability and success of co-operation with the SPD, the manner in which the Greens occupied these positions varied. The cases of Marburg and Wiesbaden exemplify the differing types of agreement reached in 1985.

The second red–green cooperation in Marburg operated on a much firmer basis than the first had done. Not only did Greens and SPD command an absolute majority of council seats as a result of the 1985 election, but divisions within the parties were less marked. The Greens had overcome their internal differences following the threatened intervention of its Land party[9]

8. In the Main-Kinzig district, which includes the site of the disputed nuclear installations, the relationship between SPD and Greens only improved in the aftermath of the Chernobyl nuclear accident which led the district SPD to reconsider its commitment to nuclear energy (*Frankfurter Rundschau* 8.2.88). For Green view of early stages of relationship with SPD, see Zierz 1986. For alliance difficulties in Giessen see Bullmann 1987: 70ff.

9. The (complicated) conflict in Marburg came to a head in 1982 with the establishment of two rival Green organisations in the town, which led the regional party to appoint three mediators to sort the dispute out. In the event the rival groups reached an understanding independently of the regional party, although the animosity resulted in the rotation of three Green town councillors, (*Frankfurter Rundschau* 2.8.83), a rarity at the local level. The

and were able to offer a more clearly defined negotiating position in talks with the SPD, based on the party's experience of local politics in Marburg.

In the publicly-held talks of 1985 the Greens insisted both upon the party's inclusion in the council executive (responsible for environmental and social policy) and the dismissal of the remaining CDU members from it.[10] A clause of the agreement which prevented the coalition partners from voting against one another on key policy matters created an interdependence between the parties and served to deflate potential crises before they became public. In addition policy co-ordination was institutionalised in the form of cross-party working groups and regular meetings of SPD and Greens before the monthly council meetings.

With Green executive representation it proved possible to influence all aspects of decision-making in Marburg, even in areas which were beyond the party's jurisdiction. Despite the placatory mechanisms of the coalition agreement, a number of conflicts have arisen between the parties, primarily on the subject of town planning. It has nevertheless always been possible for Greens and SPD to come to a compromise over such problems, if only by delaying solutions until after the next local elections in Hesse.

The Wiesbaden coalition has, however, been characterised by a series of conflicts between the two parties culminating in early 1988 in the attempts of the SPD to find a new partner to pass the 1988/89 budget. A major factor behind the friction stems from the political inexperience of the Greens in Wiesbaden, represented on the city council for the first time in 1985, which is manifest in the agreement reached with the SPD.

Whereas in Marburg and other localities the Greens had forced the dismissal of CDU and FDP executive members and had ensured that the coalition partners could not out-vote one another on policy matters, this was not achieved in Wiesbaden.

---

information on the second red–green co-operation in Marburg is based on an interview on 2.2.88 with Ulrike Kober, spokeswoman of the parliamentary party.

10. A unique feature of Hesse's local constitution allows a simple majority of councillors, in districts and towns with populations over 50,000, to dismiss members of the executive within six months of a local election (Borchmann 1986). In other regions a majority of at least two-thirds is required.

The result was that the SPD was able to maintain a facade of consensus administration. It is sometimes argued that the Greens themselves stand to benefit from participation in an all-party executive, being less reliant upon the SPD and able to seek support from other parties for its proposals, but in Wiesbaden the arrangement has tended to serve the SPD by providing them with the opportunity of seeking backing from other parties according to the measure in question. In addition, the Wiesbaden Greens were assigned executive responsibility for educational and cultural affairs, an area not normally regarded as a key feature of Green local politics. The fact that this position was then occupied by a non-party member, on the basis of her professional experience, meant that an official party opinion could not be expressed on matters raised in the executive and that the Greens were not always aware of potential conflicts. In this case it appears as if the Greens fell between two stools when agreement was reached with the SPD in 1985; the debate over whether or not they should assume executive responsibility ended in a compromise decision which achieved neither fully.

Since the Wiesbaden Greens are not held responsible for a policy area central to their programme, it will be difficult to publicly identify hard-won concessions from the SPD as Green successes. Notable Green demands have been realised in the fields of environmental and transport policy and with the introduction of traffic reduction measures and support for womens' projects (Mayer 1987/88: 21), but these areas are within the SPD's jurisdiction. The creation of a new peace committee was also regarded as a success by the Greens, but in practice the committee's function has been perceived rather differently by the coalition partners. The mere existence of the peace committee has been used by the SPD to demonstrate its openness to New Politics issues, whilst the Greens have sought to exploit it as a forum for the treatment of those issues normally beyond the scope of West Germany's local politics.[11] Green proposals in these areas rarely gained the support of the SPD however: 'Every issue beyond the verbatim text of the agreement which we

11. Such issues have included a local boycott of financial institutions with South African links, the creation of a nuclear-free zone, the US bombing raid on Libya in 1986, the creation of a city partnership with a region in Nicaragua and means of opposing NATO military exercises.

hoped to have considered in committee, was normally thrown out by SPD/CDU/FDP together. Preliminary agreements between the parliamentary groups of SPD and Greens in the committee were often disregarded when it came to a vote' (Müller 1987: 1). The tension which has characterised the Wiesbaden coalition stems less from a fundamental cleavage between the New Politics of the Greens and traditionalist nature of the SPD, than from the Greens' failure to establish themselves as equal partners in the initial agreement.

The Changed Context of Local Red–Green Coalitions

A certain degree of conflict has accompanied all local coalitions between the Greens and SPD in Hesse, but while the parties were working together in the state legislature it proved possible to resolve crises as they arose. The inauguration of a new CDU/FDP government as a result of the regional elections of April 1987 has, however, significantly altered the context under which local red–green coalitions operate (Schmitt 1987; *Frankfurter Rundschau* 7.4.87). The period since the collapse of the red–green Land government in Hesse has been marked by difficulties for the local level coalitions, indicating their great reliance upon events at the regional level.

For the Greens in particular, the political and financial support of the red–green regional government was an essential precondition for the successful implementation of their new policies. In a climate in which the financial scope of local authorities is increasingly restricted by constraints placed upon them by higher levels of government (Riedmüller 1987), the provision of state subsidies was the only means by which the Greens could gain local SPD support for their new waste management and energy programmes or for the funding of social initiatives. The future of these Green-sponsored projects has been called into doubt by the withdrawal of state subsidies by the new CDU/ FDP government. Significantly, the collapse of local red–green coalitions has not been orchestrated by the Greens. With the SPD having difficulty coping with its new oppositional role in Hesse, the latent resistance of old politics sections of the party to forms of co-operation with the Greens (temporarily overcome by Börner's actions in the wake of the 1983 regional election) has begun to manifest itself more openly.

Within days of the 1987 Land election the SPD in the Darmstadt-Dieburg district brought their coalition with the Greens to an end by affirming the party's support for the development of a former quarry and site of archaeological value (Messel) for use as a dump for domestic waste.

Ironically, the decision of the CDU/FDP regional government to save the Messel site has enabled the former partners to reconvene their alliance, albeit without the conviction of its early months. The location of new waste disposal sites has also led to friction in the Wetterau and Marburg-Biedenkopf districts. In both cases individual SPD councillors were unwilling to give their support to the siting of new dumps in their constituencies, thereby undermining the key feature of the red–green regional government's waste policy which sought to make each district responsible for the disposal of its own domestic and chemical refuse. In the Wetterau district the SPD rebels voted with the opposition to secure the rejection of the 1988 budget and brought the coalition with the Greens to an end.

With respect to the waste disposal measures the relationship between the Greens and SPD in Hesse appears to have come full circle. Whereas the Greens were once regarded as unreliable alliance partners, it is local SPD groups that have generally been less prepared than the Greens to assume responsibility for the implementation of the policies agreed by the parties at the regional level. That the assumption of such responsibility still does not come easily to the Greens is shown by an entry in Joschka Fischer's diaries:

> This whole search for locations promises to be quite something. How does one do this as a Green? For those from the established camps the answer tends to be simple enough: decide on a location and then push it through. For a Green Minister of the Environment this approach is, of course, impossible. We have to try and soften the protests through openness, conviction and information . . . (Fischer 1987: 141).

Once suitable locations were found for new dumps, local Green groups could rely upon gaining additional political support for their decision from the *Landtagsfraktion*. The formal links maintained between the Greens in the Hessian state legislature and the party's local council executive members, the so-called *Dezernentenrunde*, provided a forum in which the implementation of policy could be co-ordinated. These contacts between the system levels have been accorded a greater priority by the Greens following the collapse of the red–green regional government, as the party attempts to alleviate the pressure under which local coalitions are currently operating.[12]

Conclusion: The Integration of the Hessian Green Party

An examination of local red–green coalitions in Hesse is at the same time a portrayal of the integration of the Green protest into the state's parliamentary system and of the party's transformation from a radical oppositional force into one willing to co-operate with established parties in order to implement their reforms. The process of integration, which has occurred essentially at the local level of the party system, coincided with the Greens' movement away from its New Politics organisational structures and was accompanied by a broadening of its programmatical basis. In this respect the Greens became a suitable coalition partner for the SPD.

A first phase of red–green alliances which followed the Hessian local elections of 1981 developed at a time of great polarisation between the parties. Without the support of their regional parties, these alliances were dependent entirely upon the interaction of a series of local factors for their success; notably upon the willingness of the Greens to compromise and upon the openness of local SPD groups to the issues of the New Politics. In contrast, a second, more important phase of local red–green coalitions evolved in 1985 under the overriding influence of events at the regional level, which had seen both the SPD and Greens reconsider their relationship to one another. Only with the creation of a loose network of local coalitions between

---

12. The Green strategy in Hesse is currently aimed towards halting the 'Wende' at the local level in the forthcoming local elections of March 1989. The party hopes that a confirmation of existing red–green majorities and the creation of new ones will form a solid basis for the recreation of the regional coalition with the SPD after the 1991 state elections (Erklärung undated).

Greens and SPD was the regional government guaranteed an element of stability, since red–green administered local authorities were inevitably the most willing to implement the policies advocated by the regional government.

Whereas local level coalitions with the SPD are no longer the source of great controversy in the Hessian Green Party, the willingness of the SPD to co-operate with the Greens still varies considerably. The non-uniformity of the SPD's approach stems primarily from the uneven nature of the process of socio-economic modernisation in Hesse and the subsequent variation in the spread of new political values within its local party organisations. Whilst the Greens have moderated their new political orientation at the local level in Hesse, there is a clear gap between the New Politics left and old politics right of the SPD which was only overcome temporarily by Börner's new conciliatory strategy towards the Greens in the wake of the 1983 regional election. It is likely, therefore, that future coalitions between the SPD and Greens in Hesse, be they at local or regional level, will depend more upon the pace of change within the state's SPD than upon any further movement by the Green Party away from the New Politics.

References

Books and Articles

Alber, Jens (1985), 'Modernisierung, neue Spannungslinien und die politischen Chancen der Grünen', *Politische Vierteljahresschrift* 3

Baker, Kendall, Russell Dalton and Kai Hildebrandt (1981) *Germany transformed. Political culture and the New Politics*. Cambridge, Mass. and London: Harvard University Press

Berger, Manfred, Wolfgang Gibowski, Dieter Roth and Wolfgang Schulte (1985) 'Starke Wählerbewegungen und stabile Strukturen, kein Test für Bonn — Landtagswahlen 1985', *Zeitschrift für Parlamentsfragen* 3

Borchmann, Michael (1982), 'Gemeindlicher Aufgabenkreis und Tagesordnung der Vertretungskörperschaft. Zugleich ein Beitrag zu Erscheinungsformen "grüner" Kommunalpolitik', *Der Städtetag* 10

—— (1986), 'Die vorzeitige Abberufung hauptamtlicher kommunaler Wahlbeamter. Erste Erfahrungen mit der neuen hessischen Regelung', *Der Städtetag* 6

Bürklin, Wilhelm (1981), 'Die Grünen und die "Neue Politik". Abschied vom Dreiparteiensystem?' *Politische Vierteljahresschrift* 4

—— Gerhard Franz and Rüdiger Schmitt (1984), 'Die hessische Landtagswahl vom 25. September 1983: Politische Neuordnung nach der "Wende"?', *Zeitschrift für Parlamentsfragen* 2

Bullmann, Udo (1985), 'Rot-grüne Politik von unten?', in U. Bullmann and P. Gitschmann (eds.), *Kommune als Gegenmacht*, Hamburg: VSA

—— (1987), 'Mehr als nur der Unterbau. Die Zusammenarbeit von Sozialdemokraten und Grünen in den Kommunen', in R. Meng (ed.), *Modell Rot-Grün?*, Hamburg: VSA

—— and Peter Gitschmann, (1985), *Kommune als Gegenmacht. Alternative Politik in Städten und Gemeinden*, Hamburg: VSA

Eichel, Hans and Bertram Hilgen (1985), 'Mehr als ein Schönwetterbündnis. Bilanz einer vierjährigen Zusammenarbeit', in N. Rehrmann (ed.), *Rot-grünes "Modell Kassel"?*, Kassel: Werkstatt Verlag

Feist, Ursula and Hubert Krieger (1985), 'Die Nordrhein-westfälische Landtagswahl vom 12. Mai 1985. Stimmungstrend überrollt Sozialstrukturen oder: Die Wende ist kein Kaffeefahrt', *Zeitschrift für Parlamentsfragen* 3

Fischer, Joschka (1987), *Regieren geht über Studieren. Ein politisches Tagebuch*, Frankfurt: Athenaeum

—— (1987/88), 'Zukunft für die Grünen', *Stichwort Grün* Dezember/Januar

Franz, Gerhard, Robert Danziger and Jürgen Wiegand (1983), 'Die hessische Landtagswahl vom 26. September 1982: Unberechenbarkeit der Wählerpsyche oder neue Mehrheiten?', *Zeitschrift für Parlamentsfragen* 1

Gröbner, Thomas (1984), 'Kreistagsarbeit: Keine Angst vor der Kompetenzfrage!', *Alternative Kommunalpolitik* 4

Grupp, Joachim (1986), *Abschied von den Grundsätzen? Die Grünen zwischen Koalition und Opposition*, Berlin: Edition Ahrens, Zerling

Handbuch (1985) *Handbuch für alternative Kommunalpolitik*, Bielefeld: AJZ

Hassler, Gerd (1981a), 'Die Kommunalwahlen in Hessen am 22. März 1981. Teil I: Gemeindewahlen in den kreisfreien Städten und Kreiswahlen', *Staat und Wirtschaft in Hessen* 5

—— (1981b), 'Die Kommunalwahlen in Hessen am 22. März 1981. Teil 2: Gemeindewahlen in den kreisangehörigen Gemeinden', *Staat und Wirtschaft in Hessen* 7/8

—— (1985a), 'Die Kommunalwahlen in Hessen am 10. März 1985. Teil 1: Gemeindewahlen in den kreisfreoien Städten und Kreiswahlen', *Staat und Wirtschaft in Hessen* 4

—— (1985b), 'Die Kommunalwahlen in Hessen am 10. März 1985. Teil 2: Gemeindewahlen in den kreisangehörigen Gemeinden', *Staat und Wirtschaft in Hessen* 6

Herbers, Hans (1987), 'Grüne Kommunalpolitik. Nahbereich zwischen Rhein und Weser. Wo die Bündnisse kommen — anders als gedacht', *Kommune* 8

Kerschgens, Karl (1985), 'Gratwanderung zwischen zwei Verlockungen. Tolerierung einer SPD-Minderheitsregierung', in W. Bickerich (ed.), *SPD und Grüne*, Reinbek: Rowohlt

Kimmel, Adolf (1985), 'Die saarländische Landtagswahl vom 10. März 1985: Zwei Verlierer, zwei Gewinner, ein Sieger oder: Der Wähler hat den Wechsel gewollt', *Zeitschrift für Parlamentsfragen* 3

Kleinert, Hubert (1982), 'Marburger Koalitionen — Modell oder abschreckendes Beispiel?', *Moderne Zeiten* 1

—— and Jan Kuhnert (1982), 'Aufstieg und Fall des Marburger "Ampelbündnisses"' in J. Reents *et al*, *Es grünt so rot*, Hamburg: Konkret

Klotzsch, Lilian and Richard Stöss (1984), 'Die Grünen', in R. Stöss (ed.), *Parteien-Handbuch: die Parteien der Bundesrepublik Deutschland 1945–80*, Volume 2, Opladen: Westdeutscher Verlag

Kuhnert, Jan (1981), 'Die Grünen im Marburger Stadtparlament', in R. Schiller-Dickhut *et al*, *Alternative Stadtpolitik*, Hamburg: VSA

Loreck, Jochen (1987), 'Rot-grüne Rathaus- Bündnisse. Szenen einer wilden Ehe', *Vorwärts* 2

Mayer, Wenzel (1987/88), 'Das Ende der Fahnenstange', *Stichwort Grün* Dezember/Januar

Meng, Richard (1987), *Modell Rot-Grün? Auswertung eines Versuchs*, Hamburg: VSA

Müller-Rommel, Ferdinand (1983), 'Die Wahl zur Hamburger Bürgerschaft vom 19. Dezember 1982: Die neue Alte Mehrheit', *Zeitschrift für Parlamentsfragen* 1

Peter, Horst and Norbert Sprafke (1985), 'Rot- grüne Zusammenarbeit in Kassel: Berechtigt zu den besten Hoffnungen' in N. Rehrmann (ed.), *Rot-grünes "Modell Kassel"?*, Kassel: Werkstatt

Rehrmann, Norbert (ed.), (1985), *Rot-grünes "Modell Kassel"? Eine Bilanz nach vier Jahren*, Kassel: Kasseler Verlag/Werkstatt-Verlag

Resolution (1987), *Resolution des Deutschen Städtetages: "Städte an die neue Bundesregierung"*, 17./18 März 1987

Reidmueller, Barbara (1987), 'Die Rolle der Kommune in der Sozialpolitik' in M. Opielka and I. Ostner (eds.), *Umbau des Sozialstaats*, Essen: Klartext

Schiller-Dickhut, Reiner *et al* (1981), *Alternative Stadtpolitik. Grüne, rote und bunte Arbeit in den Rathäusern.* Hamburg: VSA

Schmitt, Rüdiger (1987), 'Die hessische Landtagswahl vom 5. April 1987: SPD in der "Modernisierungskrise"', *Zeitschrift für Parlamentsfragen* 3

Schulz, Armin and Andreas Schmitz (1985), 'Rot-grünes "Modell Kassel": Ein Trauerspiel mit magerem Ergebnis', in N. Rehrmann (ed.), *Rot-grünes "Modell Kassel"?*, Kassel: Werkstatt

Seliger, Berthold (1987/88), 'Spielacker Kommunalpolitik', *Stichwort Grün* Dezember/Januar

Swatzina, Klaus (1987), *Perspektiven Grüner Kommunalpolitik.* Düsseldorf: Grüne/Alternative in den Räten NRW e.V.

Traunsberger, Ekkehard and Herbert Klemisch (1987), 'Rot-grün in NRW — Kaum der Rede wert?', *Alternative Kommunalpolitik* 1

Weirich, Dieter (1982), '"Rot-grüne Ehe" bahnt sich an', *Kommunalpolitische Blätter* 5

Weist, Reinhold (1985), 'Rot-grün als Hoffnungsträger. Grüner Versuch in Kassel' in N. Rehrmann (ed.), *Rot-grünes "Modell Kassel"?*, Kassel: Werkstatt

—— (1987), 'Der Traum ist erst einmal ausgeträumt. Stationen grüner Realpolitik bis zur hessischen Wende', in R. Meng (ed.), *Modell Rot-Grün?*, Hamburg: VSA

Wentz, Martin (1987), 'Eine neue SPD? Sozialdemokratischer Wandel und rot-grüne Politik', in R. Meng (ed.), *Modell Rot-Grün?*, Hamburg: VSA

Woyke, Wichard and Udo Steffens (1987), *Stichwort: Wahlen. Ein Ratgeber für Waehler, Wahlhelfer und Kandidaten*, Leverkusen: Leske

Documents

Atomzentrum Hanau (1986), Atomzentrum Hanau: Tödliche Geschäfte, Hanau: *Neue Hanauer Zeitung*/Initiativgruppe Umweltschutz Hanau, November

Darmstadt-Dieburg (1985), Koalitionsvertrag zwischen den Fraktionen der SPD und den GRÜNEN im Kreistag Darmstadt-Dieburg für die Legislaturperiode 1985–89

Erklärung (1984), Kommunalpolitische Erklärung, ed. by Die Grünen Landesverband Nordrhein-Westfalen, Düsseldorf

Erklärung (undated), Erklärung der Grünen Hessen. Für eine ökologische Reformpolitik in Hessen

GAK (1986), Zusammenfassung der Ergebnisse des Rundschreibens an Kommunen mit rot-GRÜNEN Mehrheiten. Fulda: Grüne und Alternative in den Kommunalvertretungen Hessen e.V

Haushaltsdokumentation (1983), Was machen DIE GRÜNEN im Parlament? Haushaltsdokumentation 1983 der Grünen im Römer — Beispiele aus zwei Jahren GRÜNER Kommunalpolitik in Frankfurt. Frankfurt: Die Grünen im Römer

Kerschgens, Dorothea and Irmela Wiemann (1985), Die ersten 4 Jahre: Die GRÜNEN im Landeswohlfahrtsverband Hessen, Frankfurt: Die Grünen im LWV

LHA (1981), Protokoll der Landeshauptausschuss-Sitzung in Wethen/ Diemelstadt am 20.9.81

Marbach (1983), Beschluß der Landesversammlung der GRÜNEN-HESSEN am 1./2. October 1983 in Petersberg-Marbach

Marburg (1985), Vereinbarung zwischen SPD und Grünen in der Stadt Marburg für die Kommunalwahlperiode 1985–89

Marburg-Biedenkopf (1985), Eine neue Politik für Marburg-Biedenkopf. Vereinbarungen zwischen SPD und Grünen für die Wahlperiode 1985–89

Müller, Jens Christian (1987), Bilanz der Zusammenarbeit zwischen SPD und GRÜNEN im Friedensausschuss. Wiesbaden

Radikalökologische Politik (undated) Dokumentation radikalökologischer Diskussionsbeiträge in den Grünen-Hessen. Frankfurt: Arbeitsgruppe Radikalökologische Foren

Satzung (1987), Kommentierte Satzung des Landesverbandes Die Grünen Hessen, Frankfurt: Die Grünen Hessen

Vereinbarung (undated), Vereinbarung zwischen SPD und Grünen für die II. Legislaturperiode. 2. Edition. Wiesbaden: Die Grünen im Landtag

Wetterau (1985), Verhandlungsergebnis zwischen SPD und GRÜNEN im Wetteraukreis

Wiesbaden (1985), Gesamtergebnis der Verhandlungen zwischen SPD und die Grünen 1985

Zierz, Michael (1986) 'Unruhe ins Parlament, Grüne im Kreistag Main-Kinzig' in 'Atomzentrum Hanau', *Neue Hanauer Zeitung*/Initiativgruppe Umweltschutz Hanau

8
Women in the Green Party

Eva Kolinsky

The Mobilised Electorate

Women, whose traditional roles as mothers and homemakers implied that they would take a back seat in public affairs, have emerged as one of the most interesting and volatile groups in West German politics. In the founding decades of the Federal Republic, their participation in elections, parties and the political leadership kept to a conventional path: preferences tended to be conservative, party membership remained well below that of men, and only few women achieved public office (Bremme 1956; Fülles 1969). Women were usually less well educated than their male peers, and few obtained vocational or professional training since domesticity and homemaking continued to exercise a powerful influence as prescriptive social roles. Although the shortage of men during and after the Second World War had opened some avenues of employment and set a trend in motion to regard work outside the home as an integral part of a woman's life, rather than a mere stop-gap measure prior to marriage, political preferences and motivations only began to change in the 1960s once a younger generation looked towards political parties and elections with new expectations to make a personal and visible impact (Kolinsky forthcoming). The gender gap of political participation is still visible but has narrowed considerably in the last twenty years (Hoecker 1987).

Of particular significance for the emergence of the Green Party has been the mobilisation of women's electoral choices. As traditional dividing lines of social class or denomination have lost some of their definition, electoral decisions have rested increasingly on personal choices while inherited orientations have receded. Better educated West Germans, especially the new middle class, were likely to base their preferences on their

189

perception whether or not a party was competent to put certain policies into practice (Klingemann 1985). Improved access to vocational qualifications had a similar mobilising effect. Women of the post-war generations emerged as an electorate able to choose and willing to change between parties. In the 1950s, the Christian Democrats enjoyed a women's bonus as the party to generate normalisation in the socio-economic and the private spheres. In the 1960s, young women were more concerned with achieving equal recognition in society and regarded the Social Democrats as the political force that could achieve it. From a party with an endemic women's deficit, the SPD has since emerged as something of a women's party, with women constituting over half its electorate (Hofmann-Göttig 1986). In the 1980s, the Greens took over as the party which inspired most confidence among young women as an advocate of equal opportunities in a political setting where the SPD had discarded its fervour for change in the light of economic instabilities, and where CDU and FDP had consolidated their position among voters who sought a socio-economic equilibrium rather than a redistribution of rights or opportunities. In contemporary West German politics, SPD and Greens are immediate competitors for the electoral support of young and educated women (Table 8.1).

The Green Party built its electoral successes on the inability of the SPD in government to meet the expectations of innovation and equality among young West Germans who based their party preferences on personal choice (Hülsberg 1988). They made decisive gains among the under forties as the party that could draw on the new protest milieu and the New Politics and extended their support among urban and educated young women (see Chapter 2). The electoral mobility of women and their confidence to choose between parties and switch preferences between elections, has put women into a position of kingmaker whose votes could make or break the chances of either one of the big parties to lead a government and the chances of the Greens to retain or consolidate their place in West German regional parliaments and in the Bundestag.

Participatory Politics and the Women's Movement

In West Germany, turning out to vote has been widely accepted as the main opportunity for the individual to influence public affairs and policy directions. On average, 85% of the adult population take part in national and some 75% in regional elections; by comparison, participation through party membership attracts only a determined few. In 1988, two million (4%) of West Germans over the age of 16 were members of a political party, close to half-a-million (23%) of them women. Research into motivations for party membership has shown that personal reasons have superseded institutional ones. In the fifties or sixties the majority of SPD members, for instance, had joined their party in order to strengthen the organisation and never intended to hold a party office. CDU members, by contrast, were keen to hold an office and enter local or higher level politics through the party (Kolinsky 1984). In the 1980s, an increasing number of West Germans hope to influence policy formulation through their membership, and also hold a party office (Roth and Wiesendahl 1986). Party membership is closely tied in with expectations that the citizens can influence decisions in a democracy.

Women had traditionally joined political parties alongside their husbands or in the context of their socio-political environment. Since the early 1970s, political participation has taken two distinct directions: on the one hand, West German women are looking to party membership as an entry point to the political elite, they are motivated to hold political office and rise into parliamentary politics. No longer satisfied with providing background cultural or clerical support, they intend to play a role equal to that of men, and have placed political parties under pressure to respond to these expectations. The second direction of women's participation has emphasised issues and non-hierarchical modes of organisation. Since the early 1970s, citizens' initiatives and new social movements have emerged with a special focus on issues which it was claimed had been ignored by mainstream parties. Extra-parliamentary movements gained ground as self-styled correctives to the catch-all parties and also as catalysts of policy adjustments (Smith 1987). This new tier of political activity could draw on an increased willingness among

191

Table 8.1. Women's preference in Bundestag Elections 1972–87 (voting by age and gender group)

Age	Year	CDU/CSU			SPD			FDP			Greens			Other		
		M	F	Total	M	F	Total	M	F	Total	M	F	Total	M	F	Total
18–24	1972	34.8	35.9	35.3	54.3	55.0	54.6	9.6	8.5	9.1	–	–	–	1.4	0.6	1.0
	1976	40.3	40.2	40.2	49.4	50.2	49.8	8.5	8.6	8.5	–	–	–	1.8	1.0	1.4
	1980	35.6	33.0	34.6	47.6	50.3	48.9	10.9	11.9	11.4	5.3	4.3	4.8	0.7	0.4	0.4
	1983	42.0	40.3	41.2	37.6	40.6	39.0	5.4	5.2	5.3	14.2	13.5	13.9	0.7	0.4	0.6
	1987	37.0	34.8	36.0	37.5	38.7	38.1	8.6	8.0	8.3	14.5	16.5	15.5	2.3	1.9	2.1
25–34	1972	40.5	41.9	41.2	48.1	47.5	47.8	10.5	10.1	10.3	–	–	–	0.9	0.4	0.7
	1976	43.3	44.2	43.7	45.3	44.5	44.9	10.3	10.7	10.5	–	–	–	1.1	0.6	0.8
	1980	37.6	35.6	36.6	46.4	47.9	47.1	12.8	13.9	13.3	2.6	2.4	2.4	0.7	0.3	0.5
	1983	43.1	42.8	43.0	38.3	40.4	39.4	6.3	6.2	6.3	11.5	10.1	10.8	0.7	0.5	0.6
	1987	34.7	34.4	34.6	39.0	39.0	39.0	7.9	7.3	7.6	16.9	17.9	17.4	1.5	1.5	1.5
35–44	1972	41.5	43.8	42.6	48.4	47.3	47.9	8.9	8.3	8.6	–	–	–	1.1	0.6	0.9
	1976	48.8	50.0	49.5	41.4	40.9	41.1	9.0	8.7	8.9	–	–	–	0.8	0.4	0.6
	1980	45.7	44.6	45.2	40.3	40.7	40.5	12.6	13.6	13.1	0.9	0.8	0.9	0.4	0.3	0.3
	1983	50.3	50.9	50.6	35.7	36.4	36.0	8.8	8.3	8.6	4.7	4.1	4.4	0.5	0.3	0.4
	1987	40.6	42.5	41.5	37.6	36.6	37.1	10.7	10.5	10.6	9.9	9.3	9.6	1.2	1.1	1.2

45–59	1972	44.4	47.9	46.4	45.0	43.6	44.2	8.9	7.7	8.2	–	–	–	1.7	0.2	1.2
	1976	48.4	49.6	49.2	42.7	42.1	42.4	7.7	7.4	7.5	–	–	–	1.2	0.6	0.9
	1980	46.9	46.5	46.6	42.2	42.5	42.4	9.7	10.1	9.9	0.6	0.6	0.6	0.6	0.3	0.5
	1983	49.2	50.9	50.1	39.7	39.6	39.6	8.0	6.7	7.3	2.4	2.4	2.4	0.7	0.4	0.5
	1987	45.2	47.2	46.3	39.4	38.1	38.8	10.3	9.4	9.9	3.7	3.9	3.8	1.4	1.1	1.3
60 and over	1972	49.3	51.7	50.6	42.5	42.0	42.2	6.7	5.7	6.1	–	–	–	1.5	0.6	1.0
	1976	51.2	52.5	51.9	42.0	42.0	42.0	5.7	5.2	5.4	–	–	–	1.1	0.4	0.7
	1980	50.6	49.3	49.8	41.2	42.6	42.1	7.1	7.5	7.4	0.4	0.3	0.4	0.7	0.3	0.4
	1983	50.9	53.5	52.6	39.9	39.7	39.8	6.8	5.4	5.9	1.5	1.1	1.2	0.9	0.3	0.5
	1987	50.1	53.5	52.3	38.0	37.2	37.5	7.9	6.9	7.3	2.2	1.6	1.8	1.7	0.8	1.2
Total	1972	43.0	46.0	44.6	46.9	45.7	46.3	8.8	7.7	8.2	–	–	–	1.3	0.6	0.9
	1976	47.2	48.8	48.0	43.6	43.1	43.3	8.1	7.6	7.8	–	–	–	1.2	0.5	0.8
	1980	44.2	43.7	44.0	43.1	43.9	43.5	10.5	10.8	10.6	1.6	1.2	1.4	0.6	0.3	0.5
	1983	47.7	49.2	48.5	38.4	39.4	38.9	7.2	6.3	6.7	5.9	4.8	5.3	0.7	0.3	0.5
	1987	42.5	45.1	43.8	38.5	37.8	38.1	9.2	8.3	8.7	8.3	7.7	8.0	1.6	1.2	1.4

Source: Eckard Jesse, 'Repräsentative Wahlstatistik 1972–87', *Zeitschrift für Parlamentsfragen* 2, 1987: 239.

West Germans to engage in unconventional actions and to use demonstrations as a means of articulating their political intentions (Sinus 1983). Of particular importance for women was the non-hierarchical nature of the new political activities, and the concrete focus on normally one issue or a cluster of related issues. Issue politics seemed to allow individuals to see the effects of their involvement. It has been estimated that women constitute half the membership of citizens' initiatives and new social movements.

The new social movements, their political utilisation of specific issues, and their informal organisational practices have been precursors if not models of the Green Party. In the context of our discussion, the women's movement and its linkage with the Greens are of particular interest. The history of women's movements in Germany stretches back over a hundred years or so. As pressure groups for equal opportunities, women's movements were traditionally affiliated to mainstream political parties or defined themselves as members of a specific political camp (Hervé 1982). The women's movement which had a bearing on the Greens arose within the protest culture of the 1970s and has called itself 'new' to underline its detachment from the traditional women's movements or their parties (Schenk 1980; Haug 1986). Although there is thematic overlap between the conventional women's organisations and the new movement in their general concern for equal opportunities, the new women's movement regards itself as the spearhead of fundamental change while its conventional counterparts have made their mark as lobbyists for social reform.

The birth of the new women's movement can be traced to the final phase of the student movement, and in particular the 1969 annual congress of the Socialist German Student Association, SDS. The SDS had gained notoriety as a trailblazer and self-styled protagonist of the West German student movement and aimed at translating its leftist beliefs into far reaching changes of the political priorities and policy styles of West German democracy. Despite the apparently progressive overtones, the women affiliated to the movement felt excluded from its leadership and typecast as 'little women' whose only break with their capitalist surroundings and traditional women's roles should consist of a break with conventional and allegedly bourgeois morality codes to make women all the more freely available as sexual partners for the male protest elite (Becker and Burns 1987; Burns and van der Will 1988). When the SDS women articulated their demands to be treated equally in today's world and not only after some revolutionary changes had swept prejudice and restrictive attitudes aside, they voiced the expectations of the educated, mobilised young generation who faced the discrepancy between their personal aspirations and qualifications on the one side and social practices on the other which were changing at a slower pace.

The theme which, more than any other, amalgamated the mixture of aspirations and frustrations into a social movement and a visible force of the extra-parliamentary protest culture, was the theme of abortion. It was perceived as a women's rights issue. The right to decide whether or not to bear a child became identical with a woman's right to decide on who should have control over her body, her person, her social or political role. In West German politics, abortion headed the political agenda as a controversial subject of legislative change in the 1970s when the SPD/FDP government attempted to extend personal liberties by legalising abortion while the opposition insisted on restrictions. After the Bundestag had passed a law to make abortion freely available, a Christian Democratic appeal to the Constitutional Court produced a modified law which specified the conditions under which abortion could be obtained. It fell short of declaring abortion a woman's right. A decade later, the issue remains unresolved and § 218, the section in the Civil Code which regulates abortion, continues to be contested by women's organisations and also by the new women's movement which is preparing to register a complaint at the Constitutional Court against the abortion legislation as an undemocratic curtailment of individual liberties. The focus on abortion as a right and a personal issue is characteristic of the new personal dimension of political participation in the women's movement which also shaped the place of women in the Greens.

Another aspect of the women's movement which has left its mark in the Green party concerns its organisational structure. The women's movement did not develop the organisational cohesion through steering committees or a national leadership which had characterised the ecology or peace movements (Kölinsky 1987). Although it generated an active media sector with two journals, *Emma* and *Courage*, a host of bookshops and feminist publishers, none of these could claim to be the official voice of a co-ordinated movement. The women's movement remained deliberately unco-ordinated and its core consisted of local, small-scale action groups and projects. After an initial phase of mass-based demonstrations which were centred on abortion, the movement splintered into a plethora of homes for battered wives, refuge centres, workshops, each inspired by broadly similar orientations but working separately in their own neighbourhoods.

Many of the women who initiated the movement in the seventies or who identified with its causes in the 1980s, now belong to the Green sphere of voters and party activists. Although the doyenne of West German feminism, Alice Schwarzer called in 1980 on the readers of her journal *Emma* not to opt for the new Green party which did not appear sufficiently committed to the feminist cause, she had to admit seven years later that nearly 70% of *Emma*-readers voted Green (*Emma*, 1980; 1987). The women's movement and the topicality it bestowed on the issue of equal opportunities strengthened the position of women and their associations in all political parties and activated electoral support for the Greens among women. The aspect which proved the most influential in shaping the organisational role of women in the Greens was the emergence of a section in the new women's movement which called itself autonomous. These were women of the post-war generation for whom the main message of equal opportunities and women's rights consisted of the assumption that societies had, in the past, been dominated by men and shaped in a patriarchal mould which would always disadvantage women. What needed to be done was to reverse priorities, and create a climate in which female priorities, modes of behaviour and patterns of decision-making would come to the fore. The question was not merely to bring more women into positions of influence in politics, in employment or in public life; women needed to obtain such influence as women in their own organisational environments, not in channels which were created by men and whose agendas and communicative styles would favour men:

When we organise ourselves today in an autonomous fashion and include only women, we do this because we no longer fight only for equal rights, but we fight in a more fundamental sense for a new type of legislation and a new kind of lifestyle. We do not want to win the right to be equal with men in competitiveness, in war, militarism, the destruction of the environment, exploitation and the malformation of the soul [*seelische Verkrüppelung*]. Feminism is not just a political creed. It is a new lifestyle, for which we have to fight step by step. This is why we do not wish to offer ready-made solutions. Nothing shall be imposed on women from the outside, neither political knowledge nor any kind of commitment for others (!). Instead, women have to place themselves into the centre, they have to articulate their own dissatisfactions, and have to work together with other women who have made the same experiences. . . . We have organised ourselves in this way since we were thoroughly disillusioned with the practices of the sexist, male-dominated parties, associations, clubs and general organisations or institutions and because we could not recognise ourselves and our purpose in the lobbying, the party-political orientations and the competition among traditional women's associations and their representatives who have nothing in common with our own interests (*Ein Himmel auf Erden?* 1987: 63).

The Green Focus on Women — An Uncertain Consensus

Among the motley groups which converged to create the Green Party in January 1980 — environmentalists, left-wing remnants of the student movement and conservatives determined to halt technological change in the name of nature, life or mankind — the feminist perspective was just one of several. The founding programme included a section on equality, but it also stressed that the party had not reached a consensus whether to follow the new women's movement and campaign against restricting abortion or whether to object to abortion and advocate the right to life. (Document 4). While the fledgling party had resolved to defer a decision until a later date, and attempted, in the first instance, to integrate as broad a political spectrum as possible, the feminist focus soon dominated Green policies and organisational practices. Similar to the move of the party from a diverse grouping of left and right, loosely held together by a common concern for the environment, to a party with a distinct left-wing

197

profile, the feminist orientation evolved without a policy debate or an articulated consensus. While conservative ecologists and adherents of the far right, who had looked towards the Greens as a broad church, have since turned their backs on the party, diversities of focus persist among women. Although the Greens appear to have formulated a women's policy based on party consensus, internal divisions and conflicting priorities were not ironed out, and became more visible as the number of women in Green politics increased. The uncertain nature of the Green focus on women is the subject matter of this section.

The practicalities of access have been the most straight-forward component of the Green focus on women. From the outset, the party boasted that contrary to its political rivals it had no discriminatory legacies to overcome. In the first round of elections the Greens did not live up to their pronouncements, since women held less than half the seats in those parliaments where the young party gained representation. Women were, however, always included in the collective leadership of the party or the parliamentary groups and in 1984 an all-women group (*Das Feminat*) led the Greens in the Bundestag. From the outset, women in the Greens complained that their standing in the party remained lower than that of men despite the overt approval of equality. The candidacy of the *Feminat* has to be seen as a bid for full recognition of the political calibre of women. It came shortly after the party was rocked by a much publicised incident of sexual harassment of women by a male member of the Green parliamentary group. Although the culprit was forced to resign his seat (Spretnak and Capra 1985) the incident itself had soured the atmosphere. No longer content with an implicit consensus on equal opportunities, women now began to press for a more outspoken commitment of the party in its organisational practices and its policies. For the 1987/88 round of elections at national and regional level the party operated a 50% women's quota in most areas, and succeeded in having a record number of women elected to hold parliamentary seats (Table 8.2).

In September 1986, the Greens amended their statutes entitling women to hold no less than 50% of all posts in the party organisation and in parliamentary politics. The quota approach had been pioneered in 1985 when the Greens in Hesse amended

Table 8.2. Green women members of parliament in the Landtage and the Bundestag[1]

Parliament	Year	Women Total	%	Women Greens	% of Greens
Bundestag	1983	51	10	10	36
	1987	80	15	25	57
Baden-Württemberg	1980	7	6	1	17
	1984	9	7	1	11
	1988	12	10	4	40
Bavaria	1982	15	7	–	–
	1986	25	12	8	53
Berlin	1981	14	11	3	50
	1985	24	17	9	60
Bremen	1979	15	15	1	25
	1983	18	18	2	40
	1987	25	25	4	40
Hamburg	1982	20	17	4	50
	1986	40	33	13	100[2]
	1987	36	30	8	100[2]
Hesse	1982	12	11	4	44
	1983	14	13	3	43
	1987	18	16	5	50
Lower Saxony	1982	11	6	2	18
	1986	20	13	6	55
North Rhine-Westphalia	1980	13	7	–	–
	1985	26	11	–	–
Rhineland Palatinate	1983	11	11	–	–
	1987	11	11	1	20
Saarland	1980	3	6	–	–
	1985	6	12	–	–
Schleswig-Holstein	1983	6	8	–	–
	1987	13	18	–	–
	1988	18	24	–	–

1. The table focuses on the representation of the Greens but lists elections since the early 1980s to show the extent to which the share of women has increased in all parliaments, but particularly among Greens.
2. In 1986 and 1987 the Grün-Alternative Liste Hamburg (GAL) fielded an all-women's electoral list.

Sources: *Statistische Berichte* of the various Statistical Offices.

their statutes, and when the Alternative List in Berlin fielded the first parliamentary group with a women's majority (*Erfahrungsbericht* 1987: 56ff). By 1986, all regions had approved quota systems. Party lists for parliamentary elections now had to be composed according to the so-called zip-principle, alternating between women and men. In the party organisations, positions were to be filled in such a way that equal responsibilities and equal seniority for women was ensured:

> The Green Party as an employer will fill all vacancies at regional head office, at the parliamentary group or in the offices of members of parliament with women until all posts at all level of qualifications have been filled evenly by men and men. In those areas in which women are currently underrepresented, they will be employed in preference to men until parity has been reached (*Frauenstatut* 1986: 9).

After the quota regulation had already shaped the party's electoral lists for 1987 the Greens brought the quota approach into the limelight with two distinct moves. In September 1986, the party congress in Nuremberg accepted the so called Reconstruction Programme — *Umbauprogramm* — a detailed plan showing how economic policy should be reorientated to adhere to ecological principles, to cope with unemployment and also to end unequal opportunities for women in the world of work. The recommendation was curt: to introduce a 50% quota and preferential employment for women until gender discrepancies had been overcome (Umbau 1986: 60). In October of the same year, the parliamentary group in the Bundestag launched its major initiative in the field of women's policy: the Anti-Discrimination legislation of the Greens extends the same quota principle across society and demands a women's bonus until a gender equilibrium has been established (Documents 5 and 6). To monitor the transformation of patriarchal practices the legislation envisages the appointment of an ombudswoman, and a system of enforceable penalties, notably for violence against women.

At the eve of the 1987 elections, the Greens had arrived at an organisational and political formula for equality — the 50% quota approach. It was more radical than any attempted in other political parties and made the party appear in the public eye as committed to a cohesive women's policy. Could it not be expected that the women's majorities in Green parliamentary groups in the Bundestag and the regions would follow the same radical course? This has not happened. As women held the majority in parliamentary groups, the uncertainties of the Green focus on women became apparent.

To give just two examples: at the post-election congress in May 1987 in Dortmund, the perspective of the new women's movement was challenged by a so-called mothers' faction who launched a manifesto to call for the right of mothers to choose their own priorities and way of life. On one level, the manifesto was a critical broadside against the single, childless feminist minority who took it upon themselves to instruct the majority of women, the mothers in society, on the way they should think, work or organise their private lives; on another level, the mother's manifesto reflected the new diversity among women in the Greens. The quota regulation had brought more women into parliamentary politics, but their views were more disparate than those of the feminist faction who had prepared the quota approach and the Anti-Discrimination Legislation:

It is high time that other women or men stopped instructing mothers in how to plan their lives, how to regulate their emotional ties with their children and their husbands, their attitudes to employment, careers, housework, society and child rearing. . . .

The times of withdrawal, of complaining and questioning oneself have passed. Mothers no longer allow themselves to be quizzed on whether or why they wish to have children, but they in turn ask the world why it does not provide them with the legitimate, necessary and sensible support they would need: the future depends on mothers and in the final analysis mothers create the psychological and physical well-being of the whole of society.

To demand scope and room for mothers does not mean weakening the women's movement. It does also not mean excluding men. On the contrary: only strong mothers full of vitality and with self-confident children who know that there is room for them, are fully-fledged partners for those women, who have decided to lead a life without children, and for the men, whether or not they are fathers (*Müttermanifest* 1987: 2).

To the daughters of the new women's movement, the praise of mothers sounded alarmingly similar to conservative affirmations of the family and domesticity which seemed to have prevented generations of women in the past from becoming confident and self-motivated individuals.[1]

1. In an attempt to increase the birth rate and also to attract the electoral support of young

The second example of diversity concerns the core of Green women's policy itself, the Anti-Discrimination Legislation. Since it had received its first parliamentary reading at the very close of a legislative period, and had not completed its passage through the Bundestag committees before the federal elections in January 1987, the new parliamentary party had to start the process afresh and resubmit the legislation. It included more women but also more advocates of contrasting priorities on the role of women and on specific provisions in the legislation. Therefore, further progress of the bill turned out to be more than a formality of parliamentary procedure: it was a question of party consensus on women's policies itself. The issue which revealed the rift concerned punishments for rape. The ADG saw rape as arguably the worst crime of violence against women and proposed to introduce a minimum sentence of two years' imprisonment. This may have corresponded to feminist views about the severity of the crime; it did, however, conflict with the traditional championship in the Greens for minority groups and marginals including prisoners. The special section on prisoners in the 1980 programme had already implied that, regardless of their individual misdeeds, prisoners had to be seen as victims of an inhumane system of law enforcement and as deprived of their rights. The Greens had even entered prisoners as parliamentary candidates to underscore the point that they were scapegoats of an unjust social order. The feminist focus on rape disregarded these misgivings about the justice of West German legal procedures. It went unchallenged when adherents of the new women's movement called the tune; the challenge was unavoidable once their influence had weakened. After the 1987 elections, the Green parliamentary party deleted the rape-clause from the draft legislation; in order to make it easier for women to carry the motion, voting was conducted by secret ballot and the parliamentary group decided without seeking approval from the party leadership or the women's affairs experts. A letter of

---

career orientated women, the CDU/CSU and FDP government introduced an interesting legislative package in 1985 which gave women some pension rights for child care, a right to employment after a career break, a right to retraining before returning to the labour market after a career break, and allowed either men or women to claim a 'baby year'. To the authors of quota politics, the mothers' manifesto seemed to be a step in the same direction, towards government policies and away from the Greens.

protest in the national press highlights the dismay and also the impotence of the party to call its parliamentary representatives to heel:

> The latest Green party assembly had instructed the parliamentary party to retain a minimum penalty of two years imprisonment for rape, as envisaged in the Anti-Discrimination Legislation. By voting — in a closed ballot — against this resolution the majority of the Green parliamentary party has ignored the wishes of the party. Their comment that the party might as well continue discussing the issue until it could agree with the position taken by the parliamentary party only shows how arrogant and detached many of the Green members of parliament have become. . . . The majority of the parliamentary party has refused to call for prison sentences for rapists, and has thus proved itself incompetent to conduct Green politics. It leaves the political initiatives in this field to the other parties and accepts that the key issue of male violence against women falls victim to (male) power interests. In doing so, the parliamentary group has completely lost sight of the women's movement. We will not tolerate such a disregard of party resolutions and of feminist concerns!!! (*Frankfurter Rundschau* 21.5.1988).

Organisational Structures and Women's Affairs

A disdain for organisational channels and formalised processes of decision-making paired with the belief that women's affairs can only be addressed by women and for women has been one of the legacies of the new women's movement. It is an unspoken assumption of this approach that all women in a movement or party are motivated to participate actively and that communicative processes exist which render constitutional regulations unnecessary. The focus on women in the Greens suffered two unexpected setbacks: a shortage of potentially active women and the factionalised structure of the party itself.

The Greens have found it difficult to activate enough women to fill the positions which the 50% quota rule has earmarked. The prospect to hold a party office does not appear to be an incentive within the contemporary protest culture, and female membership has stagnated at around one third in a party whose overall membership has, in any case, grown much slower than the mass participation in movement politics might have sug-

203

gested. In 1988, the Greens had around 40,000 members: among the 13,000 women, no more than 3,000 can be expected to take an active role in the party. There has never been a shortage of women candidates for list places with electoral chances and unkind critics claim that women are only keen to take on political work which will generate media publicity (interview with Konrad Will-Schinneck). There has, however been a severe shortage of women lower down on electoral lists, and a shortage of women willing to hold an office in the party organisation. Some causes for this imbalance can be traced to the party's political style: women with children or in employment found it difficult to cope with the irregular hours and extended meetings which have characterised Green party politics; holding an office also does not serve a clearly defined career function as it does in other parties since entering parliament is possible without previous party service. The arduous *Ochsentour* of multiple posts is unnecessary in the Greens. The few women who are willing to take party offices, tend to be overburdened with responsibilities and barely able to cope:

> For nearly two years, we women have argued and pleaded, and have campaigned all over the country, until our proposal was finally accepted: In future, the regional executive has to include the same number of men and women. Two years ago . . . the regional party congress decided that the executive should include five women . . . but only two women could be found to aspire to so high an office. Therefore, the elections had to be postponed because nothing can be allowed to happen which is not supposed to happen. It took a lot of persuasive talent to talk five women into standing for office, but when the elections came round again, we had actually succeeded in finding five women. This was in November. The following March, the first of the women had to resign. Single parent, working in the district executive, in her local women's group, in the women's group of the region . . . she could not cope. But this was an exception — or was it? The following May, I threw in the towel. Forty hour working week, local executive, district executive, travelling for hours and often at night, always on my own, and many, many more reasons (Martens 1986: 26).

In addition most party posts are unpaid in order to ensure that the party is not dominated by functionaries. This anti-professionalism has proved a deterrent to women who often encounter additional expenses to assist with child minding and who often do not have a personal income to supplement the costs arising form their party work. The provision of child care facilities by political parties is regarded as a priority issue among women in the Greens. Most regional parties have recently begun to employ nursery nurses during party meetings, or reimburse child care expenses. However, interim reports indicate that these incentives have not produced a women's stampede for party posts.

Beyond their formal membership, the Greens have always drawn on action groups and citizens' initiatives especially for nominating parliamentary candidates and appealing to a wider electorate. The vacant slots for women parliamentary candidates have been filled by bringing in activists for related causes; one in three women who held parliamentary mandates in 1988 have gained their formative political experiences in action groups. One-third of Green parliamentary candidates in 1987/88 had joined the party as they were nominated in 1986 or had not taken out membership. Half the women candidates for the Greens were not involved in the party's women's affairs; in the SPD and CDU virtually all women candidates were active in the relevant associations (Kolinsky 1988b). This relates back to the more relaxed approach in the Greens to organisational integration, but it also helps to explain why so many of the women who were elected in 1987 and 1988 were not committed to the party consensus: they had not been close to the women's circles which formulated it and their loyalties lay elsewhere.

Given the preferences for non-hierarchical modes of participation the Greens have developed only rudimentary organisational structures for women. While SPD and CDU/CSU maintain elaborate organisations parallel to the main party and feeding into it with their own body of functionaries, policy suggestions and an involvement in the nomination of candidates, the Greens created a network of discussion groups. Since 1984, not least in response to the sexual harassment incident mentioned above, the party has a federal working group for women, based at the head office in Bonn and serviced by a full-time women's affairs officer. Membership and function have remained unclear. While the federal working group claims to be the voice of Green

205

women across the party, its meetings involved women who felt like attending, not elected representatives or delegates who might speak for cross-sections of the party. The federal working group (*Bundesarbeitsgemeinschaft*) played a decisive role in preparing the anti-discrimination legislation and the quota regulations. It has done so on its own initiative, since the working group had not been authorised by a party congress, by the executive or even the women who attended the relevant meetings. Here, the audience was confronted with ready-made agendas which were introduced and publicised but not discussed with an eye to changing them. The *Bundesarbeitsgemeinschaft* could be effective since it was the only co-ordinated voice on the issue and also because it worked closely with the women's group in the Bundestag.

The Greens in the Bundestag had also appointed a women's affairs officer in 1984. Officially, her functions were not linked to her counterpart in the party organisation but aimed at co-ordinating the activities of the *Arbeitskreis Sechs*, the special subject group for women. All women affiliated to the parliamentary group are nominal members, even those who have not been elected to parliament. Of the six parliamentary working groups, the *Arbeitskreis Frauen* has been the only one which was not directly linked to one or more parliamentary committees, and this freedom gave Green women the scope to articulate their own policies. In the eleventh legislative period, a Green woman member of parliament, Heike Wilms-Kegel, chairs the parliamentary committee on Youth, Women, Health and the Family.[2] Linked to the Ministry of the same name, the committee fulfils the normal legislative functions and also scrutinises other legislation with regard to its effect on the situation of women. Holding the chair in this committee makes the Green women at once more powerful and less independent than they had been between 1983 and 1987 when the Greens' focus on women was defined internally.

2. Heike Wilms-Kegel was first elected to the Bundestag in 1987, and took on the chair of the *Ausschuß für Jugend, Frauen, Familie und Gesundheit* which the Green Party had been eager to win, after two more experienced (women) colleagues turned it down. Heike Wilms-Kegel's background is not in the women's movement, or the Green women's groups and her style of administration and organisation appears to be more conventional than the participatory and non-hierarchical models the protest culture would suggest (*Das Parlament*, 1.7.1988: 16; also *Kürschers Volkshandbuch*, 1987).

The organisational structure in the regions is similar to that at national level. Green party organisations in the Länder have working groups on women (*Landesarbeitsgemeinschaften*), and some employ a part-time women's affairs officer. Annual meetings are intended to facilitate communication among Green women and to reach women who may be interested without being party members. The stress on informality has led to a large number of small groups — in 1988, the Greens in Hesse counted 400 women's groups. Their concerns are localised, and they have resisted attempts by the party to impose a more unified organisational structure. Although Green by name, these groups appear to be closer to the new women's movement than to the party.

As an organisational device to increase the party membership, the women's groups have not paid off. They may have been more successful in creating an environment in which women can communicate freely. Since all women's activities in the Greens have been for women only, there have been ample opportunities to speak out and take an active part. The primary purpose in setting up the women's groups, however, has been to create an inner-party pressure group to formulate a women's policy, and a forum of women which could give it popular approval. The women's groups were headed by activists from the new women's movements who tried to turn their ideas into the party's programmatic platform. The consensus on women did not arise in the party, but was imported, so to speak from the women's movement. As mentioned earlier, to seek legitimacy for their polices and present them as the consensus of Green party women, the organisers of the working groups held a number of conferences and hearings on themes of the anti-discrimination law and related topics.

The women's affairs activists in the party benefited from an unusual equilibrium between the parliamentary group in the Bundestag and the party organisation (Kolinsky 1988a). Until the federal elections of 1987, representatives of the party organisation and the women's parliamentary group collaborated in order to achieve a common platform and break what they perceived as the male-dominated party culture. Such a coalition of interests has been an exception in a party whose institutional channels such as congress (*Bundesversammlung*) or the party's

207

main committee (*Bundeshauptausschuß*) exercise policy control only on paper and whose policy agendas are frequently set by individuals through their personal contacts with the media. The co-operation from 1985–7 of the women's working groups in the party organisation and in the Bundestag brought personalities and organisational structures together into a temporary alliance which could turn the demands for equality and quotas into a core area of Green policy. Any such consensus in the Greens refers to only one issue and relates to only a segment of the party, in our case a policy on women, voiced by women, backed by women, and aimed at women. Strictly speaking, a Green policy on women across the party does not exist.

The uncertain acceptance of apparent policy priorities may explain why the numerical weight of women in the Green parliamentary party appears to have made a relatively modest impact on policy styles and priorities. In the Bundestag women have become more visible. For the Greens, women address plenary sessions on the full range of topics and have not been restricted to proverbial women's concerns like child care, health or education. However, women do not appear to determine the public profile of Green parliamentary politics sufficiently to speak of an innovation of contents or approaches. Heide Simonis, an SPD member of the Bundestag who concedes, with something approximating to envy, that Green women have it easier in their party to get to the top as members of parliament or party leaders, noted that they seemed surprisingly passive, even shun responsibilities which SPD women would dearly love to take on:

> The Green women knit while Green men dominate party congresses. Man becomes a minister, while the secretary of state for women's affairs becomes the target of men's contempt and ricidule. Women bake muesli-bread, found eco-shops, peddle wool and work in play groups, while men start a law suit against the federal chancellor, sit in parliamentary investigation committees and formulate important programmes on the reorientation of our society. . . . The 'normal political day' of men accumulating power is catching up with the Greens. It is true, women speak more frequently in parliament for the Greens than for other parties, and address important issues, but as a parliamentary colleague one does not get the impression that women in their majority occupy the power switches of the par-

liamentary party and have made a lasting impact' (Simonis 1986: 88).[3]

Quota Politics and Party Culture

The demand for a women's quota across society and its introduction as mandatory in the party has been the mainstay of the Green focus on equal opportunities. In this section we shall examine the repercussions of quota politics on the communicative styles and on the role of women in the Green Party. Women's quota are a new departure in the commitment to equality (Richardson and Michalik, 1985). Combined with the efforts to preserve the informalities of social movements in the policy functions of a party organisation and in parliaments, have the Greens developed communicative styles which could serve as catalysts for changes towards equality elsewhere? How important are quota politics in the Green party culture and to what extent have they altered the role of women in the organisation, and in the wider political environment?

The policy consensus on quotas has been a segmented consensus. The relevant themes were only developed and advocated by women. In preparation of the electoral platform for 1987 (Document 5) and the anti-discrimination legislation (Document 6), for instance, all-women conferences discussed women's issues — men who did attend had to sit quietly at the back of the hall. Disagreements which did arise about the role of housework, the need for child care facilities or the controversial theme of abortion arose between women and were discussed only among women. The one man who dared to castigate the quota regulations as a *Berufsverbot* for men at the 1986 congress in Hanover sparked off anger but no policy debate. 'If we turn such questions into a taboo and suppress criticism we lose credibility and will become an alternative party of opportunists. That we conduct ourselves in a more democratic and free man-

3. Heide Simonis refers to the appointment of Joschka Fischer as Minister for Environmental Affairs in Hesse and the appointment of Marita Haibach as the Representative for Women's Affairs, a post the Green women had hoped to elevate to ministerial rank; the other references are aimed in particular at the role played by Otto Schily in utilising the irregularities of party funding to bring court proceedings against Chancellor Kohl and the drafting of the *Umbauprogamm* by the (male) eco-socialist faction within the Green parliamentary party in 1986.

ner than other parties is not guaranteed by declarations but only by creating a climate in which opposing opinions can be articulated (Protokoll 1986: 185).

From the outset, the party has suffered from an implicit discrepancy of expectations: while members and affiliated followers were led to believe that grassroots democracy could ensure that they would be heard at any time and could influence policies from the sidelines without opting for a formalised position, the segmented factions in the party attempted to stifle debate and office holders soon realised that unrestricted discussions made their political duties unwieldy. The very lack of structure and the assumption that grassroots democracy would somehow emerge through practice meant that the work of parliamentary groups in particular was left to develop its own equilibrium (Spretnak and Capra 1985: 142ff). Since most Green activists had been affiliated to action groups, protest movements or the Social Democratic Party before their involvement in the Greens, the positive or negative experiences in these organisations served as guidelines to individuals on how to pursue their policy priorities and how to communicate them within the party or parliamentary group (Fogt 1986 and Chapter 4). The results have not been encouraging. As discussed above, on an organisational level, co-ordination has been impossible to achieve. On the personal level, frustration about 'green self-destruction' (Haibach 1988) and a sense of competitive hostility have all but uprooted the expectations that a new participatory style might govern everyday political activities:

> We have not succeeded in creating a constructive culture of relating to each other and of conducting controversies. Distrust and hardening of attitudes as well as a lack of tolerance have blocked changes and a willingness to experiment. Virtually everything gets talked to death. And everyone always ascribes bad intentions to the other side. . . . After the image of an enemy without began to recede, internal hostilities flourished. The tendency to engage in simplistic black-and-white thinking is widespread in society, and also within the Greens. The media love stereotyping, and they like conflicts and catastrophes. The tendency to stereotype people and policies makes it impossible to see that reality is much more complex and prevents further development and the changes that would be needed (Haibach 1988).

The battle lines within the Greens divide party from parliaments, members of the Bundestag from other Green parliamentarians and office holders, regional camps from one another, and protagonists of policy priorities amongst themselves and from each other. Policy debates which attempt to relate factions and explore their linkage or indeed their contrasts, are not part of the Green political culture.[4]

The culture, which does function, is that of the personal, competitive profile, untouched by the mellowing influence of a shared political mission. Half a year into his term of office as one of three parliamentary business managers after the 1987 elections which extended Green Bundestag representation from 27 to 44 members, Thomas Ebermann, a veteran left-winger and prominent spokesman of the eco-socialist faction suggested that jostling for status and marginal advantages had taken the place of policy debate:

> The most difficult problem was the distribution of rooms among the members of parliament. Because the rooms with a view across the Rhine are much more popular, hour-long debates were held to determine who had the right to sit in them. . . . Once somebody regards it as really important on which side of the building he or she is accommodated, all freedom is lost to be either tolerant or radical in politics. Whoever could find such a trivial matter important is bound to adopt positions in political life which will be to nobody's credit (Ebermann 1987: 18).

Ebermann forgot to mention that the women in the parliamentary party accused their male colleagues of claiming the best rooms and the presumably superior status.

True to the spirit of protest politics, the Greens had originally pledged that they would abolish differences in status and remuneration and give equal rights to office holders in the party, members of parliament and staff employed to assist with the political day-to-day work. For the party, the pledge has remained marginal because staffing is minimal and with the exception of the treasurer and the women's affairs officer, restricted

---

4. This view was expressed repeatedly in interviews conducted in January 1987 in Bonn with members of the Green party executive, and parliamentary group, in particular: Rita Werkmeister, 24.1.1987; Claudia Pinl, 25.1.1987; Eberhard Walde, 28.1.1987; Christa Nickels, 29.1.1987; Regina Michalik, 29.1.1987.

to part-time secretarial assistance. In the Bonn headquarters, a total of eight people are involved and they can meet informally in the pine-clad kitchen over cups of herbal tea. In the parliamentary groups, the interrelationship between elected members and employed personnel is of different proportions. The Bundestag Greens are entitled to fill at least 80 full-time posts and in fact employ 150 or more people in the *Fraktion*.

In the early 1980s, when the Greens envisaged a rotation of office, the replacement candidates would be employed full-time as a kind of political understudy by the respective parliamentary group. This practice has largely fallen into disuse. The same is true for the employment practice of the first Bundestag Greens, who recruited personnel collectively in order to allocate special policy areas to researchers and assistants as the party required. Today, the *Fraktion* still employs secretarial and administrative staff in line with public funding allocations, but individual members of parliament have begun to claim a personal support entitlement and have appointed their own support staff. In the constituent phase of the eleventh Bundestag in January/ February 1987, each Green member could control a personal staffing allowance of 9,000 Deutschmark; in the regions, the sums and staffing numbers are somewhat smaller but similar practices prevail.

At the parliamentary level, equal participation of elected members and the hundred or so paid assistants cannot be assured informally. Since a participatory culture has not emerged, the offices of individual members function as focal points of identification, policy initiatives and also as political dividing lines. Most non-elected Greens who are attached to the parliamentary group have been caught in a web of interpersonal and political rivalries which characterise Green parliamentary groups, and have tended to experience their working conditions as stressful. Job satisfaction seems all the more difficult to obtain for the Green parliamentary assistant since his or her role has remained ill-defined between clerical support and policy articulation. The comments made by one of the parliamentary assistants, who had been active in the women's movement before taking her post with the Greens in the Bundestag, expresses many similar experiences:

It is impossible to please anybody here. There are so many implicit demands, especially in the working groups how much one should contribute. Either I cut down on my secretarial duties, then my member of parliament may find herself in chaos and miss appointments, and the members in the working group will disapprove. Or I do not contribute enough to the political work, and they turn around and ask: Why aren't you doing any constructive political work? If I work in the women's group of the party, nobody takes the slightest bit of notice, but I might obtain information which could be useful for me. In general, nothing here is predictable, and nothing is acknowledged as useful (Jäger and Pinl 1985: 156).

Differentials between the elected elite and the others have crept back despite the initial instructions that everybody should receive a worker's wage, and pay the remainder to the party for redistribution to ecological causes. Meanwhile, members of parliament draw larger salaries than their assistants or substitutes. On joint business trips, Green members of parliament make ample use of the free first class travel available to West German parliamentarians and instruct their Green entourage to make their own arrangements for — second-class — transport and accommodation.

The quota regulations of employment have sharpened gender-based internal dividing lines. Appointments now are determined at least as much by the gender balance as by matching tasks to qualifications. In Rhineland Palatinate, for instance, the newly elected parliamentary party was occupied for months with a row over the appointment of a male press officer to a post which had been earmarked as 'female'.[5] Despite the quota practice, a gender mix in the Greens has not taken place. Women seem to experience mixed-gender politics as in imposition which prevents them from self-projection and self-fulfilment. Thus, a first generation woman member of parliament for the Greens reported that she needed regular breaks from an atmosphere which she described as 'self-rape' and in which she could only function by shutting out all emotions or personal expectations and functioning like an automaton (Spretnak and Capra 1985: 142). Women at all levels of Green politics

5. Interview with the business manager for the Greens in Rhineland Palatinate, Konrad Will-Schinneck, on 8.4.1988.

have opted for 'women only' activities because they suspect their male colleagues of being power-hungry. Even their language appears to set them apart. Men, it is argued, do not communicate, they dominate:

> In our society men enjoy a higher status than women. This means they have more rights than women — including in communication. They are allowed to interrupt more often . . . they correct the speaker and they decide in a debate when a women has talked enough . . . Men assume that they have something to say. The very act of communication is a statement. To be allowed to speak out is male. Although nobody gave him permission, he gives it to himself. Women are more inclined to say: 'May I add something'. Men just come out and say it (Müller 1985: 28–9).

To counter such perceived inequalities, rhetorics seminars by women and for women have been held in the Green party and in parliamentary groups. However, these seminars were not designed to make women more aggressively competitive in their use of language but aimed instead at developing specifically female styles of communication which could reflect women's perspectives on politics, i.e. to merge politics with pleasure. Even among women activists, a warped version of the age old stereotype that politics are too dry and boring for women is rampant. How else could it be explained that the organiser of the first Green women's conference called on participants to 'have a fascinating, successful and pleasurable [*lustvoll*] congress' or that the caption of a congress photo of laughing women reads 'politics can even be fun' (*Grüner Basis Dienst* 10, 1985). To introduce this emotional and personal element — it has been called fun, pleasure, libido, understanding — into all types of political participation is hailed as the innovative contribution women should and could make.

If combining politics with pleasure can be regarded as the ultimate aim of the all-women culture and if the intimate action groups give a foretaste of it, quota regulation can be no more than a short-term measure. In the contemporary political environment such regulations are regarded as a 'necessary evil' to gain some elbow room:

> It is difficult for women, even in the Greens to make an impact.

Partly because there are male specialists for all topics, and partly because women reject to make an impact based on criteria applicable to men. They therefore need quotas in order to develop their own type of qualification and to bring it into the party and into parliament (Kolinsky 1988b).

A survey among elected and non-elected women candidates for land parliaments and the Bundestag in 1987/88 showed that 95% of the Green women had been nominated through a quota system and also thought it was a good or very good system. A proportion of 5% expressed reservations such as 'women are not mature enough to fulfill these quotas' or 'they may help to overcome existing inequalities of opportunity, but often women are stigmatised as quota women — and women's qualifications are not taken seriously'.[6]

In the broader perspective of political culture change women's quotas are welcomed by Green women as a lever to coerce society into changes of attitude and opportunities. Ensuring that women have a voice in public affairs — provided 'that those who have been elected, actually make feminist politics' — is a first step towards triggering those changes:

> Only in this way can we make sure that the needs of women (and children) are taken into account to same degree as those of men, in shaping our society and therefore our lives. Women can only make an impact if they reach relevant positions and do so in sufficient numbers. In order to achieve this, we still have to rely on quotas, and we cannot dispense with them in the foreseeable future (Kunkel 1988).

For this wider change of access, impact and ultimately political priorities and communicative styles, the Green Party serves as an experimental microcosm. At least from a feminist vantage point, the party should provide the framework and serve as a model. Women's organisational and political satisfaction in the Greens rests on the ability of the party to overcome conventional

6. The survey Career Patterns of Women in Parliamentary Politics was conducted in February/March 1988 and included women who had been nominated for 1987 regional elections and women who had been elected into the Bundestag. A proportion of 58% of the questionnaires were returned; Green women constitute one in three respondents to the survey. The quotations are taken from comments on the usefulness of women's quotas and the issues which women regard as priorities for action (Kolinsky 1988b).

gender-divisions and to create a new scope for women to articulate and achieve those political and personal goals which they
see as specific to women. Attitudes in the party hamper male/
female collaboration on policy issues if attitudinal adjustments
have to precede collaboration: 'lower ranking of women has to
be overcome and their work valued equally'; 'men need to be
emancipated and take a different view of housework'. The
segregation of women's affairs that women have advocated, and
which the organisational structure of working groups and defined factions tends to underpin, also reinforces misgivings that
the party does not live up to women's expectations of democratic equality and value innovation: 'Disadvantaging women is
a deficit of justice in society, and is undemocratic.' The political
practice in the Greens is perceived as unjust and essentially
undemocratic since, as we have seen, the party did not develop
new avenues of decision-making or grassroots politics but has
slipped into a routine of personalisation and a factionised camp
mentality. The obsession with informality and non-hierarchical
politics has produced an internal culture of extensive and controversial discussion and favoured hostile camps and factions, a
'pillarisation' instead of integration. Consensus across the party
on policies and procedures has not yet developed. The party has
not created organisational mechanisms to generate such a consensus; on the contrary, the structures which did emerge tended
to strengthen factionalisation and the uncontrolled influence of
personalities. Under pressure to adapt to parliamentary procedures and standards of efficiency, the Greens have tended to
fall back on personalisation and factions. Both practices run
counter to the participatory culture which should have emerged
from the social movements, and the culture beyond competition
and patriarchy which the Green women had hoped for.

Conclusion

The focus on equality as personal rules about behaviour, speech
patterns, and the blend between political involvement and
pleasure slotted into the Green factionalised culture and has
reinforced what it had meant to overcome: the competitive spirit
of power politics and political opportunism. The bitter tone

between the male and female camps, the acrimony of 'spite and resignation' (Kunkel 1988) and the discontent of Green women with their party environment point to more than ill-tempered disgruntlement. The active core of Green women who formulated the quota policies and created the current all-women working groups, expected that the party would develop a participatory culture similar to that experienced in the small and localised groups of the new women's movement. The commitment to equality of opportunities for women which quota politics imply, has been submerged in the rivalry between factions, individuals, party functionaries and parliamentary groups which constitute the party culture of the Greens. Far from being consensus-based and participatory, the political culture of the Greens is segmented and personalised. It is an unstable coalition of party wings and issues, a broad church for the contemporary protest culture. Contrary to similar internal coalitions in established political parties, the Greens have not defined organisational structures which could moderate coalition interests and maintain a balance between them. This has to be fought for time and again; factions, parliamentary groups and personalities constantly pressurise each other to shift the balance of this coalition; the women's issue and the working groups which focus on it, are only one among several such forces in the party. To the outside world, the Greens appear committed to equal opportunities for women, underpinned by the draft legislation against discrimination, and the 50% quota regulations in the party. On closer inspection, both these policies are half-hearted concessions to the women's faction, supported mainly by this faction. The tendency of women to guard their themes against outside, notably male, interference, has squandered any chance the Greens might have had to develop a cross-party consensus on equalisation policies and consolidate the political bonus they have begun to develop among young urban and educated women across the generations and regions of West Germany.

References

Books and Articles

ADG (1986), 'Gesetzentwurf zur Aufhebung der Benachteiligung von Frauen in allen gesellschaftlichen Bereichen — Antidiskriminierungsgesetz', *BT Drucksache 10/6137* 9. Oktober

Becker, Renate and Rob Burns (1987), 'The Women's Movement in the Federal Republic of Germany', *Contemporary German Studies*, Occasional Papers, University of Strathclyde No. 3

Bremme, Gabriele (1956), *Die politische Rolle der Frau in Deutschland*, Göttingen: Vandenhoeck & Ruprecht

Burns, Rob and Wilfried van der Will (1988), *Protest and Democracy*, London: Macmillan

Ebermann, Thomas (1987), Interview, *Konkret Magazin für Politik und Kultur* No. 10, October

Emma (1980), 'Sonderband Wahlboykott, Eine Streitschrift zu den Wahlen', 80

—— (1987), 'Emma-Umfrage zur Wahl. Die Frauen verlassen die SPD', No. 1

Fogt, Helmut (1986), 'Die Mandatsträger der Grünen. Zur sozialen und politischen Herkunft der alternativen Parteielite', *Aus Politik und Zeitgeschichte* 11f

Fülles, Mechthild (1969), *Frauen in Partei und Parlament*, Cologne: Wissenschaft und Politik

Haug, Frigga (1986), 'The Women's Movement in West Germany', *New Left Review*, January

Hervé, Florence (ed.) (1982), *Geschichte der deutschen Frauenbewegung*, Cologne: Pahl Rugenstein

Hoecker, Beate (1987), *Frauen in der Politik*, Opladen: Westdeutscher Verlag

Hofmann-Göttig, Joachim (1986), *Emanzipation mit dem Stimmzettel*, Bonn: Neue Gesellschaft

Hülsberg, Werner, (1988), *The German Greens. A Social and Political Profile*, London: Verso

Jäger, Brigitte and Claudia Pinl (1985), *Zwischen Rotation und Routine: Die Grünen im Bundestag*, Hamburg: KiWi Verlag

Kallscheuer, Otto (ed.) (1986), *Die Grünen — Letzte Wahl?*, Berlin: Rotbuch

Klingemann, Hans-Dieter (1985), 'West Germany' in I. Crewe and D. Denver, *Electoral Change in Western Democracies*, London: Croom Helm

Kolinsky, Eva (1987), 'The Transformation of Extraparliamentary Opposition in West Germany and the Peace Movement in E. Kolinsky (ed.), *Opposition in Western Europe*, London: Croom Helm and PSI

—— (1988a), 'The German Greens — a Women's Party?' *Parliamentary Affairs* 1

—— (1988b) Career Patterns of Women in West German Parliamentary Politics. An empirical survey, unpublished report, Aston University

—— (forthcoming), *Women in West Germany — Life, Work and Politics*, Oxford: Berg

Kunkel, Brigitte (1988), 'Gedanken zur Quotierung', statement included with the response to the survey Eva Kolinsky, Career Patterns of Women in West German Parliamentary Politics, Aston University 1988, June 1988, typescript

Martens, Ima (1986), 'Jetzt erst recht. Parität im Landesvorstand?!', *Grüne Illustrierte Niedersachsen*, September

Müller, Andrea (1985), 'Männliche Sprachpraxis und Möglichkeiten männlichen Widerstandes', Paper delivered at the congress *Grüne Frauen Macht Politik. Dokumentation der 1. Bundesfrauenkonferenz der Grünen Frauen: Grüner Basis Dienst* gbd 10

Richardson, Elke and Regina Michalik (1985), *Die quotierte Hälfte. Frauenpolitik in den grün-alternativen Parteien*, Berlin: LitPol

Roth, Reinhold and Elmar Wiesendahl (1986), 'Das Handlungs und Orientierungssystem politischer Parteien', *Analysen und Berichte* No 17. *Forschungsstelle Parteiendemokratie*, Koblenz und Bremen

Schenk, Harrad (1980), *Die feministische Herausforderung*, Munich: Beck

Simonis, Heide (1986), 'Macht Macht Frauen männlich?' in O. Kallscheuer (ed.), *Die Grünen — Letzte Wahl? Vorgaben in Sachen Zukunftsbewältigung*, Rotbuch: Verlag Berlin

Sinus Institut and BMJFG (eds.) (1983), *Die verunsicherte Generation*, Opladen: Leske

Smith, Gordon (1987), 'Party and Protest: The Two Faces of Opposition in Western Europe', in E. Kolinsky (ed.), *Opposition in Western Europe*, London: Croom Helm and PSI

Spretnak, Charlene and Fritjof Capra (1985), *Green Politics. The Global Promise*, London: Collins (Paladin)

Selected Documents and Programmes

'Gesetzentwurf zur Aufhebung der Benachteiligung von Frauen in allen gesellschaftlichen Bereichen — Antidiskriminierungsgesetz (ADG)' (1986), *BT Drucksache* 10/6137 9 Oktober

Anti-Diskriminierungsgesetz (1986), Vorläufiger Entwurf eines ADG. Die Grünen: Bonn, January

Anti-Diskriminierungsgesetz (1986), Materialien zum Kongreß am 28 und

29 Juni 1986 in Frankfurt/M, Die Grünen: Bonn

Argumentation § 218 (1986), Sonderdruck der Argumentationshilfen zu unserer Forderung nach ersatzloser Streichung des § 218 StGB. Zusammengestellt von Rita Werkmeister und Regina Michalik. Die Grünen: Bonn

Bundestagswahl Programm 1987: Farbe bekennen Die Grünen, Bonn (broch)

Bundesprogramm Die Grünen (1980), Verabschiedet auf der Bundesdelegiertenversammlung in Karlsruhe, März 1980. Bonn (bochure; also in English: Die Grünen: the Programme of the Green Party of the Federal Republic of Germany)

Ein Himmel auf Erden? (1987), Kontroversen um eine Grün-nahe Stiftung, Bundesstiftungskommission der Grünen, 'Femmes Fatale: Warum, Wieso, Wie', Bonn, April

Erfahrungsbericht der Alternativen Liste April 1985–April 1987 (1987) Alternative Liste Berlin

Frauenstatut (1986) verabschiedet auf der Landesdelegiertenversammlung der Grünen in Baden-Württemberg 8–9.3.1986, *Grüne Blätter* 6

Grüne Frauen Macht Politik (1985), Dokumentation der 1, Bundesfrauenkonferenz der Grünen Frauen: *Grüner Basis Dienst* gbd 10

Grüne Frauen Politik (1985), Texte zur 1. Bundesfrauenkonferenz der Grünen, Die Grünen: Bonn

Haibach, Marita (1988), *Thesen zur Krise der Grünen*, Discussion paper dated 1.2

Müttermanifest (1987), 'Antrag V10 Einrichtung BAG Mütter. 9. Ordentliche Bundesversammlung Die Grünen 1–3 Mai 1987 in Duisburg. Protokoll, Bonn

Protokoll (1986), Außerordentliche Bundesversammlung der Grünen in Hannover, 16–19 Mai, *Grüner Basis Dienst* gbd no. 7–8: 127–90

Umbau der Industriegesellschaft (1986), Schritte zur Überwindung von Erwerbslosigkeit, Umweltzerstörung und Armut. Als Programm verabschieder von der Bundesdelegierternkonferenz der Grünen in Nürnberg, 26–28. September, Bonn (brochure)

Interviews in January 1987 with Regina Michalik, Eberhard Walde, Rita Werkmeister of the party organisation; also with Claudia Pinl, the women's affairs officer of the parliamentary party, with members of the parliamentary group especially Christa Nickels, Waltraud Schoppe, Bärbel Rust, Charlotte Garbe

Other documents/newspapers consulted

Die Grünen im Bundestag. Published by the parliamentary group and distributed to the press; the publication contains speeches, policy

discussions, and various statements by individuals or groups in the
Bundestag.

Grüne Illustrierte Niedersachen. Published monthly by the Greens in
Lower Saxony, this is a highly informative journal on Green policies
and activites in the Federal Republic, and in Lower Saxony.

Tageszeitung. The newspaper of the alternative movement, published in
Berlin, presents detailed and often critical accounts of Green activities. One of the best sources on the Green Party.

Frankfurter Rundschau, the West German daily gives excellent coverage
of Green policies and major controversies, but is less detailed in its
coverage than *taz.*

In the preparatory phase of the ADG, the Greens in Bonn published a
series of leaflets headed *Antidiskriminierungsgesetz,* each highlighting
a specific point. The leaflet was prepared by the women of the
Bundesarbeitsgemeinschaft, especially the women's affairs officer, Rita
Werkmeister.

9
Counterattack is Futile or the Inevitability of Green-Alternative Economic Innovation

Konrad Will-Schinneck

Preliminary Remarks

Since 1 November 1983 I have been working as the business manager of the Land organisation of the Greens in Rhineland Palatinate and could, as something of a 'participating observer' experience at first hand the tensions between the ideals and the realities of Green policy-making.* Although my own tasks 'at the centre of the cyclone' have been, according to the Green division of labour, essentially of an administrative kind, I have witnessed the many different developments within the party and in the so-called 'Green environment', i.e. in the Green-alternative movement.

I hope my readers will not hold it against me when I refrain from writing in the apparently neutral, research-based style of a social scientist or economist but present, instead, a mixture of facts and evaluations as they have arisen from my own informations and impressions.

In order to demonstrate that the various tiers of the Green environment hang together and to show how results have been forthcoming without planning co-ordination and in an apparently disparate fashion, I shall look at economic policy-making in the party and the Green-alternative movement on two levels,

| A. The Green Party | B. The Green-Alternative Movement |

and explore the following themes:

* Translated by Eva Kolinsky

1. Green Economic
   Programme

2. Alternative Economy

3. Eco-Funds and Legal Aid
   Funds

4. Eco-Bank
5. Regional Companies
6. Project 'Ecopolis' (*Ökopolis*)

7. Project 'Regional
   Conversion'

Despite the organisational duality of party and movement and the multifaceted policy areas, and despite efforts by conservative circles to prevent any advances of the Greens in creating a format for ecologically based economic policies and institutions, results have been achieved.

1. The Green Economic Programme

In the first instance we need to clarify what Greens normally regard as economic policy. Unfortunately there is a tendency to forget in everyday controversies to identify the different assumptions clearly. This produces a good many misunderstandings and all too often, people talk at cross purposes, not least when representatives of other political parties publicly accuse the Greens of incompetence in economic matters.

The major point of reference for Green economic policy is the concept of ecology. Contrary to other political parties, who use the term 'ecology' simply as a convenient formula to refer to, say, dying forests, acid rain and similar environmental problems, the Greens understand ecology in a much broader sense as encompassing human beings and nature. Although man and nature are different concepts, man is in reality part of nature and himself suffers the damage which is inflicted upon nature (Document 7). The dichotomy between economy and ecology which is widely regarded as something resembling the law of nature, is seen by the Greens as an erroneous approach which lacks or deliberately flouts deeper understanding.

True to the principle 'think globally, act locally' ('Denk global, handle lokal') the Greens make consistent efforts to breathe a new meaning into the concept of *Volkswirtschaft* — (macroeconomy; literally: people's economy). To give one example: at the end of the fifties, the Greens might have regarded the utilisation of atomic energy as the correct and ecologically sensible way to meet the projected higher demands for energy in the wake of population increases. Smoking chimneys of coal-fired power stations were a visible warning that a clean process of energy production needed to be found urgently. At the time, the cooling towers of atomic power stations appeared clean by comparison since 'they emitted only steam'. The financial calculations that it would cost several million Deutschmark to produce such power stations were regarded as economically sound, since clean energy seemed to be in reach at a price which would even make the installation of electricity meters superfluous. Today, of course, we know better!

First, the mere building costs climbed by several hundred percentage points on average since the production companies received a blank cheque in the shape of research funding paid from federal resources. These unlimited funds could be used to test any kind of flaw in the construction plans without incurring additional costs and also to develop and employ teams of technicians whose findings boosted the profits of the respective companies — from the vantage point of business administration a cost effective move; from the vantage point of public economic benefits a loss maker.

Second, other side-effects such as the increased temperature of rivers through using them as cooling water, the emission of radioactivity into the environment even at normal operation, the spread of leukaemia, the widespread death of forests or the increased occurence of cancer among the workforce cannot be quantified in terms of cost. In order to conduct a serious calculation of costs according to the criteria used by the Greens, these consequences of technology and the costs they generate would have to be considered as well: atomic power stations should never have been built because of their exorbitant cost to the country's economy.

Furthermore, the need to 'decommission' nuclear materials was simply overlooked in the calculations. But since even the most advanced technical knowhow has no other answer to the problem other than to bury exhausted nuclear materials in the soil, and since it takes several tens of thousands of years for the radioactivity of isotopes to disappear — who could even attempt to calculate the costs of protecting the population against this incessantly ticking time bomb? 'We have only borrowed the earth from our children and from future generations!' This slogan guides the Greens when they reject atomic power stations as absurd in economic terms and as nothing less than criminal.

When Greens, therefore, talk of economic policy they normally refer to a web of problems of an economic kind. In doing so, they do not confine their attention to the classical politics of cost and finance. People with different political priorities tend to react in three ways to Green analyses and suggested solutions: they may take refuge in traditional ideologies and denounce Green concepts as lacking reality; or they may hide behind notions of cost-effectiveness and claim Green policies cannot be financed; or they may smear these policies for party political and tactical reasons as ill-conceived only to adopt them in a new disguise and pass them off as their own political ideas and as evidence of their innovative capacity. In everyday politics, these three reactions may occur separately or overlap in any combination.

Let us present some examples of Green demands and typical reactions they elicited:

— Energy policy: 'Switch off atomic power stations' against 'The lights go out!'; 'Work places will be destroyed' etc.
— Social policy: 'Introduction of a basic pension for all!' against impossible to finance; unjust since achievement must be rewarded; impracticable since nobody would wish to work.
— Transport policy: 'Maximum speed 100 km!' against 'Free driving for free citizens!' 'Employment under threat!' since driving a car and the purchase of new, faster cars would become unattractive.
— Peace policy: 'Abolition of all atomic weapons!' 'Leave NATO now' ('Raus aus der NATO') against 'The Russians are coming!'

Discussions are complicated further by the fact that the Greens themselves include several groupings with differing ideas as to the root causes of economic malfunctioning: eco-socialists, eco-libertarians and others.

The theoretical discussion has generated a number of diverse programmes — the federal and regional party programme, the *Sindelfingen* economic programme named after the venue of the relevant party congress, the so called reconstruction programme (*Umbauprogramm*), and a heap of grey literature as well as the establishment of several research institutes.

2. Alternative Economy

The sector of the economy which has been called the economy of the niche or alternative enterprise has grown to provide well over one hundred thousand places of employment. It partly uses traditional markets, and has also created new markets for its products. The alternative economy includes everything from the tiny one-man business to collectives or co-operatives within broader informal networks.

I would like to present an example from the northern district of Rhineland Palatinate, the region of my administrative party activity, in order to show how such networks can emerge from modest beginnings.

In March 1985, the *Bildungswerk Westerwald* (BWW) was founded. It is a registered, charitable association aimed at 'helping to co-ordinate for the Westerwald region the many attempts to live and work in an alternative fashion'. A 'working group of self-administered businesses and projects' prepared the concept which they called *Projectadie andere Messe*, a mixture of project, academy and trade fair for alternative activities. It was first organised in 1985 and enabled the interested public to experience at close quarters various projects and initiatives in the region. The original working group spawned a broader based *Westerwälder Initiativen und Betriebe Netzwerk* (WIBeN) to facilitate co-ordination and communication between groups, and a 156-page handbook was produced, the *Westerwälder Landbuch* as an advertising and information booklet for interested parties who were not familiar with alternative culture and lifestyles.

227

A quotation from the *Westerwälder Landbuch* shows clearly how difficult it can be to operate within the alternative economy:

> To be different in the Westerwald region is hard even for local residents. Traditionally, people regard the views of those highly with whom they have grown up. Since little good had come in the past from the big cities to inhabitants of the Westerwald, the local population distrusts ideas which enter the countryside from there. The alternative scene which originated in the big cities but dared to live in the country is regarded and watched with suspicion. With so much apparently unspoilt nature about, locals eye the urban ecologist who has been sensitised through urban violations of the environment with curiosity and consider him mildly insane. . . .
>
> In order to preserve one's own identity in such a climate, it is necessary to meet with like-minded people and to strive for as much autonomy as possible within the framework of the subculture. This is only possible if more and more areas of everyday life become part of this subculture; in a truly autonomous social network one needs for instance alternative bakers, peasants, artisans, shops, artists. . . .
>
> At some stage, however, a 'critical mass' will have been reached and the subculture can no longer be ignored by the surrounding society and has to be taken seriously and recognised as part of it.
>
> In the Westerwald, this stage has in fact been reached. The original *Westerwälder Landbuch* which listed the various educational establishments, health food shops, organic farms, a collective insurance company, a printing workshop and other projects, has long been superseded and will soon have to be updated and revised. Above all, members of the alternative economy stress that 'public awareness and attitudes have really changed'.[1]

3. Eco-Fund and Legal Aid Fund

The motor behind the institutionalisation of the alternative movement has been the strong dependency on private financial resources, and on the goodwill of the established parties to pursue the new political aims in parliament. The latter, futile, expectation eventually provoked the founding of a separate political party: the Greens.

---

1. Westerwälder Landbuch und Näheres: Bildungswerk Westerwald e.V., Haus Felsenkeller, Heimstraße 4, 5230 Altenkirchen.

Compared with established institutions, the various citizens initiatives experienced a structural 'competitive disadvantage' when they tried to enter the political stage: a chronic shortage of funds. For instance, the protest movement against nuclear power had to spend considerable sums on the production of alternative scientific reports, although the real purpose should have been to enlighten and mobilise the public. Since the German public, however, is more willing to believe scientific evidence than political appeals, and since the advocates of atomic power could command extensive support from researchers, the expenditure on alternative reports was essential. It was soon evident that idealism and shoestring budgeting could only last for a limited period, not least since the financial weapons were so unevenly distributed — the private purse and small donations stood against the publicly subsidised or supplied mammoth resources of big industrial enterprises — and finding new, more plentiful financial means became a crucial precondition if the alternative movement were to survive the uneven financial contest.

Thus, the entry of the Greens into parliament was linked to the idea 'to redirect some of the copious public funds to which political parties are entitled back to the grassroots, where sensible things could be done with all this money'.[2] It was by no means a coincidence that the first application for money from the eco-fund in Rhineland Palatinate concerned a court case against granting permission to construct an atomic power station in Mülheim-Kärlich. In today's terminology, this would have been a legal aid application. At the time, in 1982, an eco-fund existed in Rhineland Palatinate more in theory than in practice: the Greens had neither entered the Bundestag nor indeed the land parliament. (In the meantime, Greens in each region had created eco-funds, albeit with widely disparate organisational structures and briefs.)

After the Greens entered the Bundestag in March 1983 and after some delay while the parliamentary group tried to organise itself and decide its business, funds begun to flow, or, to put it more accurately, the miniature money-tap began to drip a little.

2. The wording was used by the former eco-fund business manager for Rhineland Palatinate in a circular: '. . . die den Parteien reichlich zufließende Staatsknete in gewissem Umfang an die Basis zurückfließen zu lassen, auf daß dort Sinnvolles mit ihr geschehe.'

The parliamentary delegates were required to pay part of their remuneration into a trustfund and these monies were redistributed to regional party organisations according to an agreed formula. Initially, Rhineland Palatinate received 37,000 Deutschmark per quarter. Just to put these figures into perspective: in 1984, Rhineland Palatinate held 140,000 Deutschmark in its eco-fund ready to support projects outside the party organisation. This was far more than the total budget which was available to finance the political work of the Greens in the region, and cover all expenses for offices and personnel of the Land organisation.

If I earlier referred to the incoming funds as mere drops from a small tap I had in mind the discrepancy between the size of the fund and the demand for funding which was to be met from it. Once the existence of the eco-fund became more widely known, an increasing number of projects, initiatives and associations appealed for their share from the Green money pots. At one allocation meeting of the eco-fund, applications amounted to 320,000 Deutschmark while the eco-fund only had 37,000 Deutschmark at its disposal: a clear case of a drop in the ocean.

In 1982, the Land executive had dealt with the few applications for financial support of non-party work within the alternative movement. In order to cope with the vast number of applications for money which were coming in after 1983, a special committee, the *Ökofondausschuß*, was set up to sift applications and to distribute the available money in a responsible manner. Setting up a committee had also become necessary since party congresses were in danger of deteriorating to pure 'eco-fund congresses'. It appeared that party congresses were increasingly unable to serve their original purpose of political discussion and decision making.

The newly formed committee was to remove the issue of funding from party congress debates. It agreed its own constitution, and set aside a fixed proportion of the available money — the *Gesamttopf* — for legal aid. In this way the uncertain boundaries between support for ecological projects and for court cases were clarified, and the two tiers again administered by one common funding body, as had been the case at the outset (see the example of Mülheim-Kärlich above). The committee also elected its own business manager, who faced the thankless task for the princely 'salary' of 350 Deutschmark per month to scrutinise applications, to distribute them for appraisal in the party organisation, and to minimise the chaos which tended to erupt at meetings arranged to allocate funding.

From the start, the eco-fund was greeted with a good deal of hostility by the established parties. When accusations that the eco-fund was squandering tax payers money proved futile (since the means did not come from public funding of parties' electoral expenses but were donated by Green members of parliament), allegations were raised that the Greens had attempted to 'blackmail the voters'. When none of these invectives produced the desired result of stopping the eco-fund altogether, legal experts claimed that the Greens were in violation of the legislation pertaining to banks, and also in violation of the legislation which governs donations and tax liabilities by administering loans and supporting economic enterprises. These attempts to declare the eco-fund illegal did little more than provoke the creativity of the Greens. A solution was soon in sight: the eco-bank.

4. Eco-Bank

The idea of founding an alternative bank originated within the peace movement following a call to boycott financial institutions with any involvement in armament deals or trading links with South Africa. The problem with this call for a boycott was that virtually all banks were more or less deeply involved in such transactions.

A 'clean' bank needed to be created with the aim of giving not a single penny to armament deals or for atomic power, and to support instead environmental projects and alternative enterprises in a targeted way. To set the process in motion, the 'Friends and Supporters of the Eco-Bank' was founded on 17 March 1984.

Among the West German public, the idea of creating an ecologically focused bank met with keen interest from the start. Since its first public airing in August 1984, the plans were widely discussed first in the alternative press, and increasingly in established news media and also in the major economic journals.

The project had hit upon a gap in the market: even before operations had begun, some 7.5 million Deutschmark had already been paid into the relevant trustfund. By the end of 1986, the financial preconditions for founding the bank were secure.

Not everything went smoothly, however. The eco-bank was to be based on the ideals of Friedrich Wilhelm Raiffeisen, and be constituted as a co-operative bank, similar to the chain of Raiffeisen banks which provide funding for West German agriculture. Of all possible obstacles, the Federal Association of National and Raiffeisenbanks created the most formidable ones. It was openly distrustful of the potential newcomers, and hoped to delay formal recognition and membership even after the Federal Office for the Control of Financial Institutions had already approved the new bank and its co-operative status.

On 23 March 1988 the Association for Co-operative Banks finally agreed to the eco-bank, and it started to operate on 2 May 1988, again with keen interest and participation of the general public and the media.

The strict regulations contained in the legislation governing financial institutions blocked the original idea of creating a bank which would be organised in self administration and without a hierarchical structure. It also proved impossible to support alternative projects solely on the basis of political criteria. Such a political approach was all the more inadvisable since the eco-bank regards it as of paramount importance to ensure that all its funds are invested in sound enterprises, not least to prevent being swept off the market during its first phase of operation.

Green eco-funds by contrast could apply political criteria in supporting specific projects and have done so in the past. In order to avoid the problems of overspending and of exhausting the financial resources of the alternative movement, the eco-fund have now stopped giving out unsecured loans and have shifted towards secured loans which are frequently administered via the eco bank. In this way, the party can evade attacks from other political camps of its financial practices, and also ensure that alternative enterprises and projects obtain optimal business advice by the eco-bank; this often includes advice on identifying other sources of finance such as public loans or subsidies.

5. Regional Companies

In line with its policy of playing safe, the eco-bank has committed itself to allocating only 10% of its loans to projects which are not based in a specific region, and continue these cautious practices until a full network of branches has been established. In the initial phase the bank also pledged to restrict its loans to three times its capital base although current legislation permits banks to issue loans amounting to eighteen times their capital base. In the interim situation of striving for security and also for expansion, the Friends and Supporters of the Eco-Bank and their special know-how play an important role. They have created a number of companies which have essentially three main purposes: to advertise the service of the eco-bank; to execute preliminary checks on projects and prepare credit transfers and to plan opening further branches of the eco-bank.

In Rhineland Palatinate the idea has been mooted of setting up a specifically regional company of this type, the *Ökofinanz Südwest GmbH*. Shareholders and core capital had already been determined when it emerged in negotiations with the eco-bank in Frankfurt that the amount that could be spent on advertising at this stage would not be sufficient to be effective in this relative large and rural area. Facing the risk of making at least an initial loss, the founding team decided to defer a decision until a later date. As a next step, branches of the eco-bank and related companies will be created in major industrial centres and in big cities which can support the ventures with a more favourable infrastructure than Rhineland Palatinate could, and bring the Green banking venture to fruition. The *Ökofinanz Südwest* has been put on ice for the time being, but with the understanding that it will be activated as soon as the business turnover of the eco-bank is such that more funding for advertising and similar pump-priming expenditure could be forthcoming.

6. Project Ecopolis

The former business manager of the Green eco-fund in Rhineland Palatinate and yours truly came, independently from one another to the same conclusion: that there is a huge reservoir of innovative impulses within the broad sector of alternative enterprises but that business acumen or administrative skills are often insufficient to develop viable approaches or products.

Over the years, the eco-fund had to deal with an increasing number of applications by alternative businesses which applied for investment capital. It took some time for us to understand why funds were scarce although the ideas which were to be developed seemed sound and marketable. The explanation was, however, quite straightforward: most of the people involved in alternative projects knew nothing about national or regional investment programmes, about subsidies to start new business enterprises or how to exploit the scope within the corporation and taxation legislation to best advantage when building up a business.

It seemed self-evident that a company which could offer such all-encompassing advice should be founded and could free alternative businesses from the need to beg for support, cap in hand. *Ökopolis* is meant to be such a company of alternative consultants. It has been founded as a Working Group and offers services to alternative enterprises in the fields of finance, business organisation and liaison with bureaucracies and state administrations. In working with the alternative sector of the economy we noticed that far too much money is flowing 'out' and that demand for the goods and services provided by the alternative sector is not buoyant enough. We thought it would be useful to bring private consumers and alternative producers closer together through advertising, and also to persuade the traditional economic sector to extend their contacts and co-operate with alternative enterprises.

I would like to illustrate the concept of *Ökopolis* with an example:

A carpenter receives an order to renovate a roof using ecological wood, i.e. wood preserved with non-toxic substances. Since he does not normally know how he can obtain such wood, he will not be able to comply with the order in the way it was placed. In addition, rumour has it that wood which has not been made toxic by industrial processing is excessively expensive, a rumour which kills any potential demand from the public before it can even arise, notwithstanding the growing awareness in West Germany of the need for environmental protection. Since we, however, know where to obtain the wood in question, we ensure that the carpenter receives the quantities he needs to restore the roof. In this way, we assist the carpenter, we assist the alternative producer of wood, and also ourselves.

Another area of activity of *Ökopolis* concerns finance. Alternative enterprises are not normally in a position to accept large orders since they are unable to advance the necessary sums before receiving payment. In spite of adequate production capacities and a sufficient number of employees they are frequently unable to compete in the market place. In the medium term, we are therefore exploring possibilities of expanding the concept of economic co-operatives. As a co-operative, our company could undertake the necessary intermediate finance and help close the gaps between supply and demand in the alternative sector of the economy.

7. Project 'Regional Conversion'

On 6 March 1983 Roland Vogt from Rhineland Palatinate became one of the first generation of Green members of the Bundestag. As a convinced 'worker for peace' he repeatedly marvelled at the apparently high degree of acceptance of the United States Armed Forces among the West German population. All the more so since his constituency belongs to the most densely militarised region in the world including, for instance, Ramstein Air Base which constitutes the European bridgehead for the United States Air Force. He was surprised and hurt to find that during sit-ins and demonstrations against the deployment of further nuclear weapons at military bases the invectives hurled against the demonstrators by German civilians were no less aggressive than the treatment they received by the state-appointed 'guardians of public order'.

The root cause of the loyalist attitudes of the civilian population lies in the financial dependence on the military. In the area of Kaiserslautern alone some 16,500 German civilians are employed by the US army; in addition, thousands of small businesses, landlords, restaurants, etc., rely on the soldiers as their major source of income. Counting soldiers and their families together, a minimum of 72,000 military personnel are stationed in the area. Since the end of the Second World War, the occupying powers have also confiscated extensive stretches of land. Throughout the region, one constantly encounters so-called 'restricted areas'. The ubiquitous presence of the military and their economic contribution to the region appear to have eradicated all traces of thought in the population, that the military itself may be unnecessary. This apathy is exacerbated by the fact that 43 years after the end of the war, the regional government has yet to develop plans for the region which address themselves to economic restructuring and employment needs after the occupying powers have been withdrawn.

Using some of his earnings as a member of the Bundestag, Roland Vogt opened an office for Regional Conversion in Kaiserslautern. Its task is, in the first instance, to assemble a regional profile of the economic situation prior to the high military presence and subsequently examine which areas could be reactivated or developed further. By publishing data about the damage inflicted by the military upon the indigenous economy and the environment, the population of the region and all socially relevant groups should be encouraged to jointly think of alternatives to the status quo of military dependency.[3]

Conclusion

Up to this point I have briefly described a number of themes and areas whose linkage may be more or less apparent. Admittedly, I have not presented elaborate explanations or copious detail but aimed at a succinct sketch of basic issues. I wanted to show how various developments complement each other and to constitute a network of an alternative economy which has become important in society at large, and which will remain important despite

3. Further to the theme of environmental damage: it has been claimed that apart from the 'usual' damage through military exercises, close to 800 accidents occurred in the vicinity of Ramstein through oil spillage, but penalties cannot be imposed due to the special status of the US forces; wells seem to be so contaminated with oil that the Americans no longer use their waters. The number of environmental crimes committed by the Americans cannot be ascertained by German authorities since the US army does not provide any relevant information and answers accusations with summary denials. All this contributes to the anti-American views which prevail in some circles. See: Hanspeter Greger and Roland Vogt (eds.), Westpfalz Zivil. n.d. Volume 1 der *Schriftenreihe des Projektes Regionale Konversion*, Adolph Kolping Platz 1, 6750 Kaiserslautern.

the numerous conservative inspired attempts to prevent it from emerging.

My party, the Greens, have repeatedly been reproached for wanting to change society. Of course we want to change society! And many thousands are already busily engaged in doing just that!

Changing society, however, does not happen in the way suggested by the propaganda departments of the old parties to the electorate: nobody is interested in installing an inhumane eco-dictatorship or to drive the Germans into the arms of the 'evil' Russians.

The conservatives are not really afraid of the Green Party with its membership of just 40,000. They are, however, afraid that an increasing number of people are willing to doubt that economic growth and a purely quantitative way of thinking are the only meaningful value orientations in the contemporary world.

In this process of finding new values and priorities, the Greens are sometimes initiators and sometimes merely catalysts of change. The project 'Regional Conversion' had been initiated by a Green member of parliament. For the eco-bank — 'the banking house of the Green-alternative movement' as it calls itself — the party was little more than a unifying catalyst. Although only a few Green party activists were personally involved in setting it up, the bank has become entrenched in the consciousness of the traditional banking sector as the bank of the Greens.

Both cases illustrate how the old parties cling to traditional values and feel that they have to put pressure on the Greens and stop its progress; they also illustrate how this very pressure has aided the conversion of Green ideas into alternative projects, and has made the internal structure of the Green-alternative movement more differentiated and therefore better able to accommodate a variety of economic and political innovative forces. As alternative projects and enterprises gain ground, they themselves influence the world of conservative values in society: issues which emerged within the Greens as salient themes of contemporary politics are adopted: first only verbally but in the long run actions which follow the Green lead cannot be avoided.[4]

4. For instance: all established parties now refer to atomic energy as transitory energy

The Green-alternative project of economic change owes much to the strong determination of the Greens to effect such change but also to the inability of the other political forces to denounce traditional values. As the Green-alternative project becomes stronger, the Greens have less need to integrate the multifarious alternative culture and to provide a political focus for the alternative movement; they can instead resume their original and most important task of acting as the *Standbein*, as the parliamentary voice of the broader movement.

---

and signal that they hope to abandon it (without defining a time span); a regional party congress of the CDU in Rhineland Palatinate objected to low flying aircraft and openly opposed — an unparalleled occurrence — the local and national party leaderships; in open competition with the eco-bank the big German banks now offer loans for ecological projects and sell eco-bonds.

Appendix: Selected Documents

Document 1: Federal Programme, 1980: Preamble

Introduction

We are the alternative to the traditional parties, originating from a merger of green, coloured and alternative lists and parties. We feel close to all those who participate in the new democratic movements: in the associations for life, nature and the environment, in citizens' initiatives, in the labour movement, in Christian initiatives, in the movements for peace, human rights, women and the Third World. We consider ourselves to be part of the Green movement the world over.

The established parties in Bonn behave as if this finite planet earth could support an infinite increase in industrial production. According to their own admissions, they lead us to face the impossible decision between an atomic state and atomic war, between Harrisburg and Hiroshima. The ecological world crisis is looming larger day by day: raw materials are becoming more scarce, one pollution scandal chases the next, whole animal species are being eradicated, plant families die out, rivers and oceans change into cesspools, in this late industrial and consumer society human beings are in danger of being mentally and emotionally crippled; we burden future generations with a gruesome inheritance.

The destruction of the foundations of life and work and the demolition of democratic rights have reached such threatening proportions that we need a fundamental alternative for the economy, for politics and society. This was the reason for the spontaneous formation of a citizens' movement. Thousands of citizens' initiatives emerged and organised mighty demonstrations against atomic power stations, since the hazards they bring cannot be tolerated and since their radioactive waste products cannot be disposed of; citizens' initiatives have protested against the devastation of nature, against concreting over our open countryside, against the consequences and the causes of a throw-away-society which is endangering life itself.

A complete change of our short-term and economically minded pragmatic way of thinking is required. It is an error of judgment to believe that the present day economy of wastefulness could increase individual happiness and satisfaction with life; on the contrary, people

239

have become increasingly stressed and unfree. Only to the degree that we disregard material standards of living, that we again encourage self-realisation and remember again the limits set by nature, can creative forces become free to reconstruct life on an ecological basis.

We therefore think it is essential to supplement the extraparliamentary activities by working inside parliaments and assemblies at local and regional level, and in the Bundestag. There we want to ensure that our political alternatives become known in public and make an impact. In this way we will open a new possibility for citizens' and grassroots initiatives to put their concerns and ideas into practice.

Green, coloured and alternative lists have enjoyed their first electoral successes. The 5% clause and other obstacles can no longer stop them. We refuse to be part of a government which continues on the current destructive course. But we shall try to make sure that our aims influence the established parties and that we in turn back those proposals by other parties which match our aims.

In contrast to the one-dimensional focus on increased production we advocate a broadly comprehensive concept. Our policies are guided by long-term views of the future and based on four core principles: they are ecological, social, grassroots-democratic, and non-violent.

Ecological

Based on the laws of nature and in particular on the knowledge that no infinite growth can be accommodated within a finite system, ecological policies mean understanding ourselves and our environment as part of nature. Human life is also bound into the cycles of ecosystems: we interfere with these ecosystems through our actions and the changes that we cause affect us. We must not destroy the stability of the ecosystems.

Above all, ecological policies are a comprehensive renunciation of an economy of exploitation in which the wanton destruction of natural resources and raw materials goes hand in hand with the destructive interference with the laws of nature and natural cycles. We are convinced that we have to halt the exploitation of nature and of human beings, in order to control the acute and serious threats to life itself.

Our policies are those of active partnership with nature and with man (Mensch). They tend to be more successful in self-determined and self-sufficient, manageable units of economic activity and administration. We favour an economic system which is guided by the essential needs of people and of future generations, by the preservation of nature and the thrifty use of natural resources. We are concerned with creating a democratic society, in which relationships between people and between people and nature are increasingly based on thought and reflection.

In order to accomplish such changes against the existing power structures, a political movement is required which is based on human solidarity and mutual democratic recognition and on the renunciation of an achievement-orientated and hierarchical way of thinking which is based on competition and is intrinsically hostile to life. These social and economic changes can only be achieved in a democratic fashion and with the support of the majority of the population.

Social

A future social policy must aim at establishing a stable social system whereby 'social' means, above all, economic.

Through continuous increases in prices and through public tax and subventions policies, existing inequalities between rich and poor are exacerbated. We are opposed to a labour process which is dominated by economic power and which creates a situation in which a select few can determine what should be produced and even how the majority of people should live. Unemployment on the one hand and inhumane conditions of labour on the other provide ample evidence for this.

The destruction of the personal living environments, longer distances between home and work, the commercial exploitation of natural beauty and of leisure have meant that, notwithstanding rising incomes, a real impoverishment has begun to spread among low income groups especially children, young people, the old and disabled.

The competitive economy and the concentration of economic power in state-run and private monopolies have combined to produce that extortionist obsession with growth that threatens to completely devastate and pollute the human basis of life. It is here that the environmentalist and ecology movement fuses with the labour and trade union movement. This is the reason why we jointly advocate shorter working hours and humane working conditions.

Only the self-determination of those affected can avert a complete ecological, economic, and social crisis. Because we favour self-determination and the free development of every human being and think that people should be able to lead their lives creatively and in harmony with their natural environment, their own desires and needs, we radically advocate human rights and extensive democratic rights for everyone.

Conditions in our society produce social and psychological mass suffering. Sections of the population who experience ethnic, social, religious or sexual discrimination are hit particularly hard. Known consequences

241

are a rising crime rate, more suicides, drug abuse and alcoholism.

This state of society is also apparent in the fact that women have been oppressed and placed at a disadvantage in nearly all fields of social activity.

Grassroots-democratic

Grassroots democracy means putting decentralised, direct democracy into practice. We assume that the views of the grassroots (*die Basis*) have priority in principle. Compact, decentralised grassroots groups (at local or district level) are given virtual autonomy and administrative authority. However, grassroots democracy does require a unifying organisation and co-ordination, if ecological policies are to make an impact in public life against strong resistance. In all areas of politics we advocate more co-determination by the people concerned through plebiscites at district, regional and national level, and the introduction of elements of direct democracy to assist with planning in matters of life and survival.

Our internal organisational life and our relationship with the people who support us and vote for us is the exact opposite of the established parties in Bonn. These parties are unwilling and also unable to respond to the new ideas, suggestions and interests which have come from the democratic movement. We are, therefore, determined to create for ourselves a party organisation of a new type; this should combine the two strands of democratic organisation by being both grassroots-democratic and decentralised. A party which does not adopt this structure will never be in a position to pursue ecological policies convincingly within the framework of parliamentary democracy. The core of the organisational concept concerns the continuous control of all office holders, elected representatives and institutions through the supporter base (open access meetings; limited duration of terms of office) and the right to replace office holders at any time, both to ensure that the party organisation and the process of policy formulation are clear to all and in order to prevent a detachment of party officials and parliamentarians from their grassroots.

Non-violent

We are aiming for a non-violent society in which repression and violence will no longer exist. Our noblest principle reads: humane aims cannot be reached with inhumane means.

Non-violence regulates, without restriction or exception, the relationships between people, and therefore also between social groups, in

242

society as a whole, between nations and national groups.

The principle of non-violence does not impinge on the fundamental right of self-defence and also permits social resistance in its many varieties. As the example of the anti-nuclear movement has demonstrated, social resistance can be conducted most effectively in a social manner. We are no less fundamentally opposed to the use of violence between states in war.

We therefore advocate in international relations active pacifist policies. Active pacifism means that we also object to the occupation of states and the suppression of national groups but endorse the independence and the self-determination of national groups in all states. Peace is inexorably linked to the independence of states and the existence of democratic rights. There has to be worldwide disarmament. Throughout the world, nuclear, biological and chemical weapons must be destroyed, and troops withdrawn from foreign territories.

Non-violence does not exclude active social resistance and thus does not confine people to passivity. The principle of non-violence means, on the contrary, that in certain circumstances resistance against measures of the state to defend people's life-sustaining interests against a power structure over which they have lost influence can be not only legitimate but even indispensable (e.g. sit-ins, road blocs, the obstruction of vehicles).

(Source: *Die Grünen Bundesprogramm 1980*)

Document 2: Constitution of the Federal Party the Greens: Preamble

1. The Greens are the fundamental alternative to conventional parties. They aim to create a society which adjusts its development to the living conditions of natural processes and to the individual and social existence of human beings.
2. The Greens have recognised that a fundamental change of previous policies is needed. We oppose all disregard of human rights, hunger and poverty in the Third World, growing unemployment, the exacerbation of the environmental crises and military confrontations. The Greens know that this change requires the mobilisation of all ecological and democratic forces in the parliamentary and extra-parliamentary sphere.
3. The aim of the Green alternative is to overcome social conditions, in which short-term growth which benefits only segments of the population displaces the ecological, social and democratic life-needs

243

(*Lebensbedürfnisse*) of mankind.

4. In order to achieve this the economic, state-political and cultural life of society has to be recast. Within this recasting we also aim at a new form of participation for citizens and their initiatives in the processes of political and parliamentary planning and decision-making.

5. The principal direction of this innovation shall be ecological, social, grassroots-democratic and non-violent and based on the right of people to self-determination. The work of the Greens occurs within the framework of the Basic Law of the Federal Republic of Germany. If, however, the constitutional order or the regulations in the land constitutions do not provide sufficient room to put its aims into practice, the Greens will advocate the extension and further development of the constitutional provisions.

6. The method of political work emanates from the new spirit which inspires it: active tolerance is characterised by non-violence and the capacity to engage in dialogue.

7. Only through the readiness for evolution as outlined can wars and destructions be avoided in future. The Green alternative is the comprehensive expression of this readiness. By fighting for the protection of life and for human freedom, its endeavours are directed towards the welfare of the individual as well as towards the society as a whole.

(Source: Präambel from *Satzung der Bundespartei Die Grünen*, 1987)

Document 3: The Greens in the Bundestag: German–German, Bonn 1986.

Inner German Policies in a cul-de-sac

Every year on 17 June, a ritual is repeated: a celebratory hour in the German Bundestag is devoted to the 'Day of German Unity'. On this occasion, the politicians of the old parties choose to emphasise that the German question remains open, that Germany has to be reunited. The majority of West Germans, however, have long accepted as a political reality the existence of two separate German states and recognised the Federal Republic as the Western state. Today, nobody acts in the belief that the Federal Republic is something of a transitional state which would soon dissolve to make room for an all-German nation state. Most West Germans regard themselves as citizens of the Federal Republic, not as of all-German nationality; the GDR is a different country with the same language. Even for the majority of refugees and expellees, the

Federal Republic has become a second homeland.

Given this situation, it is not only unrealistic to imply that the German question remains open; amongst our political neighbours in Europe it also stirs new fears of a German nation state in the centre of Europe. Auschwitz and the dead of the Second World War have not been forgotten.

The present federal government refuses to draw the consequences from nearly 40 years of different development and to recognise the existence of the two states. Doggedly it persists with the claim to be the sole political representative in all things German and by insisting that the German question has remained open — an issue which has hardened into an ideology — it has obstructed all progress in German–German relations. Thus, years have been spent fighting over whether the border has to be drawn in the centre of the river Elbe or on the banks of the GDR side instead of looking for ways of cleaning up this same highly polluted and poisoned river. A reorientation in the politics of German–German relations, therefore, has to tackle this ideological ballast in the first instance.

Against Industrialism and Militarism — for an Ecological, Democratic and Non-violent Way of Life in Both German States

The Greens pursue their policies with and towards the GDR not from the perspective of national reunification dreams but as part of their world wide concern for a humane way of life. It is not that the German question is open, but the Greens confront existing structures in the two German states with open questions. Despite the different social and political systems in the FRG and the GDR, both face similar problems as industrial states.

The belief in the necessity of exponential growth and the ability to create technical progress has severely damaged the environment on both sides regardless of boundaries between the systems. Air pollution which knows no borders, the pollution of rivers, the problems arising from depositing highly toxic waste materials and the effect on the soil of chemical fertilizers are immediate consequences of industrialism and hinder human needs for an ecological way of life. Life-threatening nuclear technologies continue to be employed in the FRG and in the GDR even after the catastrophe of Chernobyl.

Membership of two well-armed, mutually hostile military blocs also determines policies and public awareness in both German states and societies. The focus on an assumed enemy for the purpose of mutual demarcation is as much part of this as the militarisation of social life.

Pre-military education, repressive attitudes towards pacifists and military mass rallies have become a firm component of public policy in the GDR. In the Federal Republic, on the other hand, the influence of the military on education is evident for example in the restrictions imposed on conscientious objectors by the conservatives.

On the basis of these structures we adopt a critical attitude towards both systems. This does not mean that we overlook the differences between them. We acknowledge the advantages which an open, pluralist democracy, rule of law and the separation of powers offer people in Western Europe. At the same time we observe with interest the efforts in Eastern Europe to ensure a secure living for everybody, even if we detest the authoritarian and state-dominated way in which this is done.

In both German states — albeit under different conditions — forces begin to grow which support peace and demilitarisation, environmental protection and the liberation of mankind from social manipulation and repression. The Greens regard themselves as part of this movement and consider solving the fundamental problems related to human needs as a priority issue in their German–German policies. Our aim is not a national reunification but unrestricted contacts among people, who are committed to an ecological, democratic and non-violent future. In which political structures the Germans and the other European nations will organise in future has to remain open. This can only be decided after the power blocs have been dismantled.

The Greens are in Favour of a Comprehensive Policy of Recognition

If we Greens support a policy of recognition this does not mean we advocate that things should be kept as they are. Instead, a policy of recognition means:

- to assume the existence of two German states and societies of equal importance and to overcome all obstacles which stand in the way;
- to rely not on pressure or a policy of strength towards the GDR but on dialogue and on jointly solving problems and generating confidence;
- to closely combine inter-state relations with a policy of intensifying communication among people and across the societies;
- not to shy away from clearly identifying repression, one-party government, political persecution and the lack of liberties in the GDR, to demand their abolition and to support the victims of repression.

The Policy of recognition should operate on three levels:

The self-recognition of the Federal Republic: This means to end the provisional status of the Federal Republic, as it is laid down in the constitution, to forgo the focus on a German national state and to define the FRG as an ordinary Western state.

This would contribute to end the dangerous self-deception which implies that an all-German identity exists. This self-deception has been used in particular by the nationalist sections of the CDU/CSU in order to propagate a new type of 'German' identity (*Deutschsein*). Democratic values such as pluralism, tolerance, and the protection of minorities are disregarded. Behind the emphatic support for the nation looms an authoritarian concept of society — 'the right to order' instead of democracy. By contrast, the Greens hope to link the self-recognition of the FRG with the development of a democratic identity in the FRG and encourage the emergence in West German society of a truly democratic constitution.

Furthermore, the self-recognition of the Federal Republic as the basis of German–German relations opens new opportunities of securing peace and detente in Central Europe. It is a precondition to renounce, once and for all, the territorial and political claims at sole representation which are inherent in the policy of keeping the German question open and of waiting for a peace treaty prior to any changes. Self-recognition of this kind would also dismantle the rights of political intervention which the victorious allies of the Second World War have tended to build on the claim that they are responsible for 'the whole of Germany'.

The recognition of the GDR in international law: Recognition of the GDR in international law including its citizenship without challenging the secure links of West Berlin with the Federal Republic is intended to end the political and cultural discrimination of the GDR as a 'second class state' and it will once and for all do away with an argument which has again and again been used to exert political pressure.

On such a basis of equal rights, mistrust, enmity and demarcation lines can be reduced and a neighbourly climate created of mutual trust and reduced tension. Above all, the Federal Republic could take a first step towards developing an honest dialogue which would facilitate an unprejudiced exchange of views between the people and the two societies.

In favour of dialogue in society and state: On the basis of the policy of recognition which has been proposed by the Greens a comprehensive dialogue would be possible between the two German states and societies. This dialogue would have to be focused on those questions which are essential for the future of people in Europe: questions of disarmament and the demilitarisation of societies, questions of keeping air, soil and water clean to ensure an ecologically balanced exchange with nature, questions of the future shape of work and the emergence of new technologies, questions of the boundaries of science and its ethical acceptability (e.g. gene technology), questions of putting human rights into practice and ensuring the self-determination of human beings.

A dialogue built on the assumption that both sides are willing to learn could set in motion a development of spiritual, political and ideological disarmament. This is only possible if this dialogue is not confined to high politics and delegations by associations and interest groups but if the people of both societies play an active part individually or in the shape of informal groupings such as citizens' initiatives.

Everyone should be able to articulate their experiences, views, feelings and wishes in this dialogue. People talking to each other — and this means going beyond diplomatic phrases and managerial chumminess — would enrich political discourse and could encourage a process of learning from each other. We hope to bring about such meetings and mutual interest through town twinning, the exchange of visits but also through a network of personal peace treaties and other forms of 'detente from below'.

Such a normalisation of the relationship between the two German states and societies also requires the GDR to change its policies concerning the freedom of movement and political activity of its citizens. The border restrictions between the two German states need to become more relaxed.

Berlin — Legacy of the Past, Open Future

The real measure of the relationship of the two German states to each other is the situation of West Berlin. All political, legal and economic obstacles and irritations in German–German relations resemble the wall which divides this city in two. There is one basic truth: without abolishing the bloc confrontation between the super powers and clarifying the fundamental issues between the two states, without international recognition of the GDR there is no chance of long-term detente in and about West Berlin. Its geographical position and the sensitivity of the social, economic and political ties between West Berlin and the Federal Republic make this town particularly prone to be used as a stake in the poker game of negotiations and big politics on both sides.

The Greens see all notions of Berlin as a 'border town', as a thorn in the flesh of the GDR as unsuitable notions and likely to endanger peace itself. West Berlin will only be able to find a proper role of its own when it begins to see itself as the turntable for disarmament, detente and the emergence of confidence across Europe, and actively participate in achieving them. Berlin would have to closely co-operate with its neighbouring territories without questioning the social, political and economic links with the Federal Republic.

The multifaceted agreement on Berlin from 1971 envisages a status for Berlin which could serve as a basis to further develop the international role of the town. The Greens envisage two major lines of development:

— recognition of West Berlin as the eleventh federal state of the Federal Republic, provided the GDR has first been accepted as a sovereign country of equal importance;
— the development of Berlin as an international city whose political status would have to be agreed among the four powers as well as the FRG and GDR themselves.

A first step which could be taken to bring this city of peace closer and would boost confidence between East and West would be to reduce the military presence in Berlin to merely symbolic units; a military defence of Europe does, in any case, not make sense.

(Source: *Deutsch–Deutsch. Wider die Mauern auch in den eigenen Köpfen*, Die Grünen im Bundestag, Bonn 1986)

Document 4: The Federal Programme (1980) on abortion: Section 7. Pregnancy (§ 218)

On the issue of termination of pregnancy two basic aims of the Greens conflict with each other: on the one hand the aim of defending rigorously the right of self-determination for men and women and on the other hand the aim of protecting human life in all circumstances.

The aim of protecting life, above all human life, implies also to secure the future development of mankind; it is paramount to ensure that the developing life can grow into as happy and humane a future as possible. This aim cannot be achieved through the efforts of the individual family alone but requires far reaching social and public measures of support.

Termination of pregnancy is essentially a question of ethical preference and of personal circumstances and must not be made an issue of criminal proceedings. It should be rendered unnecessary through information, through material and social assistance, and through the introduction of further methods of birth control. We demand:

— full reimbursement of medical costs for abortions within public health insurance schemes;
— safe and non-harmful contraceptives for women and men, dispensed without charge;

— no unwanted guidance and discrimination of women through the state and the medical profession;
— no persecutions and intimidations of women and doctors who have practised abortion.

(Source: *Das Bundesprogramm 1980*: 35.)

Document 5: Women's Programme — We Want Everthing!

We are Aiming at a Society Without Repression of Women, Without Authority, Violence and Prescribed Roles

We want meaningful occupations which are more than just earning money. We want to be active culturally and politically, we want to be free to decide for ourselves whether we should opt for a life with or without children, we want to determine the course of our individual lives for ourselves. We want to decide freely and without discrimination how we want to live — whether alone or with others — and whom we love — men or women.

In the patriarchal structures of contemporary society women are today defined — and often define themselves — through their men and their children. We propose to make women's policy, not family policy. Women as human beings constitute the centre of our political activity, not women in their function as wives or mothers.

One of the preconditions for putting this kind of self-determination into practice is the abolition of a gender-based division of labour, since this tends to prescribe social roles to women and men which are restrictive and leave little room for personal fulfilment. Unpaid work in home and family is the main pillar of support for the capitalist economic system. Therefore, we are not content with demanding equal rights alone. We are aiming at a more fundamental change of society. Women should be in a position to earn their own living. Men have to assume half the responsibility for children and housework.

We are fighting for the right of self-determination for women and demand, therefore, the abolition of § 218. We are fighting any kind of discrimination of women on grounds of gender (sexism). We are fighting against the special dependence and repression of foreign women and girls and in support of separate residence rights for foreign women.

An increasing number of women are no longer prepared to accept the patriarchal power structures and the male dominated social norms. They are challenging men in one of the strongest bastions of male

250

domination, politics. Many demands and views from the women's movement, the citizens' initiatives and the trade unions have been incorporated into the positions of the Greens. A visible result of this has been the so-called *Feminat* of the Greens in the Bundestag, when a team of women led the parliamentary party. In the Green party we have succeeded in winning the right to hold half the functions and offices. But even in the Greens we find male chauvinism and cock fighting. Even here we women have to fight for our rights.

It is impossible to achieve a fundamental change of society through parliamentary means. Our draft legislation against discrimination (ADG), however, constitutes a sound foundation for achieving full equality, equality of status at all levels of participation and influence for women in all areas of human existence. The ADG is a device for women here and now to demand their rights.

We have always worked with women from many different backgrounds who are affected by the situation and committed to changing it, and we have sought their advice. Together, we are fighting for the emancipation and the liberation of women.

(Source: *Bundestagswahlprogramm 1987*: 14.)

Document 6: Draft Legislation by the Members of Parliament Frau Dann, Frau Hönes and the parliamentary group Die Grünen to end Discrimination Against Women in all Areas of Society (Anti-Discrimination law — ADG)

Problem

On the basis of the current social position of women in the Federal Republic of Germany and in Berlin (West) and with the knowledge of the constitutional principle of equal rights for women and men as laid down in the Basic Law (Article 3 section 2) this law is designed to end the discrimination of women which exists in real life and thus counter-act a constant breach of the constitution.

Solution

A general clause which bans all discrimination of women on the basis of gender, their ability to bear children, their life style and/or their age;

— a general clause, which regulates the share of women in all areas of political and economic power;

251

- a general clause, which bestows upon women's association the right to start legal proceedings in the case of discrimination;
- a general clause which stipulates that the language of administration, legislation and the judiciary shall be cleansed of sexism;
- a law on quotas which makes it obligatory for all employers without exception to allocate 50% of all training places and places of work to women;
- a women's representatives' law to create as comprehensive a network of offices as possible; the women's representatives will control and promote the execution and implementation of the anti-discrimination legislation at all levels of society;
- a change of existing legislative norms such as removing without replacement § 218 from the criminal code; securing the right of sexual self-determination by declaring rape within marriage a crime; also punishing forced anal and oral intercourse as rape, abolishing the criminal category of a 'less severe case' for sexual harassment and rape, and changing the family law, the law on industrial relations and many others.

Alternatives

None.

Costs

Through the establishment of a federal office (the federal women's representative) additional costs of about 15 million Deutschmark annually will be incurred.

(Source: *Deutscher Bundestag 10 Wahlperiode*, Drucksache 10/6137.9.10.86: 1–2.)

Document 7: Principles and Perspectives of a Green Economic Policy

The reconstruction of the economy, which this programme is intended to set in motion, does contain essential directives to reverse the logic of development and aim at a humane economic future. We Greens advocate a new economic order and a new type of economic activity which honours its responsibility towards the needs of human beings here and in the Third World, of those who live today and of those who belong to future generations. This type of economic activity, therefore, has to be:

— *ecological*, since the unavoidable interference of human production with nature should occur in such a way that the indigenous
   processes of nature are preserved and nature, as the basis of ours
   lives, is protected;
— *social*, since the type of work and the distribution of the products
   have to ensure that all members of society experience equal
   opportunities to develop their personality;
— *grassroots-democratic*, since the social and cultural interests which
   people have in their everyday lives and at work can only come to
   bear fully if the rights of self-determination among employees
   and of democratic consensus about the course of the economy are
   extended to replace private and state dominated economic power
   and foreign influences.

In the realisation of an ecological, social and grassroots-democratic
economy both capitalist and so-called socialist economic systems have
failed: both systems are but variants of an alienated factory- and office-
society and based on the exploitation of human beings and nature. In
order to accomplish our long-term aims we do not propose to wait for a
day 'X' which would remodel society in one go.

On the contrary, we want to generate a process of reconstruction,
which will gradually overcome industrial capitalism and its economic
practices.

Our policies are designed to introduce fundamental reforms in those
areas where this is possible given the potential weight of social and
parliamentary forces today.

Ecological Economy

An ecological economy does not regard the unlimited supply of goods
as prosperity but aims to preserve and to reclaim nature as the living
environment of human beings. This means that processes of production and the products themselves have to fit into natural processes
without impingeing on the natural foundations of people's lives and on
the lives of other creatures. Consumer durables have to replace throw-
away products.

Growth as the production of the maximum number of goods is no
longer recognised as a worthwhile economic goal since the existing
industrial system is set to destroy its own natural foundations the more
it expands. The loose talk about qualitative growth only obscures the
fact that in the last analysis it is no different from aiming at overall
economic growth and at extending overall economic activity, i.e. the
production of goods and services. Instead, ecological economic policy
frees itself from the focus on overall growth without dogmatically

advocating zero growth, a decrease of economic activity or even a complete break with industrial society. Ecological economic policy aims at the reconstruction of our industrial system according to ecological requirements. While some areas will have to shrink, others should be encouraged to expand. We want:

— the dismantling of those branches of the economy which endanger life and environment, e.g. the nuclear industry and sections of car manufacturing industry in the wake of changes in the transport system;
— the redirection of harmful branches of production, e.g. in agriculture and large parts of the chemical industry;
— the creation of new branches of the economy in areas of social needs, e.g. renewable energy and public transport.

Ecological economy also involves the rejection of large industrial companies as far as technically possible and ecologically sensible and their replacement by ecologically favourable processes of production in small, decentralised units of production.

Environmental protection also means protection at work. Changes in the processes of production and in the labour process can drastically reduce the use of poisonous substances (dust, gases etc.) and harmful influences (noise). These aims require further technological innovations and improvements.

To run an ecological economy makes it necessary to grasp the complete impact of specific products (e.g. the production of pesticides) or of a specific style of life or consumption (e.g. the use of a motor car); if at all possible, producers and consumers should carry the full cost of the overall expenditures for which they are responsible (causation principle). An ecologically centred system of production and consumption will attempt to avoid the cost of destructions and repairs altogether (preventative principle). They are, thus, much more acceptable and also cheaper than an economy which abides by the slogan 'After me the deluge'.

An ecological approach to the economy also includes an ecologically sound style of life and consumption. An ecological type of construction and living does not tally with the wishes of the masses for a home of their own in the green belt and the urbanisation of the country side that goes with it. To protect the soil and the towns from being altogether sealed and covered in cement it is paramount to put a halt to further growth of vehicle traffic and the use of private cars. Many areas of life and of leisure have to be reconstructed in an ecological way from substituting dangerous chemicals in the home to developing ecologically compatible forms of tourism (e.g. avoiding damage to forests and mountains through mass tourism).

In an ecological economic system, new consumer policies are of central importance. Ecological consumer policies are concerned to inform consumers as comprehensively as possible about modes of production, the product itself and its composition, and they aim to extend the influence of the market on the producers, i.e. by increasing the range of goods on offer, by restricting cartels and by introducing the right to inspect business files. We still have to find ways of involving the consumer directly in decision-making on company production and investments.

A standard of living which is measured only against the quantity of goods and services consumed, has to be seen as a substitute satisfaction for people who are destroyed in work and in leisure and driven by forces beyond their control. A free and socially balanced society will make such substitute consumerism redundant; standardised consumerism will be displaced by a quality of human life which unfolds in free time and in self-determined activity.

We Greens are in favour of all efforts to practise this new life style.

Social Economy

A social economy serves the material, social and cultural needs of the individual and society, and is guided by them. We Greens reject the claim of the present day economic order that it is a 'social market economy'; persistent unemployment, the destruction of health through work, increasing poverty and the systematic discrimination of women characterise this economic system just as much as the excessive power of private ownership and the priority interest of profit making. A social economy, on the contrary, grants all members of a society, women and men, young and old, foreigners and Germans the right to sensible work and a secure basic income. It is essential for us Greens that work and the division of labour should no longer be alienating experiences.

The main device to overcome unemployment is the just distribution of work through drastically reducing working hours. For ecological reasons, a policy of increased economic growth is unacceptable as a means of increasing to total available work.

We Greens call for an end to a gender based division of labour between women and men. Women and girls have the right to an even share with men of the work and training places that are available. In addition, man and woman should assume an equal share in the socially necessary work in the home and in bringing up children. This can only be achieved if working hours are drastically reduced.

In paid employment, the most boring and debilitating aspects of the labour process tend to be accepted for financial reasons, in order to earn a living wage. The structure of authority in capitalist but also in so-called real-socialist societies militates against making the labour process more humane. A social, ecological, and democratic economy does provide several opportunities to turn work into a free and self-determined activity: there is no imposition of decisions by employers and no exploitation of the workforce in self-administered enterprises; science and technology seek to make work easier. The shift towards an increasingly differentiated division of labour has been stopped; new technology is used to create interesting units of work by fusing separate segments of the labour process which would be meaningless if they remained separate; monotony is being reduced and the working people are able to plan and control their own work.

Provided working hours are radically reduced people can engage in self-determined activity in the free time which they have gained.

The social remodelling of the economy also involves the abolition of social classes as well as of sexist and unjust differences in income and wealth in our society. The basic material needs of people have to be met. People who do not earn a sufficiently high income from their employment have to receive a basic supplement which will enable them to live in dignity.

The principle of social distribution of the value which has been created, has to apply also on a global scale and has to guide our relationship with the Third World.

We oppose the centralised and bureaucratic administration of people by social institutions. Instead, we intend to create self-administered, communal social services and self-help centres. Our focus is not to repair people by building more and more hospitals, drug clinics and sanatoriums, but to abolish those conditions of work and life which make people mentally and physically ill in our society.

The dominant international division of labour between industrial states and the Third World is dominated by the interests of the industrial states and only serves to exploit the countries kept in underdevelopment and seize their raw materials. In the framework of a just world economic order we advocate equality in our relationship with the countries of the Third World and aims to end their economic dependence.

The Federal Republic violates the aim of balanced exports constantly: through massive export surpluses she exports much of her unemployment to the detriment of employment in other countries.

Grassroots-democratic Economy

It is an important facet of working lives in our society that those in paid employment are excluded from the decision-making process surrounding the most important questions which affect their activities and their lives — the questions what is produced, how it is produced and for whom. The contemporary forms of co-determination including that in the steel and coal producing industries barely suffice to protect the workforce from the everlasting efforts of capital to intensify the labour process and to rationalise without regard for the people involved. Today it is important to defend co-determination against the attacks from employers and to extend it on all levels. Co-determination on the shop floor and in the board room has to apply to all decisions which affect the workforce: from the introduction of new technologies to investments and general entrepreneurial policies.

However, even the most extensive type of co-determination, full parity without a neutral additional person, is indebted to the social partnership of capital and labour and is, in the last analysis, a subjugation of labour to capital. The experiences with parity-based co-determination (steel and coal) have shown that the employees lacked the power to decide on the future of the enterprise and of work. Extending co-determination on the shop floor can, therefore, not lead to truly democratic company practices. For this reason, a number of attempts have been made to establish self-determination among the workforce.

Alternative economic projects are a response to the continued existence of alienated labour; in contrast to these alienated structures they have created their own structures, based on self-administration and self-determination. The new approaches which have been tried in alternative projects, the new types of communal property, the preference to cover costs only rather than maximise profit, the claim to produce wholesome goods and services, the chances for women's groups to win free scope to set their own priorities, the preference for decentralisation and also for establishing a network of alternative enterprises — all these approaches we Greens regard as steps in the direction of realising our aims of 'working and living differently'. Despite all the flaws which can be found in these many approaches, we fully support the movement for alternative economic projects.

(Source: 'Grundsätze und Perspektiven grüner Wirtschaftspolitik' from the economic programme *Umbau der Industriegesellschaft*, Bonn 1986: 9–11)

Select Bibliography

Alber, Jens (1985), 'Modernisierung, neue Spannungslinien und die politischen Chancen der Grünen', *Politische Vierteljahresschrift* 26/3

Ammon, Peter and Peter Brandt (eds.) (1981), *Die Linke und die nationale Frage*, Reinbek: Rowohlt

Baker, Kendall, Russell J. Dalton and Kai Hildebrandt (1981), *Germany Transformed. Political Culture and the New Politics*, Cambridge/Mass.: Harvard University Press

Bickerich, Wolfram (1985), *SPD und Grüne. Das neue Bündnis*, Reinbek: Rowohlt

Budge, Ian, David Robertson and Derek Hearl (eds.) (1987), *Ideology, Strategy and Party Change. Spatial Analyses of Post-War Election Programmes in 19 Democracies*, Cambridge: Cambridge University Press

Bühnemann, Michael *et al* (eds.) (1984), *Die Alternative Liste Berlin*, Berlin: Lit Pol

Bürklin, Wilhelm (1981), 'Die Grünen und die Neue Politik. Abschied vom Dreiparteiensystem?', *Politische Vierteljahresschrift* 4

___ (1984), *Grüne Politik. Ideologische Zyklen, Wähler und Parteiensystem*, Opladen: Westdeutscher Verlag

___ (1985a) 'The German Greens. The Post-Industrial and Non-Established and the Party System', *International Political Science Review* 6/4, October

___ (1985b), 'The Split between the Established and the Non-Established Left in Germany', *European Journal of Political Research* 13/4

Bullmann, Udo and Peter Gitschmann (1985), *Kommune als Gegenmacht. Alternative Politik in Städten und Gemeinden*, Hamburg: VSA

Chandler, William M. and Alan Siaroff (1986), 'Postindustrial Politics in Germany and the Origins of the Greens', *Comparative Politics* 18/3, April

Cotgrove, Stephen and Andrew Duff (1980), 'Environmentalism, Middle-Class Radicalism and Politics', *Sociological Review* 28/2, May

Crewe, Ivor and David Denver (eds.) (1985) *Electoral Change in Western Democracies. Patterns and Sources of Electoral Volatility*, London: Croom Helm

Dalton, Russell J. (1988), *Citizen Politics in Western Democracies*, London: Chatham House

___, Scott Flanagan and Paul Allen Beck (eds.) (1985), *Electoral Change in Advanced Industrial Societies. Realignment or Dealignment?*, Princeton:

Princeton University Press

Dräger, Klaus and Werner Hülsberg (1986), *Aus für Grün? Die Grüne, Orientierungskrise zwischen Anpassung und Systemopposition*, Frankfurt: IPS Verlag

Fischer, Joschka (1987), *Regieren geht über Studieren. Ein politisches Tagebuch*, Frankfurt: Athenäum

Fogt, Helmut (1986), 'Die Mandatsträger der Grünen. Zur sozialen und politischen Herkunft der alternativen Parteielite', *Aus Politik und Zeitgeschichte* 11

—— (1987), 'Zwischen Parteiorganisation und Bewegung. Die Rekrutierung der Mandatsträger bei den Grünen', in Heinrich Oberreuter (ed.), *Wer kommt in die Parlamente?*, Baden-Baden: Nomos

Gluchowski, Peter (1987), 'Lebensstile und Wandel der Wählerschaft in der Bundesrepublik Deutschland.' *Aus Politik und Zeitgeschichte* B12

Gotto, Klaus and Hans-Joachim Veen (1984), *Die Grünen — Partei wider Willen*, Mainz: Hase & Kohler

Gransow, Volker (1987), 'East German Society at the Turning Point?' *Studies in Comparative Communism* 20/1

Grupp, Joachim (1986), *Abschied von den Grundsätzen? Die Grünen zwischen Koalition und Opposition*, Berlin: Edition Ahrens, Zerling

Guggenberger, Bernd (1986), 'An den Grenzen von Verfassung und Mehrheitsentscheidung oder: Die neue Macht der Minderheit' in Heinrich Oberreuter (ed.), *Wahrheit statt Mehrheit?*, Munich: Olzog

Hallensleben, Anna (1984), *Von der Grünen Liste zur Grünen Partei*. Göttingen: Musterschmidt

Hofmann-Göttig, Joachim (1986), *Emanzipation mit dem Stimmzettel*, Bonn: Neue Gesellschaft

Hondrich, Karl Otto and Randolph Vollmer (eds.) (1983), *Bedürfnisse im Wandel*, Opladen: Westdeutscher Verlag

Hülsberg, Werner (1988), *The German Greens. A Social and Political Profile*, London: Verso

Jäger, Brigitte and Claudia Pinl (eds.) (1985), *Zwischen Rotation und Routine. Die Grünen im Bundestag*, Hamburg: KiWi Verlag

Kallscheuer, Otto (ed.) (1986), *Die Grünen — Letzte Wahl?*, Berlin: Rotbuch

Kelly, Petra (1984), *Fighting for Hope*, London: Chatto and Windus/ Hogarth Press

Klotzsch, Lilian and Richard Stöss (1986), 'Die Grünen' in Richard Stöss (ed.), *Parteien-Handbuch: Die Parteien in der Bundesrepublik Deutschland*. Opladen: Westdeutscher Verlag, 2 vols

Kluge, Thomas (ed.) (1984), *Grüne Politik*, Frankfurt: Fischer

Kolinsky, Eva (1984), *Parties, Opposition and Society*, London: Croom Helm

Kolinsky, Eva (ed.) (1987), *Opposition in Western Europe*, London: Croom Helm and PSI

Kolinsky, Eva (1988a), 'The German Greens — a Women's Party?' *Parliamentary Affairs* 1, Winter

Langguth, Gerd (1986), *The Green Factor in German Politics*, Boulder: Westview

Langner, Manfred (ed.) (1987), *Die Grünen auf dem Prüfstand*, Bergisch-Gladbach: Lübbe 1987

Livingston, Robert G. (ed.) (1986) *West Germany–East Germany and the German Question*, Washington DC American Institute of Contemporary German Studies

Lüdke, Hans-Werner and Olaf Dinné (eds.) (1980), *Die Grünen. Personen — Projekte — Programme*, Stuttgart: Seewald

Malunat, Bernd (1987), 'Umweltpolitik im Spiegel der Parteiprogramme', *Aus Politik und Zeitgeschichte* 29

Meng, Richard (1987), *Modell Rot-Grün? Auswertung eines Versuchs*, Hamburg: VSA

Mettke, Jörg R. (ed.) (1982), *Die Grünen. Regierungspartner von morgen?*, Reinbek: Rowohlt

Mez, Lutz and Ulf Wolter (1980), *Die Qual der Wahl*, Berlin: Olle & Wolter

Müller-Rommel, Ferdinand (1985a), 'New Social Movements and Smaller Parties. A Comparative Perspective', *West European Politics* 8/1

_____ (1985b), 'Das grün-alternative Parteienbündnis im Europäischen Parlament' Perspektiven eines neuen Phänomens', *Zeitschrift für Parlamentsfragen* 3, September

_____ (ed.), (1989), *New Politics in Western Europe. The Rise and the Success of Green Parties and Alternative Lists*, Boulder: Westview

Oberreuter, Heinrich (1983), *Parteien zwischen Nestwärme und Funktionskälte*, Zürich: Edition Interform

_____ (ed.) (1986), *Wahrheit statt Mehrheit?*, Munich: Olzog

_____ (1988), *Wer kommt in die Parlamente?*, Baden-Baden: Nomos

Papadakis, Elim (1984), *The Green Movement in West Germany*, London: Croom Helm

Plock, Ernest D. (1986), *The Basic Treaty and the Evolution of East–West Relations*, Boulder: Westview

Poguntke, Thomas (1987a), 'New Politics and Party Systems: The Emergence of a New Type of Party?', *West European Politics* 10

_____ (1987b), 'The Organisation of a Participatory Party — The German Greens', *European Journal of Political Research* 15

_____ (1989), 'The New Politics Dimension in Western European Green Parties', in Ferdinand Müller-Rommel (ed.), *New Politics in Western Europe*, Boulder: Westview

Rehrmann, Norbert (1985), *Rot-grünes 'Modell Kassel'? Eine Bilanz nach vier Jahren*, Kassel: Kasseler Verlag/Werkstatt Verlag

Richardson, Elke and Regina Michalik (1985), *Die quotierte Hälfte. Frauenpolitik in den grün-alternativen Parteien*, Berlin: LitPol

Rüdig, Wolfgang (1985), 'The Greens in Europe. Ecological Parties and the European Elections of 1984', *Parliamentary Affairs* 1, Winter

Schiller-Dickhut, Reiner *et al*, (1981), *Alternative Stadtpolitik. Grüne, rote und bunte Arbeit in den Rathäusern*, Hamburg: VSA

Schmitt, Rüdiger (1987), 'Was bewegt die Friedensbewegung?', *Zeitschrift für Parlamentsfragen* 1 (March)

Smith, Gordon (1987), 'The Changing West German Party System. Consequences of the 1987 Election', *Government and Opposition* 22/2

Spretnak, Charlene and Fritjof Capra (1985), *Green Politics. The Global Promise*. London: Collins (Paladin)

Veen, Hans-Joachim (1984), 'Wer wählt grün? Zum Profil der neuen Linken in der Wohlstandsgesellschaft', *Aus Politik und Zeitgeschichte* 35–6

—— (1987), 'Die Anhänger der Grünen', in Manfred Langner (ed.), *Die Grünen auf dem Prüfstand*, Bergisch Gladbach: Lübbe

List of Contributors

Dr Helmut Fogt is Research Co-ordinator of Comparative Government and Institutions at the *Sozialwissenschaftliches Forschungsinstitut* of the Konrad Adenauer Foundation, St. Augustin near Bonn, West Germany.

Prof. Volker Gransow is Professor of German Studies at the University of California, Berkeley, USA.

Dr Eva Kolinsky is Senior Lecturer in German Studies at Aston University, Birmingham, England.

Dr Norbert Kostede is Privatdozent in Political Science at the University of Hanover, West Germany and *wissenschaftlicher Mitarbeiter* of *Die Grünen im Bundestag*.

Dr Ferdinand Müller-Rommel is *Akademischer Rat* in Political Science at the Hochschule Lüneburg, West Germany.

Dr Elim Papadakis is Lecturer in Sociology at the University of New England, Australia.

Dr Thomas Poguntke is a researcher in Political Science at the European University, Florence, Italy.

Mr Thomas Scharf is a Research Student at Aston University, Birmingham, England.

Dr Hans-Joachim Veen is Director of the *Sozialwissenschaftliches Forschungsinstitut* at the Konrad Adenauer Foundation, St. Augustin near Bonn, West Germany.

Mr Konrad Will-Schinneck is Business Manager of the Green Party in Rhineland Palatinate.

Translations: Eva Kolinsky with the assistance of Lindsay Batson.

Index

265